UNDERSTANDING BHAKTI

UNDERSTANDING BHAKTI

H.P. Sah

PUBLICATIONS

KALPAZ PUBLICATIONS

DELHI-110052

Understanding Bhakti

Rs. 750

ISBN: 81-7835-597-3

Published in 2007 in India by
Kalpaz Publications
C-30, Satyawati Nagar,
Delhi-110052
Phone : 9212729499
E-mail: kalpaz@hotmail.com

Lasser Type Setting by: Rudra Computer Graphics, Delhi
Printed at : Salasar Imaging System, Delhi

Contents

Preface

> "Look at me, Arjuna! If I stop from work for one moment the whole universe will die. I have nothing to gain from work; I am the one lord, but why do I work? Because I love the world"
>
> **- Srimad Bhagawad Gita -**

Where should man go to prove the existence of God? Love is the most visible of all- visible things. It is the prime force that was moving the sun, the moofi at- the other stars, manifesting itself in every human beings and all beings everywhere and everything. It was the infinite love, the only motive power of this universe visible everywhere - and this was God Himself. We read in the *Upanisads: '/savasyamidam sarvam yatkincit Jagatyam Jagaf,* 'whatever exists in this. universe is to be covered with the Lord". We have to cover everything with the lord Himself, not by the false sort of optimism, not by blinding our eyes to the .:'evil, but by really seeing God in everything. One can realise the divine everyone, the Self in all and all in the Self, the universal *sakti* doing all things, one can feel merged in the cosmic self, full of ecstatic *bhakti* or *pramananda.*

If you want to love, love extremely something beyond this world, something above all material forces, almighty God. This extreme love for God is *bhakti.* A *bhakta* leads his life in the light of his experience of *bhakti* and the only aim of his life to live in this world is love for lord.

It gives me great pleasure in introducing Dr. H.P. Sah's book on this marvellous subject *bhakti,* real existence, real knowledge and real love - the three aspect of the one, entitled "understanding *Bhaktl'.* Dr. Sah has laboured hard on the book, having consulted a wide variety of rich source-material on the theme, and has produced a scholarly treatise, which must be of the great benefit to all students of philosophy of religion and to Indian philosophy, Psychology and Indian culture, in general. I derived a great deal of benefit after perusing through the work, the value of which lies in the wide range of the problems covered by Dr. Sah and his criticism on each aspect of problem as deal with by the traditional and modern thinkers on the subject.

Putting aside the both familiar ways - the way of the interpretation of traditional text and the way of understanding *bhakti* in the light of modernity - Dr. Sah has adopted the simplest but peculiar way of making the attempt to understand *bhakti.* This is an attempt of a common man who is free from the rational complexities and finds something very significant and charming in a *bhakta's* life. Since *Bhakti* is the purest and highest form of emotion ever experienced by the human beings as purest form of love, no any further scholarship and specific training are required to understand it. So a most uneducated man has a right *adhikara* to talk about it. In the realm of *Bhakti,* uneducated and illiterate Gopis attain the highest place as a culmination of *adhikara* to love their Divine beloved.

The readers would find very valuable and special insigts in this scholarly presentation. Dr. Sah has qealt with Subsidiary conceptual problems and significant issue, like 'a level of understanding *bhaktf,* 'whom do we call a *bhakta',* 'transformation of the doer', 'why the world has come into being', why the laws operate the way the operate', '*bhakti* as a power', etc. which have mostly been ignored by the scholars, in a manner not only an expert scholar but also a true believer and a devotee, *sadhaka.* Dr. Sah has explored new avenue of knowledge, which must receive a very wide attention of students and scholars in the field of philosophy of religion. I congratulate Dr. Sah on his excellent achievement.

TvadTyam vastu Govind! Tubhyameva Samarpyate

Dharmanand Sharma

Introduction

Kṛṣṇa! At the first glance any discussion about *bhakti* may appear to be a talk about a particular school of Hindu philosophy that teaches a path of God realization through love. If it is so then it is an ethnocentric talk that could be meaningfully grasped and elaborated only within the beliefs and practices of Hindu religious community. This is an acceptance of the view that the subject matter of *bhakti* could not be of any vital importance for people of other religious communities. A non-Hindu may have only an interest in it to enhance the boundaries of his knowledge about other religious communities but this knowledge can't play the role that his own beliefs and religious practices play in his life. This view is widely in currency among the Sociologists. This view has a merit. It concentrates on all or most miner details of the beliefs, customs and rituals of religious communities. But there is great demerit in it. It presupposes that items of religious beliefs and practices loose all their significance if they are taken out of their system. Truths dawned on the mind of a person of a particular religious tradition is, thus, reduced in this view to mere metaphysical assumptions to preach particular social norms and the *sâdhanâ* to achieve these truths is reduced to methods of self control or self purification that is encouraged by the authority to maintain discipline.

Despite the fact that religious truths, unfortunately, degenerates into sectarian belief system, there is no reason to accept that this view is universally true. In reaction this view is, at times, rejected as universally false. There seems to be no good reason to do that either. It could be and must be accepted to be true in its particularity. We can understand *bhakti* in more than one ways. *Bhakti* could be seen as a social phenomenon within the Hindu socio-religious beliefs and practices. It is a particular type of understanding about it. A serious study is required to gain this sort of understanding and it enriches our information and understanding both. But this is not the only way to understand *bhakti*. It is also possible to understand *bhakti* as the purest and the highest form of sublime emotion that human beings ever experience. The Hindu association of the word *'Bhakti'* does not come in the way of this sort of understanding.

It is a fact that anyone, irrespective of his religious faith, can understand that human beings feel the emotion of love and reverence not only for worldly persons but also for some supra earthly centre of consciousness whose presence they feel in and through this emotional encounter. Despite our cultural differences we understand well that we are all humans who have similar feelings towards the happenings of the world around us and feel pain and pleasure in similar conditions. Despite many visibly important differences a black man can and does understand that a white man, whom he does not know, feels pain if he shrieks on getting his finger cut with a knife. He also understands that despite his unfamiliarity with the white man's way of welcoming someone a white man before him would be able to understand sooner or later that he welcomes him (the white man) if does so, and his expectations come to be true mostly. Similarly a person brought up in a particular religious tradition does understand that a person of an alien culture is doing what he calls worship or prayer in his own language if he watches him doing some thing that is not visibly directed to any earthly person or entity. This does not mean to say that like many other human feelings and emotions the feeling of reverence for divine is also a natural feeling. Fundamental emotions like fear etc. are often held to be the seeds that germinate into the feeling of reverence for an unknown power. Such explanations fail to explain how the feeling of sublime enters into the feeling of fear for an unknown power. Fear generates hatred. It can make the people bow their heads before the object (known or unknown) of fear. Can it also generate or evolve into the feeling of desire-less dedication towards that object? Even if some empirical research reveals that it happens in many cases, it can neither logically nor empirically rule out the case where reverence for the unknown power emerges in the heart of the people not for fear but for the feeling of unbound gratitude for the gift of life and the abundance of the food, water and other things for it sustenance: gratitude for the offspring and their survival, for the capacity to reason that gives knowledge and for the sensitivity to feel others pain and pleasure.

Fear is a fundamental emotion found in animals too. No evidence is found as yet that could show that in any animal species this feeling made them do something that we can recognize as worshiping or praying. Even those animals, which have some sort language, don't give indication of any act of that sort. The question, therefore, becomes relevant—why and how do these special emotions directed to an unknown centre of consciousness emerge in human heart? Every religious tradition, somehow or the other, reflect the human belief that in this happening a supranatural divine will manifests itself and the persons who feel such an emotion, feel the presence of divine in and through this feeling. .The emotion of reverence in the form of complete dedication towards the unknown centre of consciousness that prompts from the sense of gratitude makes the human beings aware for the first time of what they recognize as supramundane –as contrasted with the mundane in which they grow, live and die. It is the simplest emotion although, because of its varied content, it appears to be most complex one. It is the purest form of experience of love. Since it is simplest, it can't be made further simpler. This is the emotion that is named also as '*Bhakti*'. Our socio-religious conditionings don't create any problem in understanding *bhakti* in this way; rather they help in it. It is not the *only* way but *one way* to understand *bhakti.* As it is stated in the above discussion, there is no reason to rule out either the logical or empirical possibility of understanding *bhakti* in this way. This work 'Understanding *Bhakti*' is an attempt of understanding *bhaqkti* in this way.

It is not possible to explain *bhakti*. Since it is the purest form of experience, it becomes only contaminated by any attempt to explain it in terms of any other experience. Blessed is the species of man who has been gifted with this experience because there is no method or technique to attain it if it would have not been gifted.

These are all very simple statements about the experience of *bhakti* and need no explanation for understanding what they actually mean. But we are not simple. We have learned so many complexities in course of the growth of civilization that all simple things, now, appear to be most difficult; almost impossible. So there is a need for explanation. We have to make special effort to understand what *bhakti* is Two sorts of efforts are made, ordinarily, to understand the experience of *bhakti*. One is the way of the interpretation of traditional texts that usually begins from etymological analysis and proceeds along the accepted traditional lines. Another is the way of understanding it in the light of modernity that implicitly but categorically deny any cognitive importance to any religious experience. Both the ways of understanding *bhakti* are good as they give us valuable insights about it. Can there be yet another way of understanding *bhakti*? Perhaps someone can question about the very need of another way of understanding it. The reply to this presumed question is negative. There is no *need* of any further attempt in this regard if '*need*' implies any urgency either at the cognitive or at the practical level. We can lead our life as usual without making further attempt to understand *bhakti*. Nothing will be lost in not doing so but we will definitely miss some special insights that this attempt of understanding could give us. Hence there is some acceptable reason for a further attempt to understand *bhakti* although there is no need for so doing. This book is a humble presentation of that another attempt. This is an attempt of a common man who finds something very significant and charming in a *bhakta's* life.

Legendary *bhaktas* like Narad, Druva, Prahlada can be put aside as mythological characters. But Raidas, Meera, Tulsidas, Surdas, Chaitanya and others are historical personalities and a common man finds something very charming in their life despite knowing well that they did not possess any powerful position. An ordinary man understands that their love for their dear Lord was their only support and this uniqueness alone makes them something extraordinary.

A common man does not begin with the doubt about the *bhaktas'* love for their Lord. There is no doubt that the *bhaktas* are in love with their Lord. They are all intoxicated with *bhakti* (love of

Lord). The question arise in a common man's mind about the object of their love, i.e. about their Lord because He (the *bhaktas'* Lord) does not come in any common man's experience. This question is not an atheist's doubt about God's existence. It is a curiosity to know what the Lord is like etc. It is not a presumptuous question like –how can any person or thing like God exist? It is a sort of hidden desire to see Him, to talk to Him as the *bhaktas* seem to do. We are all common people and have such a desire in our hearts. We are not quite clear what exactly we are desiring for when we find ourselves in such a desire. However, if this condition does not force us to close our minds and hearts and to declare like the atheists that the behaviour of the *bhaktas* is abnormal and their Lord is a construct of mere subjective projection then we find a deep urge to understand *Bhakti* the way the *bhaktas* understand it. An atheist may have good reasons to make such declaration but that is not the sufficient reason to prove the *bhaktas'* experience of love for their Lord as hallucinatory. We all know that the *bhaktas* are *really* in love with their Lord (despite our ignorance about the person whom they love). We can't doubt that they are *in love*. Love is a very strong emotion and it is almost impossible for anyone to hide it if one is in love. To pretend to be in love is equally impossible if one is not actually undergoing it. At least in involuntary responses it is disclosed very clearly in both the situations. It is difficult to find a *bhakta* whose life is completely submerged in love for his Lord but most of us at times (while listening a devotional song or reading a passage from the life of a *bhakta*) find ourselves overwhelmed by the emotion of *bhakti* temporarily and this enables us to understand the difference between the actual feeling of this emotion and its pretension. It can be admitted that it is not always practically possible to make such a clear difference but that does not prove that it is all pretension rather it only shows that *bhakti* is really an emotion felt by human beings and on that ground one can make a live-like enactment of it. A pretension necessarily presupposes the genuine prior presence of that of which it is a pretension. Pretension of *bhakti* also presupposes that *bhakti* is a genuine human emotion. So it is natural to feel the urge to understand this genuine human emotion because we can't deny it and at the same time we are not very clear about the nature of its object towards which this emotion is directed. This we can understand only by understanding it the way *bhaktas* understand it since they directly, vividly and permanently know the object of *bhakti* and call Him their dear Lord.

We, as common men, can understand *bhakti* the way *bhaktas* understand it. There is no conceptual or practical problem involved in it. Ordinarily a distinction is made between the understanding of first person and that of third person. In the light of this distinction it can be said that a third person like us can't have the *bhakta's* (the first person's) understanding. But this objection is baseless because its base is not rationally tenable. The very ground for making a difference between first and third person's understanding presupposes a common undifferentiated understanding. If the first person's understanding of a phenomenon is actually different from the third person's understanding then how do I (as first person) understand what does the other person (the third person) understand about any phenomenon, and how do I understand whether he is referring to the same phenomenon? If my way of understanding were really different from that of other's then it would never have been possible for me to find out that both of us are referring to the same phenomenon, and it would not have been possible for us to agree upon our understanding about that phenomenon. Bu we do agree that both I and some other person understand a phenomenon. This shows that we don't accept any radical division in understanding regarding any phenomenon. Moreover, the frequent cases of our understanding that someone is not understanding what I intend to make him understand shows again that it is possible for me to know whether someone understands or does not understand me. There is no mystery involved in it. By the response of the other person we can definitely decide whether he is understanding me or not. Frequent use of sentences like —'You don't understand me' or 'Now you followed what I wanted to say' leave no room for any radical difference between two person's understanding about any phenomenon. This does not mean that misunderstanding never takes place in our life. It only shows that despite our failure to understand each other we *come to understand* that we do not understand each other. The availability of this deeper level understanding to all of us is the bedrock that makes this world an intelligible world where we not alienated from each other but can and do understand each other. The difference between the first person and third person's understanding is acceptable only at the psychological level but not at the epistemic level.

In the light of above discussion it is, now, clear that there is not (and could not be) a radical difference between the *bhaktas'* understanding of *bhakti* and that of any common man. We can't say that the *bhaktas'* understanding is accessible to them only and not to any non-*bhaktas*. In the light of above understanding we should make ourselves prepared to accept that if any phenomenon is experienced and understood by any human being then every other human being can understand it the way that person understood it. If the *bhaktas* have experienced *bhakti* (the love of Lord) the every other human being also can understand it the way they understand it. At the epistemic level an actual experience is not necessary for understanding some other person's experience either. I can and do understand that some woman is having labour pain although I (being a man) can never experience it. However, that sort of problem of unavailability of experience does not lie with understanding of *bhakti*. All of us have experienced temporarily this divine emotion. So it is not at all difficult for any common man to understand *bhakti* the way the *bhaktas* understand it.

In the light of above discussion some questions arise about the general impression regarding the spread of *bhakti* in a particular period of medieval India (about 15th century) as a social movement. It is held that certain socio-political factors of that epoch gave rise to this movement. It is seen as sort of reform movement that brought Hinduism out of its dogmatic beliefs and the evils of social injustice emerged from its casts system etc. It was indeed a movement that brought about a social reform but the attempt to understand the reasons behind this movement eventually contradicts the spirit of this movement if it is seen to be confined to mere socio-political factors of that period. The view that this movement was the result of the explicit and implicit demand of the people for a social reform to liberate a big section of Hindu community (especially the lower caste and women), which was very much oppressed with some of its inhuman system of discrimination and dehumanizing practices, and the coming of Islam to India facilitated this movement to gain momentum, is to hold implicitly that there was nothing spiritual about it or that its spiritual aspect could be ignored as something quite personal. We fail to see, ordinarily, that the idea of reform towards which this view indicates derives its ethical import and practical significance only if we give some importance to what happened in the emotional experience of the *bhaktas'*. This point needs serious attention from all its aspects. An attempt is made in this regard at the end of this work This could be done properly only after many philosophical issues of both philosophical and practical importance are made clear. Obviously that could be done only at the end of this work. That is not the central task of this work and for some people it may not be needed at all. Others may find some interest in that, or perhaps find that more interesting than the central theme of the work. However, that task is not completely disconnected to the task of presenting the main theme of this work.

This work is an attempt to understand *bhakti* as it is experienced and conceived by the *bhaktas*. Only for the sake of avoiding confusion that it is some sort special or privileged understanding it is said in the above discussion that it is an attempt to understand *bhakti* from a common man's point of view. A *bhakta's* way of understanding *bhakti* and a common man's way of understanding can't be different radically or even substantively. So this work, which is a common man's attempt to understand it, is entitled as '**Understanding *Bhakti***' instead of 'A Common Man's Understanding of Bhakti'. It is already stated earlier that this work is not an attempt of interpreting any particular text on *bhakti*. Traditional and recent treatises on *bhakti* are quoted on various places but not for the sake of interpretation but only as a way to show how they become appropriate in our understanding of *bhakti*. There may be various interpretations of the texts of *bhakti* and some interpretation may not accord with our understanding. In such a condition this work should be seen as one possible way of understanding *bhakti*. This work is not a bold claim that this the only correct understanding. The author has no intension to defend this work on any ground of textual scholarship if it appears to someone as completely foolish or childish. Understanding of love does not require scholarship even the most illiterate person can understand it. It is true of love for the Lord also. It is felt in the heart even by the most uneducated and that is perhaps his right (*adhikār*) to talk about it. This work is being presented with this very humble sense of '*adhikār*'.

The work is spread over eight small chapters. They are not logically connected to each other but an interlink among them can be noticed easily. This is formed by the singularity of approach and emphasis. A sort of realism is emphasized about *bhakti*. *Bhaktas* do not explicitly lay emphasis on the reality of their experience of *bhakti* because they take it for granted and don't find it necessary to make explicit claim about it. A lover never finds it necessary to claim that the person whom he loves is a real person. A *bhakta* also has the same feeling about his dear Lord. But in a world that is guided by pragmatic considerations and defended by the tall claims of rationality and practical proof, *bhaktas'* this attitude is knowingly misinterpreted. *Bhakti,* for a 'practically successful and rationally calculative' person is a game of pure subjective projection that gives the person an emotional satisfaction but does not permit him to make any truth claims about his experience. It is, therefore, necessary to emphasize that no *bhakta* can ever agree with any *good and useful* interpretation of *bhakti* if it is based on the assumption that the Lord of their love is a fictitious entity and their assertions about Him can't be taken as a truth claim. No *bhakta* can ever make any compromise on this point. Any rationally consistent and practically useful interpretation of *bhakti* can be rated intellectually as very high but can't be accepted as the *bhaktas'* understanding of *bhakti*. Every chapter of this work emphasizes this implicit truth claim. Attempts made to do so may appear to be attempts of giving justification for the cognitive status of the assertions made by the *bhaktas* .At least there is no explicit or implicit intension behind such attempts. There seems to be no need for doing that since it is enough to understand that *bhaktas* mean by their assertions about their Lord that they are talking about a real state of affairs. If I mean to state an actual state of affair by making an assertion about it then at the most it can be shown to me that it is false but it can't be shown that what I mean is something other than what I mean to mean. My assertion about anything may be factually false and grammatically wrong but what I intend to is best known to me and others can understand it but can't know it better than me. My decision is final in this regard. *Bhaktas* intension in making assertions about their Lord is not to give vent to their feeling only but also to hold that what they talk is a real state if affairs. It is a different matter that we can prove in our own way that what they state is false but we can't prove that they don't mean that if they hold that they do so.

The First chapter is about the *bhaktas.* Whom do we call a *bhakta*? An attempt is made to answer the question in terms of *bhakti* that is a matter of experience and we all have some experience of it. As an emotion of love for the Lord it is difficult for anyone to hide it if he actually undergoes it. So the answer is simple. A *bhakta* is one who leads life in the light of his experience of *bhakti*, and we all understand what *bhakti* is since we all have experienced it.

The second chapter is an attempt to elaborate that point that is mentioned in the above paragraph. It is shown that the sympathetic treatments given to the *bhaktas'* understanding of *bhakti* in which the implicit truth-claim of the *bhaktas* is not taken into consideration is not a *bhaktas'* understanding of *bhakti.*

Third chapter is an elaboration of the theme of the second chapter. In order to understand what *bhakti* is for a *bhakta* we should carefully distinguish it from those interpretations of *bhakti* that don't consider it necessary to take into account *bhaktas'* understanding about it.

A *bhakta* never considers himself as the doer of any action. For him, His dear Lord alone is the doer of everything and he is merely an instrument in the hand of the Lord. *Bhakti* is a transformation of the doer into an instrument of the Lord. This is the content of the fourth chapter. For the *bhaktas* there is only one thing important in this world—to remember his dear Lord constantly and to try to attain His constant contact. A *bhakta* does not desire for any thing else. In his love for his Lord he wants to become worthy of his Lord's affection. He wants only what his Lord wants him to do. So the doer-ship gets easily transformed in the attitude of being an instrument of Lord. The hidden ego that flourishes in the garb of the doer disappears from the *bhaktas'* life.

The *bhaktas* live in this world not for any big or small aim except for Lord's love. This world, for him, is not merely a planet evolved out of certain natural laws just per chance. He finds the will of Lord operating in all natural phenomena. The question – *why did they world has come into being and why do the laws operate the way they operate?* — is a very significant question and can't be answered merely by explaining *how* things occur. His love for his Lord enables him to look at the world from an angle where divinity is seen to be manifesting from every particle of it. This is the subject discussed in chapter five. Chapter six is, in a way, an extension of chapter five. It shows that this world becomes a place worth living only because of the presence of Lord in it. There is no charm in living a world where material laws govern not only the material domain but also the psychic dimension of man. In *bhakti* the *bhakta* could see the divine presence behind every alleged material event of his life and those that are occurring around him. He gets extremely delighted over this.

Love is praised by the poets of all ages and *bhakti* is also seen a divine experience. *Bhakti* as a power (a *shakti*) is mentined in some *Śākta* texts but not very often explained from that point of view. Chapter six is an attempt to bring to fore this aspect of *bhakti.* Love itself is a force – a psychic force that is felt by the lover that keeps him attracted towards his beloved. The same force of attraction is felt by the *bhaktas* that draws his attention towards the Lord and keeps him attracted towards Him. This chapter delineates the function of this force at various levels of *bhaktas'* life.

The last chapter is about the *Bhagvan* of the *bhaktas.* God – the dear Lord of the *bhaktas* is not a metaphysical principle: He is the Supreme Person whom the *bhaktas* directly experience in *bhakti.* The attributes of Lord don't put limitation on His being but manifest His infinitude in various ways and forms.

An understanding of *bhakti* completes with a bit of understanding of the dear Lord of the *bhaktas.* So much is said about God in theologies and philosophy of religion. Both the attempts are good in many respects. Philosophical approaches to God try to look at this object of discussion as an independent ontological entity and its existence is either a matter of proof in the logical or mathematical sense or it is a presupposition for moral life. Faith in God is out and out a question of finding some rational support for it. This approach helps in casting a fresh glance over the entity that is called God in the practice of religious faith and enables us to make an effort to understand what it is or what it is like.

God in theologies of different theistic religions is an object of devotion. God in different religion is seen in some specific relation /relations. In actual practice of religion this relation, ordinarily, takes a ritualistic shape and makes some room in the life of every member of that religious community. Ritualistic worship or prayer is generally looked down upon in the light of modernity. However, this is what gives a practical significance to God in human life that could have been only a matter of speculation for a few. Going to temple and worshiping an idol, or going to church, bowing head before the cross and reciting some fixed prayers may appear to be an irrational act of superstition to a man of modern outlook. It is true also to some extant. But this is how God – a supra mundane entity of faith gets some space in the mundane routine of in human life. While condemning ritualistic worship we forget this practical aspect of it.

The attempt to understand the Lord of the *bhaktas—The Bhagvâna* God is made an object of understanding as He is experienced in an intimate emotional relation with man. In above discussion attempt is made to make it clear that this is not necessarily a way of understanding God in Hinduism but to understand primarily and essentially a human experience that provides us with a sort of direct reference for terms like 'Divine', 'Holy', 'Sacred', 'Transcendent' etc.. All these words will loose all the experiential significance without it. To understand *Bhgvâna* – the God of *bhakti,* is a way to remind ourselves that this word has an experiential significance also for us. Despite all our ignorance about the entity to whom this word refers to and all the modern or old attempts to make this word meaningless we all know that at some moment in our life we get a glimpse of that for which this word acquires perfectly appropriate meaning. We may later forget that or convince ourselves that it was just a weak moment but it can't be completely denied that all humans suffer from this weakness if at all it is a weakness. The *bhaktas* with all their humility admit all their weaknesses and surrender at the feet of that Unknown and open their hearts for Him. The Unknown at once begins to unfold in their life in the forms of inner contentment, ecstasy and fearlessness. These are not hidden from anyone's eyes. The experience of the *bhaktas* is not a proof of the existence of God; it is much more than that. They come to realize that how could not he feel the presence of his dear Lord earlier who was always with him so distinctively that makes the question of evidence just irrelevant. The last chapter of this work is an attempt to take this human experience seriously and to understand what the term '*bhagvâna*' refers to, to understand who the Lord the God of the *bhaktas* is! It is an attempt to point to a definite human experience whenever we use the term 'God'.

A discussion of *bhakti* remains merely a formal exercise unless it is related to the actual life of human being in historical condition. Bhakti descends or emerges in the heart of the *bhakta* and transforms him from inwardly. Not only the *bhakta* gets transformed by the emergence of *bhakti* but also the people who come in the contact of the *bhaktas* feel the touch of divine and get influenced by it. *Bhakti* is an experience that is personal like any other experience but it does not remain personal and tends to spread beyond the psychophysical existence of the *bhakta*. When a flower blooms its fragrance goes much beyond the spatial confinement of the tiny flower. When *bhakti* emerges in the heart of the person it cannot remain hidden in his heart; breaking all the limitations and boundaries of the individual confinement it reaches other individual also. It is therefore natural that a movement is felt by the people who come in the proximity of the *bhaktas*. Such a movement was registered by the historians in the history of medieval India as *Bhakti* Movement. 13th-15th century A.D. is regarded to be the period of *Bhakti* Movement. There may be controversy about the period of rise of *Bhakti* Movement. However, there is no dispute about the fact that such a movement was felt by the people of India.

Bhakti Movement is regarded by the historians as a movement of social reform of Hindu Society. It brought with it a kind of liberating effect. Discrimination on the ground of caste system and gender bias that was prevalent in Hindu society got a silent but effective, blow from this movement and the age-old orthodoxies lost its hold to a very large extent. Historians underline these features of *Bhakti* Movement, which is true of it, but it is very strange that hardly any attempt is made to show that this was an effect of the experience of *bhakti* that *bhkatas* felt in their hearts. On the whole it appears that most historians try to understand *Bhakti* Movement either by denying *Bhakti* completely or by giving some account of it that makes it anything else. The reason of it is intelligible. To admit *bhakti* as *bhakti* is to acknowledge indirectly the presence of divine in human life. Divine is a notion that necessarily brings with it the notions of supra mundane, eternity etc. All these terms go beyond the reference of sense experience and the scope of physical laws. So, some substitute for these terms are necessary to be postulated, to understand the history of a community in the so-called rationalistic framework. Either the historians have to turn a blind eye towards the experience of *bhakti* or leave it for the psychologists of modern times to find a suitable substitute for it. The reference to mystery that the experience of *bhakti* necessarily involves is not acceptable to the modern rationality. All the attempts to achieve this task bring forth certain theories of human psyche that make human mind more mysterious than any God of *bhakti.* We ordinarily fail to see that not only the *bhaktas* but also a common man understands without difficulty that a mystery manifests time and again in human life. The acceptance of this mystery does not really pose any rational problem either for the *bhaktas* of for the common man. Postulating new theoretical terminology does not help us in overcoming this peculiar fear from the presence of mystery in human life rather it makes it unnecessarily more problematic.

To understand *bhakti* as *bhakti* is the proper understanding of it. To understand *bhakti,* as anything else cannot be called a correct understanding of it. *Bhakti* Movement is a movement of *bhakti.* It was a mass movement that got its impetus from the powerful experience of love for the Lord that the *bhaktas* felt in the depths of their heart. *Bhakti* Movement, if understood properly, must involve reference to this powerful experience. Without this reference an attempt to understand *Bhakti* Movement could be an attempt to denature it if not pervert it. An attempt is made at the end of this work to understand *Bhakti* Movement as a movement of *bhakti*.

Poetry, music and other works of art directly or indirectly bring forth an element of mystery present in human life. This attempt is seen as an attempt to understand beauty of the sublime. We find no difficulty in talking about beauty or the sublime in our day-today life because the reference to mystery is not overtly given in them. However, if we try to capture the locus of beauty we find that it easily evades our physical space and time also. We call a work of art beautiful and also believe that it (beauty) is there in the work out there and not in the beholders imagination but we fail to point to the place where it is located. Our spatial references only become an occasion to make a link with our talk of beauty in artwork but that never really becomes the locus of it in the sense that a colour is located in a coloured object or hardness is there in a hard substance. Despite being something that involves sense organs beauty is not that perceived just by the opening of our sense organs to any object. This is a great wonder that we perceive beauty but cannot catch hold of it, and we cannot belie our experience either. This is what is called mystery. If we are susceptible enough we can find the presence of mystery in our most mundane activities. Aesthetic experience is a variety of experience in which mystery of human life manifests itself. We have no hesitation and fear in accepting it with the name of experiencing beauty. But this is merely a change of nomenclature. We should not hesitate unnecessarily or feel frightened irrationally to admit the presence of mystery in human life. If we liberate ourselves from this fear (there is no difficulty in so doing) then we can see the actual face of *Bhakti* Movement. As it is stated earlier this movement was guided by a force of divine that was actually felt in the heart of the *bhaktas* as *bhakti*. In the light of this acknowledgement we can see the function of divine force actually operating behind this mass movement that brought about a reform in Hindu society. It is made clear in course of discussing *Bhakti* Movement that the age-old religious imperatives and injunctions that were believed to be given by divine command directly cannot be challenged or even thought to be challenged if an equally strong divine force was not believed to be operating in the heart of the challenger. *Bhaktas* never challenged directly the superstitious and dogmatic practices of Hindu society but they never felt any fear to choose their path for themselves and their followers, which did not approve these practices at all. This fearlessness is never explained in course of discussing *Bhakti* Movement. Any discussion about *Bhakti* Movement about its explanation is an explanation to talk about a mass movement without referring to the actual reason or force operating behind it. Chaitnya, Ramananda, Kabir, Nanak, Namdev, all the *bhaktas* could lay their impact on the society just because of their experience of *bhakti.* Understanding of *bhakti* not merely as theoretical scaffolding but as an actual lived human phenomena, is necessary to understand *Bhakti* Movement as a historical reality. This understanding remains incomplete unless we bring in the reference of that experience that is called *bhakti.*

1

The *Bhakta*

Kṛṣṇa Who is a *bhakta*? The answer is plain and simple. One, who has *bhakti* in his heart, is a *bhakta*.

We as human beings have the intelligence and sensitivity to identify love. Love manifests in the look and in the behaviour of the person in love. It manifests in his look even if he tries to hide it in his overt behaviour. It is very difficult; almost impossible, to hide the feeling of love for someone. Often the attempt to hide the feeling of love becomes the reason for its disclosure. It is not difficult to notice such attempts of the person. By noticing it we come to know that he is in love with someone. The identity of the beloved also is disclosed in the look and behaviour of the lover. The deliberate attempt of hiding the fact that he is in love with a particular person becomes the reason for others to notice that he is in love with that person.

Love is not anyone's personal feature. Only when it emerges in someone's heart for someone then he becomes a lover. Through his look and behaviour a person's love manifests. So it is clear that through love we recognize a lover.

Bhakta is a Lover: Lover of Lord

Bhakta also is a lover- a lover of his Lord the God. A *bhakta* also is recognized by the presence of *bhakti* in his heart. A *bhakta* can never hide his *bhakti* since it is the purest and most intense form of love. Several characteristic behavioural features of a *bhakta* are stated by different *rişi* who have written the *Sutras* of *Bhkati*. Narada states that one, who attains *bhakti* becomes stunned, gets intoxicated with the bliss and tears flow profusely from his eyes due to excessive joy. Shandilya also has given many characteristics of the *bhaktas*[1]. A *bhakta* does not try to do these things. These are the spontaneous manifestation of his love for his dear Lord. So there is no problem in recognizing a *bhakta*. A false problem arises only if we try to define *bhakti* through the features of *bhaktas*. Although *bhakti* manifests in and through the look and behaviour of the *bhaktas* it is not *their* specialty. Love is not the specialty of the lover. To define *bhakti* as the specialty of *bhaktas* would be as fallacious and foolish as it would be if love is defined as the specialty of the lover. As we recognize that someone is in love with someone, we also recognize that someone is in love with a supreme person—whom the tradition teaches us to name Lord the 'God'.

A *bhakta* is a common man like anyone of us, yet he is very different. The Object of his *bhakti* — his Lord acquires the central place in his life. Everything else falls on the periphery. In this respect he is very different from others. A non-*bhakta* has nothing to place at the centre of his life, and even if he has some object or objective to place at the centre, it is not, ordinarily, the object of (emotional) love. All lovers don't give central importance to their love affairs. For the *bhaktas*, however,the emotional love for hisLord is everything[2]. For *bhaktas bhakti* is valuable since in and through it he comes in the contact of his dear Lord. This contact gives him tremendous emotional joy that makes him forget everything else including his earlier identity. The typical bliss of *bhakti* that makes him lose his identity is the temptation of the *bhaktas*. In love of his Lord the *bhaktas* gets himself completely dissolved. He gets this joy only in the emotional relation to the object of his *bhakti* (i.e. his dear Lord). Hence *bhakti* acquires central place in his life. It does not mean to say that other people don't have anything of central importance in their lives. Others may have an objective in life that acquires central place in their lives but their relation with that objective is either purely rational or even if it has an emotional aspect then it is not given central importance.

Bhaktas have a peculiar sort of identity and it is very dear to him. His identity emerges from his personal relation with the object of his *bhakti*—with his Lord. A *bhakta* either dilutes his socially constructed identity completely or makes it completely subservient to his relational identity that he develops with his dear Lord. He gets himself involved emotionally with his Lord in some personal relation such as servant, companion, beloved etc. and this relation becomes his identity. He does all his work keeping him in this relation and likes to be recognized and addressed by this very relation. A *bhakta* may be a teacher or a student, he maybe an officer or a subordinate but he is essentially a *bhakta.* Although this identity also is a constructed identity but this is not his false identity since he feels it from within and does not just carry it subconsciously as a borrowed load. If you ask a *bahkta* about his identity the most expected spontaneous reply is something like — 'I am the servant of my Lord'. Only after a second thought or on a further enquiry he would tell about his social position or status.

The *bhakta* gets new friends and new enemies due to this identity. He at once enters into friendship with the people who also love his dear Lord. No other considerations regarding such a person come in the way of this suddenly grown friendship. Caste, creed and gender don't come in the way of this friendship. Even if the person is socially condemned but loves the Lord he becomes lovable to the *bhaktas.* He wants the company of all those who love his Lord. He enjoys this company very much and aspires to pass more and more time with them since this helps him come closure to his Lord.

Bhaktas don't want to come in the contact of the persons who talk ill of his dear Lord but he does not enter into active confrontation with them. This is not the sign of his weakness. This point needs elaboration.

Bhaktas Avoid Confrontation with The Persons Who Talk Ill of Their Lord

The *bhakta* does not actively oppose them who oppose his Lord but tries to keep himself away from them. He himself does not make enemies but can't stop others to make enmity with him. He, however, remains indifferent to them. Narad Bhakti Sutra states——'*Tadwirodhiṣudasintāī*'. In this respect the *bhaktas* are different from ordinary lovers of mortal persons. A lover can't tolerate a word against his beloved and resorts to an active confrontation with the opponent. He, at least, wants to oppose strongly the critic of his beloved even if he can't practically do so. A *bhakta*, on the other hand, does not do that and does not even want to do that at all. He knows that by so doing he will engage himself in a brawl that is not only useless but also injurious to his *bhakti*. He understands that such a quarrel can't yield any good fruit and it would waste his valuable time that he could have used in remembering his Lord. So he abstains from such confrontations. This is ordinarily looked at a sort of escapism on the part of the *bhakta*. This is a valid criticism of the *bhakta* for all those people who give central importance to the affairs of material world. For a *bhakta* his *bhakti* for the Lord alone is central to his life. A *bhakta* would abstain from any act that disturbs him from his *bhakti*. Hearing ill of his Lord is unbearable for him, but confrontation is not only disturbing but also more sinful because by so doing he engages the critics more in committing a great sin (of talking ill of the Lord). He knows that the critic is corrupting himself by saying dirty things against the most benevolent Lord Who is the source and sustainer of his (critic's) life too. But he also knows that if he will try to stop him then he will react more vehemently and speak more ill of the Lord. Confrontation with the critics of the Lord is doubly injurious from a *bhakta's* standpoint. So he abstains from all such confrontations. This is not escapism. It is pity and compassion for the opponents.

Avoiding confrontation with his opponents is not at all a sign of the *bhaktas'* weakness of intellect or that of will. They deliberately choose to avoid such confrontation for above reason only. On appropriate occasions it is proved from their overt behaviour also that they are not weak either of intellect or that of will. When they find that their opponents want to stop him from singing the glory of his Lord or remember His holy name or doing anything of the sort then they come up clearly (but not violently) against such obstruction. On such occasions the *bhaktas* never hesitate in paying any price for it.

Bhaktas' attitude to avoid confrontation is inspired by their intension to save the opponents from wrath of his dear Lord. This wrath could be rationally intelligible as the fire of anger and hatred that burns the critic when he speaks ill of the Lord. But the *bhaktas* are not rationalist thinkers. They are the lovers who believe and speak what their hearts make them speak Their are dedicated to their Lord, *Bhaktas* strongly believe that their dear Lord never minds the words spoken against Him. Their Lord never becomes angry with any one who talks ill of Him but never forgives anyone who oppresses His dear *bhaktas*[3]. This belief discloses the *bhaktas'* unbound love for the Lord. But along with that it also reveals a truth that only the *bhaktas* could understand or they can understand who understand *bhaktas'* love for the Lord. A *bhakta* could see that one, who speaks ill of him due to his *bhakti* and obstructs his ways of offering his love, actually tries to close the possibilities of manifestation of divine grace in and through human consciousness and behaviour. Such a person does not close only his heart for divine descend but wants to chock the way of that descend in all hearts. He puts himself in direct confrontation with the power of divine grace that has descended in the *bhakts'* heart. He does not believe in the existence of any such power and thinks that it is all the *bhakta's* own imaginative creation. But that, which gives unbound ecstasy to the *bhakta's* heart, is a real power. Although it manifests through the *bhata's* life, it is not a product of his psyche. Obstruction in the way of this independently existing power results in very many ways and its consequences surface in the life of his opponent definitely. Ordinarily such adverse consequences are not noticed by the opponent and other people but *bhakta* can at once see it. He could see that the opponent has deprived himself from the divine grace and rendered himself into a puppet in the hand of blind material forces. How painful this situation is –only a *bhakta* can understand; or they can understand who understand *bhakti*. To distance oneself from the grace of the Lord is to reduce oneself into a lifeless material object. This is the wrath of the Lord. *Bhaktas* are very sensitive people. They can't tolerate that any one should become a target of Lord's wrath. When obstructed by the opponents of the Lord, they definitely do what the opponent stops him to because he can't tolerate to see that he (the opponent) becomes a target of his dear Lord's wrath due to him. Talking ill of the Lord also, in the eyes of the *bhaktas,* is to deprive oneself from the Lord's grace. However, it does not make the opponent an actual destitute untill he resorts to obstruct the *bhaktas'* way of performance. By so doing he only impoverishes himself at the level of speech and thought. When a person starts obstructing the *bhaktas* in performing *bhakti* actively then his life becomes actually affected By actively engaging himself in opposing the manifestation of divine grace in and through the *bhaktas'* life he actually chooses to close all doors of his life for divine grace His life (not merely thought and speech) becomes an instance of Lord's wrath in the eye's of the *bhaktas*. To save him from becoming the target of Lord's wrath the *bhaktas* do positively from what the opponents wants to stop. If the opponent is determined not to allow the *bhakta* to sing the glory of the Lord then he (the *bhakta*) tries to manage the situation so that he could sing his Lord's glory without making it noticeable to the opponent. If he finds that it is not possible at all by any means then he sings before the opponent and gets ready to face the consequence and leave everything on the will of his dear Lord. So the *bhaktas'* abstaining from active confrontation with the opponents can't be regarded as any form of escapism or his weakness. There are number of examples of *bhaktas'* sacrifices in the *bhaktas'* biography and in the history of *Bhakti* Movement of this land

Bhaktas Avoid Confrontation with The Social and Scriptural Laws

Bhaktas are above the reigns of customary social conventions and ritualistic injunctions. They are absolutely free. No lover ever fears violating any social laws that come between him and his beloved. He does not bother for the consequences. He is prepared to pay any cost for it. Love liberates a person from fears. *Bhaktas* also are not bound by social or Vedic imperatives[4]. His love for his Lord overrides all other conventional considerations. They don't desire for anything either of this world or of the other worlds for which Vedic *yajnâs* are performed. Love for the Lord is the only thing that they want to remain engrossed in and don't care to obey the social laws and Vedic injunctions. They follow only those laws that suits to their *bhakti.* Although they don't actively engage themselves in opposing these laws they have to pay for not following them and sometimes very heavily too. But they don't want to come in direct confrontation with social or scriptural laws. This is also a point of difference between an ordinary lover and a *bhakta.* A lover never likes to accept any binding over his relation with his beloved. A *bhakta*, on the other hand, avoids deliberate violation of the social and scriptural laws as far as possible. He knows that in following the conventional injunctions he would have to suppress natural expression of many of his feeling to his dear Lord but he also knows that by deliberately violating them he would engage others to stand against himself and make them the targets of Lord's wrath, which he can't tolerate. He does not want to deprive either himself or other from the grace of the Lord. He enjoys this invaluable grace directly in the form of blissful *bhakti* and wants to keep its scope open for others. By a clear proclamation against some social and scriptural laws he does not want to make others (the defenders of these laws) sinful and make himself doubly sinful. That is why we find that although the *bhaktas* have surpassed the boundaries of such laws in their words and deeds but didn't give a call to abolish them. They preach only that in *bhakti* of Lord, observance of these laws are not necessary and can be dispensed with. If someone is being oppressed by these laws a *bhakta*, inspired by his *bhakti,* can come to rescue him or her but he does not set it as his agenda. It is all because being a sensitive creature he does not want to harm even them who oppress others in the name of implementation of these laws. All the *bhaktas* have categorically said that caste does not come in the way of Lord's *bhakti* but none of them have ever clearly waged a war against caste system. They did not said anything against the age-old tradition of caste system but by their words and deeds they proved that it can't be allowed to debar human beings from the grace of the Lord. From the point of view of social reform it may appear to be an implicit Conformism that maintains status quo. From the *bhakta's* standpoint it is the only possible effective way to save himself and to the defenders of the system from losing the opportunities of *bhakti* – the greatest gift of the Lord.

Present day scenario shows that movements against caste system and other scriptural injunctions create an anti-current which seems to resist the oppression against a group pf people but very soon they themselves result into an oppression against the former oppressors and become instruments to perpetuate the system of oppression. Social scientists can defend this situation as an essential process of war against oppression and they can prove it to be progressive too. *Bhaktas* are not concerned primarily with caste system or any other system of discrimination practiced in the name of scriptural injunctions. Their sole concern is the love of the Lord and they say and do seriously all that help in achieving it and removing obstacles in its path. *Bhakta's* way to avoid direct confrontation with the age-old social and scriptural laws and to initiate people into the path of *bhakti* where these laws become ineffective can be seen as an alternative solution to end the tyranny of such laws. .*Bhaktas* are not primarily social reformers. It is needless to say that their primary interest is not in the change of a prevailing social order. Their concern is to change radically the world-centered way of life into the Lord-centered way of life. Certain social changes are bound to take place in this process as unintended consequences. The *bhakta* wants to save himself and others from the hazardous effects of these unintended consequences. He, therefore, avoids confrontation. But by his intension and its implementation he definitely raises a way of life that results into a new social order.

Bhakta is The Living Abode of Divinity

The most appropriate description about the *bhaktas'* identity is to state that they are the living abode of divinity although due to our over occupation with our mundane affairs we can't perceive this plain fact and habitually project them as abnormal, impractical, overly introvert, escapist creatures. A critical glance at this attitude of ours would help us realize that such descriptions are not the judgment of our reason. We make such comments either due to certain ideology that we adhere to or due to the habit of passing any mean comment against any one who does not enjoy any powerful social position. *Bhaktas* are ordinary simple persons who have made their hearts fully open for the satisfaction of one single desire – to get the love of his Lord. Love is a sublime emotion that overwhelms the person. Divine love –love for the Lord is a heavenly gift which very few people avail. We usually fail to notice this simple fact about the *bhakta.* Undoubtedly we understand that this person (*bhakta*) is in love because we can't fail to understand that someone is in love if he is in love with someone. But when we come to know that this person is in love with Lord the God then we only laugh and think that he is lost in his imagination. We take the lovers seriously (at time very seriously too) but, ordinarily, we don't take the *bhaktas* seriously. As a person's love for some one is an emotion that is actually present in his heart, a *bhakta's* love for his Lord also is an emotion that is *actually* present in the *bhakta's* heart. We give importance to the love of the former but don't give importance to the latter. It is peculiar that we hardly ever feel to reflect upon this uncritical attitude. Only the lovers of the *bhaktas* could see this peculiar irrationality, or anyone, who could see this irrationality, becomes a lover of the *bhaktas* and can understand him and his *bhakti.*

It is necessary to perceive that a *bhakta* is experiencing the same emotion for his Lord as a lover experiences for his beloved. The kind of psychic attraction felt by a lover for his beloved is also felt by the *bhakta* for his Lord. This is something that no one can generate by his sheer will. A lover feels attracted towards his beloved but he does not generate this feeling; he can't do that. No one loves any one because he willed to love. It just happens out of one's control that one falls in love with someone. A *bhakta* also *falls* in love with his Lord; he does not first decide to love the Lord and then loves him. It just happens beyond his control. Seeing a *bhakta* in love with Lord someone may yearn badly to have that sort of experience but can't produce it within him. If we notice this fact then we can understand that a *bhakta* also is a real lover. Despite our ignorance about the person whom he loves we have to admit that he is actually in love.

A *Bhakta's* love is, quite obviously, not a mundane affair. His beloved Lord is not a physical body. Hence he can't have any physical kind of relation with the Lord even if the *bhakta* aspires for it. A *bhakta* may love his Lord tying himself in any worldly relation wit Him (his Lord) but can't actually translate it into bodily satisfaction. He enjoys the bliss of this relation at the pure psychic and supra psychic levels of his being. Despite being perplexed by the questions as to what sort of enjoyment is this and how is it possible we witness (if we don't overlook him) that he is lost in a peculiar enjoyment.

Doubt is not The Way to Ascertain Who is A *Bhakta*

The question – 'Who is *bhakta*?'— is a straight question and its answer also is straight. One who feels the emotion of love for Lord is a *bhakta*. Practically also there is no difficulty in identifying *bhaktas* since as it is already stated it is very difficult for any lover to hide his emotion may he be a lover of ordinary mortal or that of the supreme person –his dear Lord. This simple question does not remain a simple one when it takes the form of a doubt that tends to fix the identity of the *bhakya* within certain conditions. We want to ascertain the identity of the *bhakta* in terms of our personal or collective evaluation about his social behaviour. We want to see that a person, who is said to be a *bhakta*, should not be a condemned fellow in our personal or collective judgment. We can't expect from a *bhakta* to be a thief. In a way this is a right expectation. A *bhakta* desires for his Lord's love only. He should not have the desire for someone else wealth that motivates a person for committing theft. So we want to draw the strong conclusion that a *bhakta* can't be a thief. But this strong conclusion can't be practically acceptable due to following two reasons.

(i) Love for the Lord is necessary for a person to be called a *bhakta*. There should only one desire in the heart of the *bhaktas* – the desire for Lord's love. This the state of that *bhakta* who has reached very high stage of *bhakti*. This is that stage of a lover who has forgotten everything else in the love of his beloved. But there are lovers who truly love their beloved but desire for so many other things also in their lives. Some of these desires may be socially commendable may be condemnable. That does not prove that he does not love, his beloved. A *bhakta* also may have, at a lower stage of *bhakti* genuinely love for his Lord and at the same time he may have some good and some socially condemnable desires in his heart. It is his love for the Lord present at that moment in his heart that makes him a *bhakta* and not the future possibility of this love that would one day make him forget everything else. The future possibility, if realized, would make him a *bhakta* of highest order but the presence of Lord's love at that moment is the decisive factor about his identity as *bhakta* right now.

(ii) A *bhakta* of a high stage also may, in some situations or with some special purpose, do something socially condemnable like theft but such acts only make us review our social structure and the standards of evaluation of human acts. A saint, with a purpose to help the prisoners to alleviate their wounded conscience and show them light of divine, may commit some theft and .may go to jail. This act does not prove by any means that he has no love for his Lord. He may do such acts with a divine inspiration. In some such cases we can understand the special purpose of the *bjakta* but it is not always possible to understand his purpose within our rigid system of evaluation. A *bhakta's* life and purposes are guided and controlled by his love for his Lord. This is totally independent of our accepted system of evaluation of a deed. The former may partly concord with the latter but even that concordance is accidental. Hence it is possible that a *bhakta* might prove to be a thief according to our evaluation but it can't be taken to be a reason to reject that he is a *bhakta.* This does not amount to making room for allowing the *bhaktas* to be corrupt, or relaxing the moral rule for him. A *bhakta* might be a thief in the beginning but can't continue to be so till end without sacrificing his love for the Lord. If he will pursue the path of *bhakti* then after sometime he will reach a stage where he would forget everything completely except the love for his Lord. The desire for other's wealth that motivates a person for stealing is bound to be abandoned by the *bhakta* sooner or later. This transformation, however, is completely independent of personal or collective evaluation by others. It is needless to say that a *bhakta,* who happened to be a thief earlier, drops stealing not because he comes in agreement with the social evaluation that stealing is wrong but because he because with the increase in the intensity of his love for his Lord he just forgets everything else.

In the light of above discussion about the two reasons it is clear that an attempt to fix the identity of the *bhakta* according to our system of evaluation is a wrong move. But it would be wrong to draw the conclusion on this basis that a *bhakta* may be a bad person too. As it is stated in the beginning of this discussion, it is indeed a doubt about the *bhakta* that gives rise to such a problem. It Is not a simple curiosity of identifying who is a *bhakta* but a doubt the *bhakta's* character that leads to such problems. The situation of identification of the *bhakta* is not a problematic situation. It is our attitude towards this question that makes it problematic. The same problematic situation becomes a solution to the problem if we reverse the statement –'A *bhakta* may be a thief'. By reversal we get the statement – 'A thief may be a *bhakta*'. This reversal, however, is not a verbal reversal. It is reversal of attitude. By saying that a *bhakta* may be a thief—we doubt not merely the character of a *bhakta* but also express our doubt about the possibility of any person's character. On the other hand, by saying that a thief can be a *bhakta* we keep a rational possibility open for a radical change in his life. As a thief he must be prosecuted and punished according to the socially adopted law. But the fact that he is a socially proclaimed thief does not necessarily deprive him from the divine boon of *bhakti* (love for the Lord). A thief is not debarred from the divine gift of *bhakti*. It is possible that *bahkti* may emerge in the heart of a thief but a socially proclaimed good man's heart may be empty of it. By an actual investigation about the truth of the former statement we come to know that the person under investigation is/is not a thief. We can't know anything else. By an actual investigation about its truth of the latter we come to know that in the heart of the thief under investigation love for God is/is not present. In the former we come to know something about an ordinary fact about this familiar world. In the latter we come to know something extra-ordinary about this familiar world. We must make an actual investigation of the former statement but we should not overlook the latter. We must take the latter statement also into consideration and should make an honest investigation about its truth too. The former investigation enables us to know that he is a thief if he is that. But to know whether a person, be a thief or non-thief, is a *bhakta* we will have to investigate the truth of the latter. We can know a *bhakta* by accepting the possibility that anyone, even a thief, can be a *bhakta*. To ascertain who is a *bhakta* we should begin our search with this attitude. With this attitude we can accept anyone as a *bhakta* who feels some emotional attraction for any image of God. It is not of much importance what sort of image he has. His emotional attraction for it is the only important thing. This emotional attraction can take many different forms. This point needs some elaboration.

A person in distress looks for someone's help to come out of it. Ordinarily he expects that someone mortal being like him would help him. If he has lost all hope from a mortal agency then either he sinks in the state of utter despair or he hopes for a supra natural help. In case he hopes for a supra natural help in the form of a miracle then if he has got any image of God from his tradition, his attention gets emotionally connected to it in search of help. Even if he has never remembered God about whom his tradition told him so much, he expects help from Him. This can be called selfishness but it shows undoubtedly an emotional attachment of that person with the God of his image. A selfish son, who is in distress, exposes himself if he expects some help from his father whom he had forsaken long ago but it undoubtedly also shows that at least in those moments he sincerely feels that he is his father. An emotional attachment that a son feels for his father becomes alive in his heart at that moment. A distressed person's cry for help from his God also shows his true love (in those moments) for Him. His other acts of selfishness can't belie his that moment's love for his God. We must take it as one of the forms of love for God that manifests in human life.

A person with an objective in the mind may also seek help of others for his success. The other may be an ordinary mortal but if he knows that it is not possible then he may expect help from a supra human agency—from the God of his belief. This sort of emotional attachment also can be blamed for selfishness but, as it is explained in the above paragraph, it also shows the presence of love for God in the heart of the believer at least in those moments when he sincerely expects for the help. Hence this also is to be taken as another form of love for God.

A seeker of worldly knowledge also may expect help for the success in his pursuit from a supra human agency. In order to find a definite direction or the solution of a puzzling problem one may beg help from the God of his belief if one is frustrated in one's efforts. One may seek this sort of help even if one is not frustrated. One can from the very beginning of one's endeavour pray to God for revealing the truth one is seeking. So a sincere seeker also may enter into an emotional attachment with God. This should also be taken a third type of manifestation of love for God.

A wise person, who has attained knowledge of ultimate truth, who has attained knowledge of his real self, may attain it in the emotional attachment with the God of his belief. Knowledge of ultimate truth can be attained by many other ways but an emotional attachment with one's Lord definitely gives this knowledge. A *bahkta* in the love of his Lord loses himself and regains himself as one with his Lord. Hence some seekers of real self may also enter into an emotional attachment with God of his belief. This is different from the love of the seekers of worldly knowledge and from all other forms of love for God. In all other forms God is loved for something else. As it is stated earlier the love is not false although it is not an end in itself. The love for God for the attainment of real self in Him is a love for God Himself. It is an end in itself. In fact, in *Âtma Jnâna* (knowledge of one's real self), from whatever way is it attained, one becomes aware of it essential identity with the supreme unbound absolute consciousness and it essentially manifests in a very high level of emotional attachment for it[5]. *Âtma Jnâna* is not a bare conceptual knowledge. It is an existential enlightenment that manifests at all dimensions of one's being. An emotional manifestation of this knowledge is quite natural. This may take many forms like reverence, devotion, surrender etc. But all that are forms of love sublime. This forth type of sublime love is deemed to be the highest form of *bhakti*[6].

Bhaktas and *Jnânis* are not necessarily opposed to each other. A *bhakta* essentially is a *Jnâni. Bhakta* without *jnâna* is a practical impossibility. However, the difference between the two is meaningful for all practical purposes. Not everyone could be called '*bhakta*'. The tradition to which the person belongs makes a significant role in this nomenclature. It is necessary to understand this difference for avoiding the confusion that it is only a matter of collective decision by a community to call itself with this or that name.

The *Bhkta* is Ontically The Same with The *Jâni* but Epistemically He is Different

Ordinarily we divide human life in its three dimensions – cognitive, emotive and active. Although each one affect the other dimension to some extent it is regarded that the cognitive dimension should remain unaffected with the other two— especially with the emotive dimension. Since emotional adherence to any view comes in the way of its unbiased critical examination it is seen as a hindrance to the pursuit of truth. Hence in common or rational pursuit of knowledge we keep away our emotional inclinations. In the search of one's real self also emotions are regarded as obstacles. The seekers of *Âtma Jnâna* are supposed to have renounced all emotional attachment. A seeker of *Bhakti* does not necessarily renounce his emotional relations but he tries to develop some emotional relation with God. A *bhakta* puts his emotional relation with his Lord at the centre and all other relations fall on the periphery. This experience grows very fast and soon the *bhakta* is placed at that level in which emotional attachment with Lord transforms into the emotional attraction for his emotional attachment with the Lord itself since he comes to realize that it is in this very experience that he comes in contact with his Lord. Growth of *bhakti* eventually yields this realization to the *bhakta*. This realization is an essential aspect of *bhakti*. A *jnâni*, on the other hand, does not give any importance to emotion either in the beginning or in the end of his journey not because he does not find any emotional content in his realized state. It is impossible for any *jnâni* not to experience the bliss which is a very high emotional state of being. His attention, however, is drawn to the cognitive content of this experience and the emotive dimension of it falls on the periphery.

Although in the life of a *jnâni* emotional dimension of self-realization falls on the periphery he does not remain ignorant of its relevance or significance. He does not overtly give importance to it for various reasons. There is pragmatic reason for it. He observes that emotions keep a person tied to objects and persons of physical world. Even the emotion of love fixes the attention of the lover on his beloved. The sublimity of the experience of love, which is present in every ordinary experience, also is left unattended in ordinary cases of love. The non-physical essence of one's being, thus, can't come in attention. So a *jnâni* avoids and instructs others also to avoid emotional attachment in general.

There is another reason also for so doing. To attain the state of self-awareness in the condition of complete detachment with all that is not an extension of consciousness is the aim of a *jnâni.* This is fundamentally and essentially a cognitive endeavour. If the emotive dimension of this endeavour, which necessarily ensues in the form of bliss at its every step, is given any attention then complete attention to the process of cognition would be just impossible. Hence in the path of *Jnâna* the seeker is instructed not to be infatuated by the blissfulness of the intermediary stages at all. This is the reason for a *jnâni's* abstain from emotional attraction in the world without and in the world within.

Afore stated reasons distinguish a *bhakta* from a *jnâni.* Despite their ontic sameness they are epistemically very different from each other. This difference at times result into an unfortunate confrontation of a *jnâni* with a *bhakta.* Although it is true that it shows the ignorance left as a residue in the *jnân* and such incidents become an occasion for flushing out that residue form his life in this world, this confrontation is not on a superficial issue of superiority of knowledge over emotion. The *jnâni* despite the presence of some residue of ignorance in the affairs of his worldly life is not an easy pray of ordinary mundane matters. He falters only in the situation where he thinks a supra mundane issue of pure consciousness is involved in a mundane affair. A *bhakta's* repeated emphasis on the emotional attachment with an image of God becomes such a situation where a *jnâni* can easily falter since he (the *bhakta*) also talks of the supra mundane state of consciousness. However, this is an unfortunate situation, history tells us that ordinarily it results into a happy ending in which the *jnâni's* last residue of ignorance is washed away and the *bhakta* also gets enriched by getting a friend of his level of experience with who he can have a direct heart to heart dialogue.

In the light of above discussion the identity of a *bhakta* emerges in both its aspects—positive and negative. In the positive aspect of his identity the *bhakta* is a lover of his Lord for the sake of His love alone. In the negative aspect—despite his ontic sameness with the *jnâni* he is not a *jnâni* procedurally or epistemically.

Some Unfamiliar Manifestation of Love Sublime

Bhaktas are in love with their Lord. But at times this emotional attraction, which is a supra-psychic force indeed, arise in human heart in a strange form of feeling that is not easily identified as love. A sense of mystery often generates a feeling of awe. This feeling, however, is not a repulsive one. It is somewhat so huge or intense in its magnitude that an ordinary person can't bear it because he is not used to come across it regularly. Because of its unfamiliarity it is very strange for a person in the negative sense. But it is not merely unfamiliarity that generates awe in him. Unfamiliar experiences, if they are or have to become the part of regular encounter, become familiar and the sense of awe also vanishes completely or reduced substantively. They no more remain mysteries. The vision of an ocean without any visible shore, the endless expansion and depth of clear sky at night and many other sights of similar strangeness attract our attention and fill our heart with awe. These sights gradually loose their strangeness if we regularly see them and we become insensitive to their hugeness also. But there is a positive element of strangeness in some of human experiences that never disappears despite its regular occurrences. Although such experiences are not very common because they are not available to all of us as a routine phenomenon of our life yet they are human experiences due to the simple reason that they occur to human beings as far as our knowledge goes. These putatively known mystical experiences are experiences of those persons who entered (or made to enter) into them very often and despite its frequency of occurrence it always remained strange and unfathomable for them. A person, who undergoes this experience, individuates and recognizes it due to its content but this content is uniquely identified because of its uniqueness only, i.e. the person identifies it as something unearthly. He realizes that he has never experienced anything earlier in his life. So the strangeness is never lost. The tremendous expansion and power of this experience also makes him perplexed every time because it happens at a point beyond which human sensitivity ordinarily doesn't go. Naturally such an experience is awe-inspiring because before its expansion makes the person feel himself extremely dwarf. This is awe-inspiring because of its hugeness but it is not frightening for him. This experience does not tend to destroy the person's existence. The person rather finds himself safe and secured in this experience. This results into a natural feeling of reverence. A huge power that can at once destroy any one's existence, if does not even indirectly assert its power to demean the person, naturally becomes an object of utmost reverence. This is a form of emotional attraction towards this power in which the person desires to be in its protection. This is a form of love. It may be difficult for the person to acknowledge in the beginning that it is a form of love but all his descriptions and behaviours show that he feels a great emotional attraction towards that power and wants to remain in its protection which is assured when he experiences it. The excessive power may come in the way of the person's explicit acceptance that he loves it but sooner or latter by the same person or by some other person having undergone the same variety of experience it can be acknowledged explicitly. What for Moses was an experience of a Lord of tremendous power, became an experience of the Lord of love. If it is not an experience of a love sublime then it can't be religious or divine since then it would be leaving the person unsecured and frightening and reverence can't rise in his heart. Reverence is a typical human feeling that shows simultaneously that the person finds divinity in the object towards whom his feeling is directed and that he loves it.

At the end of this chapter we develop an understanding about the identity of *bhakta*. We have come to understand that a *bhakta* is one who has unbound love for his Lord. Through the presence of *bhakti* i.e. the love for the Lord, a person is identified as the *bhakta* and it is not difficult to know that someone s in love with Lord. However, certain questions regarding the reality of Lord, Who is the object of *bhakti*, make common people puzzled and in the absence of a definite answer they form either a pervert superstitious view or prefer to buy a so called fashionably rational view. It becomes, therefore, necessary to understand *bhakti*. We have to understand *bhakti* from the stand point of the *bhaktas*. That is the subject matter of the next chapter.

References

1. *Ka Kthâvardharomâncâúrubhih paeasparam lâpmânâh pâwayantikulâniprithvin c.Sutra —68, Narad Bhakti Sutra*

2. Some great thinkers like Spinoza talk about God's rational love. They are *jnanis*- the followers of the path of Knowledge. They would not like to be recognized as *bhaktas* since they take the emotional love as a sort of weakness, call it 'passive emotion' or passion and advise to shun it. However, Spinoza also talks of an active emotion of joy that one gets in intuitive knowledge in which one finds oneself connected to God. This point will be explained later.
3. There are many stories in Sri Mad Bhagvat that states that Lord never minds for the *Devâparâdha* but never forgives *VaishKavâparâdha*. The story of Durwasha's anger against *bhakta* Ambareesh is well knon.
4. *Niridhastu Lok Vedavyâpâmyâsah* – 8, Narad Bhakti Sutra.
5. Spinoza calls it a rational love for God (*Amor Intellectualis Dei*). This is an emotion that arises not because of any weakness or desire for anything but due to the tremendous spiritual strength that one gains by knowing one's inextricable connection with God.
6. In *Bhagvad Geetait* it is strated- *Catur vidhâ bhajante mâmjanâh sukritinorjunah Ârto jgnâsurathârthi jnâni c bhartar°bha, 16, chapter -7*

2

Difference in the *Bhaktas*' Understanding of *Bhakti* for the Lord and that of a Non-*Bhakta*

Kṛṣṇa! Before making an attempt to understand the difference between the *bhakta's* feelings for his Lord and that of a non-*bhakta* it would be helpful to understand the difference between a lover's feelings for his beloved and that of a non-lover. Ordinarily a lover, who is mad after his beloved, complains that others don't understand his feelings and laugh at him. This complaint is not taken seriously from an epistemic point of view. It is ordinarily ignored as a kind of emotional exaggeration or delirium. Something very important is missed in this sort of irrational preoccupation regarding lover's statement about the ineffability of his feelings. Due to an irrational adherence to the model of factual statements resulting from sense experience we miss an opportunity to explore the non-rational component of the meaning of an important kind of statement—statement about one's emotional experience.

If a person, on looking at an object, finds it red and states that it is red then most of us don't doubt the truth of his statement. If the same person falls in love with someone and states something about some quality of his beloved then most people don't readily accept the truth of his statement and think that it is either false or exaggeration although the person says only what he actually feels. We make such discrimination on the assumption that in the state of emotion a person fails to see the real attributes of the object of emotion. It is assumed that normal sense experience is purely objective i.e. free from subjective influences resulting from emotional attraction or aversion etc. Although most of us implicitly hold this assumption and never cast a critical glance over it, it is not rationally acceptable. What a person perceives in sense experience is not purely objectively given. Personal psychic conditions directly influence person's perception. Out of several stimuli present at any point of time a person chooses only one to attend at a time and rest are left in the backdrop. This choice of the person is determined not only by external factors but also by his personal likings. A person's likes and dislikes, his emotional attachment to an object etc. indirectly determines both the content and form of perception. It needs some elaboration.

Certain Features of an Object can be Known Only in Emotional Attachment with it

When a person perceives something certain objects remain in the fore ground and many objects form its backdrop. The interchangeability of foreground (figure) and backdrop is an accepted psychological fact and in case of Gestalt pictures this interchangeability is easily noticed. However, in ordinary instances of perception also the content and the form of perception undergo a substantive change (even if not radical change) if certain items of backdrop are assimilated in the foreground figure and this is done by an active decision of the perceiver. An example will make this point clear. Let us suppose that a person is watching a scene of a movie in which the hero is dancing with his beloved and so many character artists also are dancing in the backdrop. Suppose, suddenly the person decides to look at one of the character-artists who is present in the backdrop. Just on will he can focus his attention on that artist by withdrawing it from the main artists. Since it is a scene of a movie in which the figure and backdrop are placed rigidly on their positions, the backdrop doesn't change into figure and the figure doesn't recede into backdrop but perception of that person definitely changes substantively-it does not remain same.

Suppose the above stated scene is not a scene of a movie but that of a stage performance. In this case if the person decides to look at the dress of the artist forming the backdrop. Then, in his perception, the main artists will recede into the backdrop and the artist standing in the backdrop, whom he is interested in, will emerge as the main figure. It is noteworthy that this perception will be different from the perception of that possible scene in which the character artist would have actually been placed in the forefront. In a stage performance the main artist remains in the forefront. Through the focusing of light and other arrangements he or she is made distinctly visible to the spectators. Other character artists are placed in low intensity light and made to remain away at a distance from the spectator's vision. If the director wants to bring some of the character-artist and the focus of the spectator's attention he will make similar arrangements for him that he does for the main character. Either that artist will be brought to the fore and others, including the main character, would recede in the backdrop for a while or he will focus light on that very artist exclusively keeping him on his own place. In any case what is to be in the foreground or what in the backdrop is, in a sense, readily given to the spectator. However, if one spectator decides to focus his attention on one of the character-artist in the backdrop nothing change in the above sense of what is readily given to him. The light arrangement, placing of the artist etc. all remain the same. Yet, the scene is qualitatively changed for that spectator. That character-artist comes to the fore and everything else despite the intensity of light etc. becomes hazy in his vision.

Above examples make it clear that human decision shapes the content and the form of perception. In general, we can say that a decision to attend some stimuli (as contrasted to some others) is necessary to make sense experience possible. Despite the role of human decision the objectivity of sense-experience is not affected since what a person perceives is *given* to him and not projected or imagined by him to be so. Others also, by a similar application of his decision, can see the same or similar object or event. This decision implicitly functions in all instances of sense-experience. But especially in those instances of sense experience, which become the basis of some cognitive endeavour, the role of decision becomes explicitly clear.

Very often when a person undertakes the task of some new research a non-rational adherence to the decision to stick to some stimuli becomes necessary. In an unfamiliar field of experience one does not know anything in advance that can arouse one's interest to keep attending some stimuli for long that is necessary to discover some new feature of the object of that experience. Hence one has to keep oneself engaged in attending certain stimuli (i.e. to keep observing a phenomenon) just by the power of decision taken on non-rational ground (since a rational ground can enlarge only after the discovery). This non-rational decision is, often, emotional in nature. A researcher often continues his effort with a sort of emotional attachment with his assumption to do so. It can be seen as a mild form of emotional attachment that anyone feels for some of his belongings. At times it becomes intense enough to be equated with the emotional attachment of a person with his child (theories, ideas, invention etc. are called the brainchild of the thinkers and the scientists in this sense also). Ordinarily it is not intense enough to be easily recognized as an emotional adherence. Only when someone. Comes to oppose a hypothesi's or an idea of a scientist or a thinker he feels offended. He does not like it although he does not have at that moment enough evidence or reason to support his hypothesis or idea. His emotional adherence beconles evident in his feeling of being offended on the opposition of what he thinks to be true. This emotional attachment to a particular assumption is the force that helps the researcher to continue in his effort. It is needless to say that this sort of emotional attachment is necessary for any new research that is deemed to be purely cognitive.

Emotions not only give a non-rational positive force to the researcher to continue his research till evidential confirmation is obtained but also it helps in finding out some elements of the object of his research that can be overlooked without it. Emotional attachment to a particular assumption instills confidence in the researcher about his research project as it gives him strength to undermine the objections and criticisms and move forward in his chosen direction. This may prove to be counter-productive for truth-seeking aspiration of the research since the chances of turning of this confidence into obstinacy or rigidity about one's own assumptions are many. Due to this negative feature the philosophers and epistemologists regard emotions as a hindrance in the path of achieving truth. The exaggerated fear of this negative feature results into of the philosophers' and epistemologists' non-acceptance of cognitive importance of emotional experience. This, however, is only one aspect of our cognitive quest. Emotional attachment with the object of research also discloses certain features of the object that can't be found otherwise. Due to emotional attachment with the object (it may be a thing or a person) a person can see some features in the object that is either missed completely or neglected badly if he does not feel that attachment. In the quest of purely material realm this may be true. After all if someone is studying the physical and chemical properties of any new compound his emotional attachment (if any) with that compound can hardly gives him any new infomation and he does not miss anything important, from the cognitive point of view, about that compound. However, this is not the case if someone were working to understand the experience and behavioural responses of person who gives an emotional significance to something or someone. In order to study the emotional value of a thing in a person's life one has to see that object in the colour of that emotion. What that person feels about that object could be conceived by someone only if one looks at that object with that emotional relation that the person has with it. This becomes the *objective condition* for understanding what that person feels. It is important to note that in the absence of this condition (i.e. if one dies not have any idea of emotional relation with that object) then one can't even imagine or think what the person feels and can't actually understand what that person feels. If one puts oneself in an emotional relation at least imaginatively to that object then one can also *feel* that which is, in general, felt by any human being in that emotional relation. The empathetic approach to the object of a person's emotional attachment makes one *aware of what happens to that person:* one becomes aware of what is *given* in that situation as the content of emotional experience. Anyone, by placing himself (imaginatively) in that emotional relation to that object, can feel what could be felt in that condition. This (empathetic approach) helps one understand what a person feels in an emotional relation to an object. This is a psychological fact that is experimentally established too. But for our present discussion it has much deeper implications.

If one wants to understand what a person emotionally feels about an object then one has to make it an object of one's understanding as an emotional phenomenon and should not make it an object of understanding of any other phenomenon. In other words —in order to understand someone is emotion one has to understand it as a content of emotional experience. Figuring up of an object in a person's understanding as an object having an emotional content means that he takes it as object that is necessarily related to *feeling* something about it. If one understands it as an object that is not necessarily related to feeling something about it then it is not an understanding of the content of emotion. And if it is not an understanding of the content of emotion then to take it as an understanding of emotion is nothing but a misunderstanding. It is very important to note that to understand an object as something that is necessary related to feel something about it is to *feel* something about it at the deepest level. So it becomes clear that to understand the emotional attachment of a person is to *feel* that emotional attachment at a deeper level. To understand a feeling is, at the deepest level of understanding the meaning of the word 'feeling', is to feel it. This realization discloses the *cognitive significance* of understanding a person's feeling emotionally since if it does not happen at the deepest level then it will result into complete absence of understanding about the feeling of other person, or we will only misunderstand it and to understand it correctly would be a matter of chance only. The fact that it is not so (that means it is not the case that we are unable to understand other's feeling) implies that we also feel at the deepest level something what a person feels about it. We may be wrong in exactly capturing the content of that feeling but we don't fail in feeling something about that if at all we understand it as feeling of anyone. A matter of someone's feeling can be said to be known properly only if it is known as a matter of feeling and not as a matter of thinking or anything else. If a person has some emotional attachment with someone then to understand it as that is the only way to know what a person knows (feels). Denial of cognitive significance of emotional states completely only precludes the possibility of knowing the truth content of that state.

In fact the notion of intrinsic significance of some quality of an object (a person or a thing) becomes properly intelligible only under the feeling of a non-rational attraction with that object that is seen as the embodiment of that quality. Those qualities that generate a feeling of glory, majesty, dignity, grace or beauty generate a feeling of sublime and attract a person's attention towards that object which embodies them. This attraction manifests in an emotional attraction of low or high intensity and due to this felt attraction reason judges them correctly as valuable for not any reason but for themselves i.e. intrinsically valuable. If such an emotional attraction is felt for certain qualities of human character then those qualities are deemed as intrinsic values. Intrinsic value of a quality cannot be rationally proved: they are deemed as intrinsic only because they are to be postulated as valuable to prove the value of so many other qualities. But that is merely a rational postulation and their practical intrinsic significance manifests in the emotional attraction that human beings qua humans feel towards the persons who possess them. It does not mean to say that emotional attraction for a human quality is the criterion of its intrinsic worth. Intrinsic worth of a quality is not a matter of proof either rationally or emotionally. Rationally they are accepted to be intrinsic since value of other qualities are proved by presupposing their value and emotionally they are felt to be the sources of sublime feeling.

Adding the above discussion with the theme of our discussion (in last chapter) regarding the implicit truth-claim present in expressions of beauty of an object we may come to the realization that emotional attraction towards an object need not be necessarily taken as an obstacle of genuine knowledge about it. It rather helps in gaining a deeper look of it. Emotional attraction does not hide any quality of an object indeed. Due to this attraction another aspect of it becomes predominantly noticeable that can't be seen at all without emotional attachment. The warmth, the joy of being in the proximity of a person can't be experienced without being in love with his/her. To say that we can't know the ecstasy of love without being in love— may appear to be a tautology but it is not empirically vacuous. It has an *actual* experiential content due to which it can be contrasted clearly with imaginary assertions about love. A lover actually *feels* he warmth of love: he *does not imagine* about it. And it is very important to note that this distinction itself becomes a matter of experience (i.e. verified in a sense) in the experience of love only. There is no way to verify (i.e. experience) it with an attitude of doubt or with a neutral objective attitude of a disinterested beholder. The misunderstanding regarding the lover's expressions arises basically due to the attempt to taste it from the standpoint of sense experience. Although in rational discussion people agree that so many truth-claims can't be verified on sense experimental ground but due to habitual inertia most people tend to undermine other sorts of truth-claim completely and do not take interest in the attempts of those persons who take these claims seriously in the right perspective. They not only don't take interest in such attempts but also habitually argue against these attempts. Knowing full well that their argument can never conclusively prove the futility of these attempts their efforts only disclose their irrational rigidity. In view of this normal human rigidity it is necessary to understand the experience of love afresh.

Understanding (Human) Love

A person in love (with another person) feels attraction towards his/her beloved. This attraction, as it is stated above, is psychic in nature: it is not physical. It is felt in the form of attraction for the beauty of the beloved. This beauty may not necessarily be physical: it may be behavioural, dispositional or that of character. However, it is connected to some overt physical behaviour of the beloved and the person in love gets stuck to that. The person's love is not for that behaviour but it is natural that he is drawn to physical features and behaviours of the beloved since an ordinary person's attention is drawn always towards external objects and behaviours. In love, attention of the person in love is drawn to some features or behaviours of the beloved, and love, which is *per se* a pure psychic force of attraction, degenerates into physical and bodily attraction. At this point it is necessary to understand the tendency of the movement of human attention.

Our attention is drawn, ordinarily, to a more intense stimulus. The intensity of the stimulus marginalizes the effect of other lovv intensity stimuli and attention is easily drawn to it. This is almost a physical law like tendency of attention that operates without exception in ordinary situations. It is almost impossible for a person to withstand the intensity of a stimulus and remain unmoved before it. Thus the sublimity of love relation is, generally, lost in the physicality of relation.

Although a stimulus functions at a particular level of experience but its intensity is comparable to the intensity of stimulus of any other level of experience e.g. the experience of intensity of a physical force and the experience of the intensity of psychic force are comparable by the person who faces the intensity of the pull or push of these two sorts of forces. If the intensity of a psychic force is greater than the intensity of that of a physical force the former will draw the attention of the person and will marginalize or dilute the effect of the latter. If on the other hand, the intensity of the physical force is greater, the opposite will be the result. Ordinarily the person experiences the intensity of the physical force as greater than that of the psychic force. That is why the experience of attraction of love, which is purely psychic, gives way to the physical attraction for the beloved. The attraction of love that draws the person's attention to his beloved and which is distinctly felt as different from physical attraction habitually draws his attention to the physical features of his beloved. When the attraction for physical features is aroused then its intensity dilutes the effect of the psychic attraction of love. It is not the case that psychic attraction of love is always weak in intensity in comparison to the intensity of physical attraction. But due to an innate habit our attention, ordinarily, gets drawn to the physical forces more easily. Hence an additional effort is needed to feel the force of psychic attraction even if it is moderately strong. Our attention gets drawn to the psychic force easily only if it is exceptionally strong. So while it is true that attention normally gets drawn to a higher intensity stimulus, the intensity of any stimulus is to be considered along with the fact that the inertia of habit affects the total intensity with which it pulls the attention of a person. It means that if a stimulus from the psychic level draws the person's attention with some degree of intensity and some another stimulus of the same degree of intensity also is working at the physical level then the attention of the person will be drawn to the latter since the total intensity of the physical force (i.e. the intensity of the pulling force of the physical stimulus the force of habitual inertia towards physical stimulus) becomes greater than the intensity of the pulling force of the stimulus-of psychic level. This law like truth about human attention helps in understanding a large number of psychic phenomena since it explains why attention is drawn in one direction or in the other. Without understanding the tendency of attention most explanations regarding human behaviour remain mere gross approximation.

Human beings have some control over their attention and they can choose to focus their attention on one thing rather than the other. However, this free choice can function within a certain limit of intensity of stimuli. An excessively intense stimulus doesn't leave room for such choice practically because one's attention can't help getting attracted by it. In the cases of very weak stimulus also this choice can't practically function since such a focusing can be done with power of sheer will that exhausts very quickly due to relatively strong stimuli of the surrounding. In principle it is possible to keep ones attention focused on a very weak stimulus by sheer power of will but practically it is not possible due to the enormous difference between the intensity of the force of attraction the stimulus in focus and that of the surrounding. Any method of mental disciplining has to take note of this fact. No desired result can be achieved by merely preaching to keep the attention focused on the weak stimulus without devising ways either to make the weak stimulus strong or to dilute the effect of strong stimuli of the surrounding.

In human love the person's attention, due to its habitual inertia, gets drawn to his beloved's physical features and the attraction of love itself is missed. A person in love *does feel* the attraction initially as a pure psychic attraction and can revive this distinct feeling at any stage but normally he never finds any occasion to do so. Fallen in love, a person gets absorbed in the ecstatic feeling that results from seeing his beloved and to be in his/her proximity. In this raptness one gets no opportunity to be internally aware to distinguish between the forces *of* physical attraction for his beloved's physical features and that of pure psychic attraction of love itself that brings him close to her. The psychic attraction of love operates through the attraction of the individuality of the beloved. It is in this very way love manifests at the physical plain. Love does not reveal itself forcefully before the lovers. On the contrary it hides itself behind overt attraction toward the beloved. Love itself does not make the person aware of its own pure psychic attraction. In order to be internally aware of pure psychic attraction of love the person in love has to make effort to remind himself about it. The habitual inertia attracts the person's attention towards the physical features of the beloved and he *mistakes* it as love. Thus the pure psychic charm of love manifests itself in the physical realm and opens the possibility of realization of its unearthly attraction but hardly ever is it realized. It is left unattended and the attention of the lover gets absorbed and degenerates, unfortunately, in the attraction of the beloved's bodily features and personality. A divine experience is lost. Every occasion of human love presents an occasion to experience its divinity and it becomes *bhakti* (a divine love-experience) if it is attended properly. In Sufi tradition isq mazajee is accepted to be substainially the same as *isq haqeeqee*. But ordinarily it is mistaken as an ordinary physical attraction. Not only others mistake it as a physical attraction and think that the lovers only exaggerate what they feel but, as it is stated earlier in most cases lovers also fail to notice the beauty of love. Very rarely some lover, who has a very serene temperament, can see the beauty of pure love. If a lover could see the beauty of love (as contrasted to the beauty of the beloved) then his statement about the experience of love becomes a more refined sort of a knowledge claim despite its high emotional over-tones. An ordinarily lover's assertions about his experience of love also has a truth content in it but it is about the love 'of' or 'with' (or 'through') his beloved. It is never independently about love. The lovers whose attention is somehow switched from his beloved to the experience of love itself; experiences its truth content without containing with the qualities of his beloved. His statement therefore, becomes a more refined truth claim about this experience. However, his account of his experience of love and his intension to give that account can't be captured by others since they fail to see what he sees. Such a lover gives a true account of what he feels but others, not in a position to see that, thinks that this is only his fancy.

Love for human being is not inferior to love for the Lord. It is the same as the love for the Lord. The difference lies in the fact that in the former the attraction of love gets *hidden* behind the attraction of the beloved's personality and physical features whereas in the latter this gets *manifested* in the specific form of attraction for the Lord. In *bhakti* the object that attracts the attention of the *bhakta* is not seen to be out there: He is felt inwardly within the ecstatic experience as the centre of the very phenomenon of attraction. The *bhakta* feels the ecstasy of love for Lord only in the *bhakti* of the Lord. There is no other way to enter into that experience. Only in and through the love for the Lord its own attraction (i.e. attraction of *bhakti)* gets manifested.

Understanding Divine Love - The *Bhakti*

In order to attain *bhakti*, a *bhakta*, in the initial stage, has to learn to be receptive to the ecstatic experience of love for his Lord. Given the old habit of getting easily disturbed by external stimuli it is very difficult for a person to attend to the ecstatic experience of love itself. But in *bhakti* it becomes possible and easy too. As an ordinary person the *bhakta's* attention gets easily focused on the image of the Lord or any of His physical representations. By envisaging the beauty (including extra ordinary power and exceptional virtues) of his Lord in devotional songs and by other such means he experiences the ecstasy that any ordinary person feels in imagining the glorious deeds and beauty of the person whom he respects or loves. But since he knows very well that his beloved Lord is not out there (in external space), soon he becomes aware that remembering Whose name and imagining Whose beauty gives him ecstasy, comes in contact through the experience of *bhakti* only. In human love the beloved is present physically before the lover and his experience of pure psychic bliss is suffused by her (his beloved's) physical attraction. Pure psychic bliss is missed almost totally by the lover in making a variety of physical responses to his beloved's physical attraction.

Above stated accident does not take place in case of *bhakti* since the *bhakta's* beloved Lord is not physically present before them. *Bhaktas* become aware of the beloved Lord, as the source or center of *bhakti,* only within this experience of *bhakti.* This is not a problem for the *bhaktas.* For him it is not a matter of suspicion for the Lord's reality. The ecstatic experience of *bhakti* connects him directly to his dear Lord and he finds no reason to doubt it. *Bhakti* takes the *bhakta* in the world of *bhakti* where Lord's presence is marked on each and every event.

In this spatio-temporal world there is nothing that can arouse *bhakti* in the *bhakta's* heart. Mundane affairs of this world prove to be distracting for *bhakti.* Hence the *bhaktas* take the most valuable experience of *bhakti* as a delightful divine gift that only his Lord can give. A *bhakta* can't accept that his *bhakti* for his Lord is a matter of chance because he sees the presence of Lords will in every event and *bhakti* being such a divine experience that can never take place without his will and grace. He feels that Lord Himself has graciously given him the experience of *bhakti* and enabled him to come in His contact. Thus the physical absence of the Object of *bhákti* (i.e. Lord) not only saves it from degenerating into a physical relation but also elevates the *bhaktas* at that height of self-awareness that detaches him from the physicality of the world and transports him into the sublime world of pure psychic experience.

Bhaktas feel getting connected to the Lord while passing through the enjoyment of remembering His name and envisaging His beauty. This realization gives a depth to his emotional experience. He begins to feel the presence of his Lord in the experience of joy of remembering Him. He becomes internally aware of this ecstatic experience. This is obviously an experience deeper than the mere experience of emotional joy of remembering his Lord. Remembering the glory and beauty of the Lord for getting joy of ineffable beauty and glory makes the acts of *bhakti* a means of enjoying beauty and glory of the Lord who was a character of past or in mythology. But with the awareness of the beauty of *bhakti* the *bhakta* becomes aware of the Lord Who enables him of being aware of it at that very moment. So He is not a glorious character of mythology or that of past but an actual conscious agent helping him directly at that moment to be aware of the beauty of *bhakti. Bhakti,* thus, becomes a means through which the will of Lord functions directly. Earlier it is the means of the *bhakta* to get connected to his dear Lord and later it becomes the means of the unknown conscious agent (Lord Himself) who makes the *bhakta* aware of His presence in his experience. The *bhakt,* who got joy in chanting the name of Lord or singing beautiful songs for his Lord, later gets a great joy on attaining the awareness that he is already connected to his Lord in the very ecstatic experience of *bhakti.* The awareness of the divinity of the experience of *bhakti* (compare it with the beauty of the experience of love) is different qualitatively from the bliss that the *bhakta* gets in chanting his Lord's name or singing songs for Him, and this difference is felt actually by the *bhaktas.* This is what could be called the turning of *bhakti-act (kriya- bhakti)* into *bhakti*-result'*(fala- bhakti).* Both are inseparable: they are not two yet the earlier and the later are felt different.

This shift brings about a radical change in the outlook and quality of experience of the *bhakta.* In the farmer the *bhakta* does not feel connected to his Lord. He only gets a pure psychic joy, and that also he realizes only afterwards. In the latter he feels to be connected to Lord in and through the experience of' *bhakti.* In this stage *bhakti,* for him, is not means: it is a sort of end since his beloved Lord operates through it and he can reach his Lord within it only (not by means of it).

An objection can be raised against the actual possibility of the awareness of an experience (or experiencing of an experience). One can doubt whether there is any such experience at all. It can be said that a person can be aware of (i.e. can experience) an object but can't be aware of its experience: it is merely an empty conceptualization. But this objection is not tenable. One can swallow his meal hurriedly without having a taste of it. His hunger will be satiated and he will still get some taste of it since the taste buds of his tongue are functioning. So he will not miss the taste of food completely. However, he may decide to eat his meal with taste and just with this awareness a qualitative difference is marked clearly between the former and the latter modes of eating. Same happens with the experience of *bhakti* also. Most religious people get some joy in singing devotional songs but few enjoy it *tastefully.*

Bhaktas say that *Bhakti* is a *Rasa.* Ordinarily the joy of *bhakti* is experienced by most religious persons as a form raptness that most musicians, singers and other performing artists enjoy during their performance. Enjoying its *rasa*-its taste, however, requires an internal awareness. This joy is similar to the joy that a serious artist and connoisseur enjoys. Enjoying the experience of *bhakti* with internal awareness is an actual experience that is not ordinarily given to every human being but can be achieved by every normal person. Any one can experience something and simultaneously be aware of the phenomenon that is going on within him: The person notices a qualitative difference in so doing. The person finds actual differences in passing through an experience with awareness and without awareness. It affects his behavioural responses also and others can also discover it by close observation of his behaviour. But he himself can directly distinguish between these two types of experiences. This point needs some elaboration.

The Source of Ecstatic Experience Can't Be Made an Object of Experience but Can be Experienced

Emotion is an experience. We experience it by undergoing it. It is not experienced as an object standing out there independent of the emotional experience (as it happens with objects of sense experience). Where is no way to experience the phenomenon of experiencing as an object. It is not possible practically because if one tries to fix one's attention on the experiencing the attention is withdrawn from the object of experience and with that the phenomenon of experiencing also is lost. But an internal awareness during an experience is quite possible and any one can easily do that. We see something without being aware of the fact that we are passing through an experience of seeing. But just by remembering that *I am passing through the experience of seeing* this or that object, the person becomes aware of the phenomenon of experiencing. Internal awareness of an experience brings about a qualitative change in the phenomenon of experiencing. The intensity with which the object was being attended decreases. Awareness consumes a portion of attention and it is lost if the person tries to remain exclusively attentive of the object of experience. The effort to be more aware (of the phenomenon of experiencing) affects adversely the experience of an object in case of sense experience. It also affects some emotional experiences adversely but does not so affect some other emotional experiences. To be aware of anger, without decreasing its intensity, is just not possible but to be aware of emotion of love and to maintain this awareness is easier.

It is a fact that it is easier to become internally aware of the pure psychic experience of love. The joy of this experience helps one to be aware that one is passing through the experience of love. It is true of all forms of love (not merely of conjugal form). If the attention is not allowed to be distracted by the habitual inertia of physical responses then the awareness of the ecstasy of pure psychic experience of love becomes more vivid and strong. As an ordinary person enjoys listening music but a person with taste enjoys it in a qualitatively different level the experience of love also is enjoyed at a qualitatively different level by those who make them internally aware of its pure psychic ecstasy. A person, who loves someone, may miss the joy of pure psychic experience if he becomes overpowered by the habitual desire to give it a physical expression. His attention is, then absorbed in those responses only and he misses the pure psychic joy of the experience. If, on the other hand, he allows the physical responses to manifest to that extant only so that his attention is not distracted from the pure psychic experience then love becomes an extraordinary joyful experience for him. It does not remain earthly: it becomes sublime. For them, who never care to enjoy the ecstasy of pure psychic experience of love by becoming internally aware of it, love means nothing more than a fine way to respond physically to certain physical features of the beloved person. Most people pass through this rare earthly experience without noticing its beauty and think that they, who talk about the sublimity of love, are non-realist romantic people. But the *romance and sublimity of love is a matter of experience* and not a matter of fanciful imagination. Romance and sublimity of love can't be made an object of experience but in experiencing love for anyone a person can definitely experience its romance and sublimity. This is a commonly available experience and for it no spiritual discipline is required. Just an internal awareness is needed that anyone can attain only by reminding oneself to be aware of it. The talk of the beauty of love (not of the beloved), its sublimity etc. is ordinarily regarded as a poetic talk that tends to highlight the glory of love. Such talks are, generally, not deemed to be meant for giving any truth of this experience. For most common people to say that love has an unearthly beauty of its own is only a way to say high and good things about it, which is not actually true. For a lover such assertions are really true report about the experience of love, which can be actually tasted by any one in that experience. If lover is not interested in giving proof of what he says about the experience of love and avoid entering into a debate on this matter. It is not difficult to understand the reason behind his attitude. For him the joy of experiencing the beauty of love is so great and the attempt to give proof for it is so trivial and worthless that he would prefer to keep away from it. But it is important to note that he does not willingly concede to the view that there is no truth in his assertions: he only avoids entering into such debates. To accept that his assertion is empty of truth -content will render his assertion into a baseless glorification of love. A lover does not want to underline the glory of love for the sake of human welfare. He is not interested in any such program primarily. It only intends to express his feeling honestly. Love is a common human experience and any ordinary person can understand the actual intension of the lover and can also understand that there is a truth-clainl implicitly present in his assertion. But the habitual inertia to attach the talk of truth-claim only to the sense experiential events makes him close to understand it as a truth-claim of a different order of experience. This closure is not due to any logical or factual reason. It is only due to the very old habitual inertia. To break this inertia one only has to remind oneself that the lover in having the taste of the experience of love very clearly *sees* its beauty and anyone else also, can *see its beauty,* if he is also tries to have its taste while in love. To understand this much one need not actually pass through this experience. It is obvious that to understand a lover's claim about the beauty of love that he experiences in the proximity of his beloved one need not actually fall in love with someone. Just by recollecting any of his own past or present experience, such as his mother's affection, a person can understand how beautiful, gracious and sublime this experience itself was/is! The beauty of pure love is not separable from the beautiful responses of the beloved but the two are clearly *distinguishable* from each other and any one can easily do that by becoming aware of this distinction. This is an intelligible distinction and by noticing this distinction one can understand that the lover is giving a true account of what he actually feels. He can understand that there is a sense in talking about the truth or falsity of the lover's experience and also understands the conditions of its truth or falsity. If a lover is enjoying not merely the physical charm of the beloved but is also the *aware of beauty of this experience inwardly* then he is telling truth. If he is giving this statement without enjoying the charm of awareness then he is lying. This point will become clearer in ongoing paragraphs.

A person, who has enjoyed the romance and sublimity of love in his life, can easily understand the pure sublimity of *bhakti* also, and to understand the romance and sublimity of love is not difficult for any ordinary person. The object of love has a limited physical identity and the sublimity of love experienced in his love delimited by that. The object of *bhakti*-the beloved Lord of the *bhaktas,* is neither limited nor conditioned by any limitations. So in *bhakti* alone the pure sublimity is experienced. This is the central point of difference that separates ordinary human love from the divine love or *bhakti.*

Bhakti — A Gift of Lord The God

Bhakti begins with the feeling of blessedness for the gift of ecstasy that one achieves in love for the Lord. In ordinary human love one enjoys the ecstasy of love but misses the feeling of blessedness to be in love. If this feeling is achieved in ordinary love (at times it is actually achieved) then it also becomes *bhakti.* For this reason the love of the *gopis* is called *bhakti.* Krishna was contemporary of *gopis* but their love for Him was filled and dominated with the feeling of blessedness for His love. Hence their love, even it was a passionate love affair for them, was not out and out physical. Krishna personality and His deeds dominantly manifested that sort of charm that attracted people very strongly but made them respond vvith a fine sense having inclination towards sublimity. Although a *bhakta* can realize only through *bhakti* that Krishna is God Himself and before that his love for Him may have passion to enjoy sensually His physical charm but this gets necessarily transformed into the sublime feeling of blessedness. It is this transformation that makes a lover of Krishna realize that is not an ordinary person but God, that there is nothing material in him (in Krishna). *Gopis'* love for Krishna is revered only because it is pure sublime love-a form of *bhakti.* Many people still follow this way of Lord Krishna's *bhakti.*

People experience love in one form or the other but rarely someone becomes aware of its blessedness. In love everyone passes through a blissful experience but, as stated in above discussion, the habitual inertia degenerates it into a gross or refined physical attraction. The emotion of love itself doesn't make the person (in love) aware of its blessedness. The emotion enables a person to experience bliss and gives him an opportunity to witness it beauty but does not *take* him aware of its beauty. Two persons may spend a very long period in love experiencing the beauty of love initially but eventually mistaken by them for a physical charm. Persons in love by themselves may never be aware of its pure psychic charm. To be aware of that is a very rare happening. So if one becomes aware of its beauty then one also sees that it has happened due to the grace of the Lord the God. He finds no agency other than God to whom he can accredit for this gift. The awareness of sublimity of the experience of love that fills his heart with a sense of thankfulness also makes him aware of His hidden presence in his *bhakti.*

The Deeper Layer of *Bhakti* : Experience of *Bhakti* as *Rasa*

Bhakti is an emotion - a *bhava.* But it deepens only when it becomes a fully conscious experience - becomes a *rasa* for the *bhakta. Bhakti* is a *rasambhuti* also. In other words when a *bhakta* doesn't merely get carried along the overwhelming experience of love for the Lord but also becomes aware of its taste then he gets the *rasa* of it. It, then, remains not merely an emotion: it becomes a *'Rasa'.*

'Rasa' literally means taste, or that could be tasted. Our food has very many *rasa.* Fruits like banana and cooked food like pudding is sweet. They contain *mist* or *madhura rasa.* Lemon and

pickles are generally sour. They have *amla rasa* in them. When we eat them we get their taste or *rasa*. To get the taste of a food is a cognitive experience. If our tongue is functioning properly then the taste of a food is immediately known to us. However, proper functioning of tongue alone can't give us the knowledge of the taste of food if our attention is in some other direction. If one swallows the food in a hurry to go for some work then one doesn't remain aware of the experience of eating and one either misses its taste completely or can't clearly know it. To know the taste vividly it is necessary to be aware of it. This is normal condition for clear perception of any event. Ordinarily when we perceive something our attention is focused on it and we don't have to make additional effort to be aware of it. However, under distracting conditions of perception an additional effort to be aware of the event under perception becomes necessary. In the perception of an unfamiliar situation also an additional effort of awareness is felt to be necessary. To have the taste of an emotion i.e. to know it in its vividness — also is unfamiliar situation of perception and requires additional awareness. The power of an emotion tends to overwhelm the person completely. It tends to take away his awareness also. If an emotion is strong enough then it becomes very difficult for a person to remain aware of it-to keep himself at a distance from it to watch it. At times it becomes almost impossible for a person if the emotion is very strong. Although in course of appreciation of an artwork this kind of distancing is easy, but there also to keep oneself at a distance from a powerful presentation of emotion is difficult. To keep oneself at a distance from an emotion that occurs in one's actual life is still many times difficult. So ordinarily aesthetes talk about *rasanubhuti* only in context of a work of art. They, generally, don't talk about the *rasanubhuti* of live emotional experiences. To have a distancing from emotions in actual life would require a sort of moral desciplining. In *bhakti* also this problem arises and a *bhakta* finds that with the kindness of his Lord only he can achieve this state that brings him closer to Him. The awareness of the love for the Lord that makes it a *rasa* itself is His boon for a *bhakta*.

The joy of remembering the name of dear Lord is given to almost everyone. Since it is given to almost all its importance is not realized. But this commonly available joy also is *given* and is not within the capacity of any person to produce it. So it is a valuable experience. However this is a fleeting experience. This arises in remembering the name of Lord and subsides after that. A *bhakta* enjoys it but ordinarily he does not remain aware of it while he enjoys it. When he begins to be aware of it while enjoying it then it becomes a *rasa* for him. The joy of it, then, acquires a stable significance in his life and a journey of serious and deeper involvement with beloved Lord begins.

Bhakti as *rasanubhuti* is different from the experience of joy of *bhakti* as *bhanubhuti*. This cannot be achieved by any method. There is no method to be aware of any happening. This is so commonly available to all of us that we can't think that it is something very special gift. Only the *bhaktas* can realize its specialty since they can see that not having any method to be aware proves to be a great difficulty to become aware of it. This is a very old habit of ours that to achieve anything we think of making some effort. To make effort is only thing that most of us have learnt in course of our upbringing and education. We just don't know to remain effortless. There are some valuable, enriching and energizing experiences that are availed only when we are effortless. Sleep is one such commonly available experience. Relaxing is another such experience but, in fact, most of us don't understand how do we relax. For relaxing also we need some technique. The techniques provided for this by many masters are the ways to help us reach a situation or to create conditions in which all efforts come to a pause. To have the taste of *bhakti* also we have to bring all efforts to a pause since for its awareness we only have to be aware and stop doing other physical and mental activities This is something like just to be placed in our own being. As such it is very simple but despite being simple it is not easy since we are constantly engaged in this or that mental activities (thought, imagination etc.) and we don't know just to drop them. A person, who starts his journey on the path of *bhakti* knows this great difficulty very well. So he also knows it well that there is no way to come out of it: only the grace of Lord can bring anyone out of this constant engagement of mental activities and make him have the taste of it. That is why they hold that it can be achieved by His grace only.

In other words one can have the *rasa* of *Bhakti* only if Lord gives it to one. To say so is not a trivial truism and it is made clear in above discussion. A little elaboration of that point from a different perspective is not inappropriate.

The *Rasa* of *Bhakti* is Lord's Gift

To have a taste of *bhakti* is not an ordinary achievement. In Indian Philosophy *Dharma, Artha, Kama* and *Moksha* are accepted as four *Purusarthas. Moksha* is the highest of them. But: in *Bhakti* tradition *Moksha* is despised in clear words and *Bhakti* the love of Lord itself is accepted as the highest. The reason is clear. The absolute state of pure consciousness that is regarded as the very nature of self becomes practically available to *bhaktas*. The essential condition of complete ego-lessness is fulfilled by the *bhaktas* alone in a natural manner. A *bhakta* has not to make any explicit cognitive clams about his state of being. He only talks like an intoxicated person and his cognitive intensions are expressed implicitly through them only. A *Jnani* asserts explicitly about his absolute state of consciousness, he has no other way to do that. Either he will pass in silence or he will made explicit assertion about it. A subtle sense of ego is needed for that. A *bhakta,* on the other hand, has to say nothing about himself except the tremendous joy of being in the *bhakti* of his beloved Lord. In *bhakti* his ego gets completely dissolved and what then he utters is so spontaneous an out come of his state of experience that it cannot be called his deliberate intension. He does not in fact, want to make any statement: some utterances, about what he feels, just effortlessly come out of his mouth. So not a bit of ego is needed for that. A *bhakta* talks only about his Lord and by so doing his inner state of pure ego-less consciousness gets clearly, unmistakably reflected. A *Jnani* wants to state that he is ego-less but in so doing he gives a chance to his ego to rise again.

Ignorance about one's knowledge means one's ignorance. If x is ignorant about. i.e. does not know that he knows P then it only means that he does not have knowledge about P. If x knows P then it is just impossible that he does not know about it. This is a kind of truism and necessarily true for every kind of knowledge except for self- knowledge — *atma jnana.* In *atma jnana* complete ego-less-ness is necessary and if that happens then the knower shan't explicitly know that he has attained self-knowledge. His attainment of self-knowledge will reflect from his behaviours but he himself shan't have a direct awareness that he has this knowledge. To know that I have self-knowledge is an unmistakable egoism and a proof of the fact that self-knowledge is not attained. This peculiar (paradoxical) condition is fulfilled in *bhakti*. Every behaviour of a *bhakta* speaks of his ego-less-ness but he never says explicitly about it .In fact he is not bothered about it. It is only concern is his love for his Lord. If he will be least interest in self-knowledge he will lose his love for his Lord and lose self-knowledge too. That is why in Bhakti Rasamrit Sindhu it is said that the *bhaktas* should not be influenced by the two witches-*bhoga* (pleasure seeking) and *moksha* (liberation seeking). *Bhakti* is impossible till either of the two reigns a person's mind. Although *Bhakta,* are not supposed to aspire at all for the liberations but that is naturally attained by the proximity of Lord. So it is intelligible to accept it as a great divine gift. What is aspired by *a jnani,* a *yogi* and others is very easily achieved in *bhakti.*

The taste of *bhakti* can't be experienced just by desiring to have it. As it is stated in above discussion there is no method to achieve it so there is no direct role of effort either. A person can have a taste of *bhakti* only he is gifted with it. Not everyone is so fortunate and gifted with its taste. In the tradition of *bahkti* some instructions are given to achieve it. These instructions, in fact, and the ways to attune one's mind and to create an environment in which the taste can evolve in one's heart. The word 'evolve' seems to suggest a mechanism. But that is not something that can be caused or made to come up. These instructions are only ways to wait eagerly to receive it as Lord's boon.

To have a taste of *bhakti* is to be aware of the love of the Lord for a considerable period of time. It is not a momentary or even a very short duration phenomenon. One can't have the taste of food if one is in haste. Hastiness is not conducive for awareness. Doing something very fast is different from hastiness. In haste one can't remain aware of a phenomenon for long. So in haste one can't really have the taste of food since he can't give enough time to watch all its aspects. Similar is the case with the taste of *bhakti.* It requires more time. Unless one remains aware for a considerably long period's one can't have its taste. But that requires the persistence of *bhakti-bhava* for long. This is not at all within a person's *(bhakta's)* control. To arouse any emotion is not in our direct control. To keep it alive for a desired period is doubly difficult. *Bhakti* is a rare emotion so to get into it is itself very difficult and to keep it going for long is excessively difficult and not within human control. To have this ecstatic experience of *bhakti,* therefore, is said to be a gift of Lord, and to have a taste - *rasa* of *bhakti* is a still greater gift.

The most important aspect of this happening is the actual, clear and intense feeling that it happens only with Lord's grace. It is a complete shift in feeling from *doing* something to achieve it to the feeling of *getting* it absolutely as grace. These two are radically opposite feelings. This is not merely a conceptual difference: it is a difference in actual feeling of the *bhakta.* This is the feeling that reaches its optimal realization in the *'Madhura Bhakti'.* In this form of *bhakti,* irrespective of one's, gender, one aspires to reach that state of feeling that Lord is one's lover and one is His beloved. The *bhakta* desires most intensely to get the love of Lord-to be loved by Him. In the tradition of *bhakti* this state is discussed very tastefully with great elaboration. To understand *bhakti* from the *bhakta's* point of view it is necessary to understand this state of emotion and this very special *rasa* in its depth and in its extension. But that is the content of the next chapter. At the end of this chapter we can summerise the present discussion as follows:

A *bhakta* experiences and understands his *bhakti*-his love for the Lord as a gift as in the form of an ecstatic emotion *(bhava)* and also in the form of the taste (rasa) of this ecstatic emotion. By saying that these are great divine gifts he makes a genuine assertion about what he feels and thereby he also makes a genuine assertion about the beauty of the *bhakti* in the form of a normal *bhavanubhuti* and also in the form of a very special *rasanubhuti.* His assertions are genuine assertions since this is his actual experience and he says only what he actually experiences he does not exaggerate or lie. A *non-bhakta* habitually tends to deny it. This is the difference between the *bhakta's* understanding of his *bhakti* for the Lord and a non-*bhakta*'s understanding of the same.

At the end of this discussion we corne to note the difference between a *bhakta's* understanding of *bhakti* and a *non-bhakta's* understanding of it. Not to understand the truth content of emotional experiences as a matter of general preoccupation against emotions is the fundamental reason for this difference.This preoccupation is unfounded at least it can't be rationally acceptable if its propounded as a general principle that all emotional experiences lack cognitive or truth content. Preparing ourselves to come out of this unfounded irrational preoccupation helps in understanding *bhakti* the way *bhaktas* understand it.

References

1. In Sanskrit and Hindi Grammar *'Rasa'* is explained as a generalized literacy experience having in its base as one stable emotion (sthāya bhāva) with some emotions that support it (ānucāri bhāva) and some that accidentally come and go *(vabhicāri bhāva).* This shows the span of the experience, 'which is different from a mere emotional experience due to its complex content despite all its contents are emotions *Rasa* can't be equated with emotions due to its content and also due to the fact that it can not be experienced without'having an internal awareness that is not necessarily present in emotions since they are aroused almost instinctively in specific situations. Both the reasons to distinguish *rasa* (taste) from *bhālv a* (emotions) are interconnected. In present discussion *rasa* is taken as an awareness of the taste of emotions only since it is needed to explain the point under consideration. However, the other aspect of its meaning i.e., its span is not ignored and will figure in another chapter.
2. 2/1/11-Bhakti Rasāmrit Sindhu.

3

Understanding *Bhakti* from the *Bhakta's* Stand Point

Kṛṣṇa! To understand '*Bhakti*' properly means to understand it as *bhakti.* To understand it as any thing other than *bhakti* is to misunderstand it completely or not to understand it properly. It is primarily and essentially love - love for God. In Nârada Bhakti Sutra also it is described as love for the Lord -'*Sâ twasmin parama prema rupâ'*[1]. This love manifests in the life of the *bhakta,* influences his life overwhelmingly and becomes his way of life. *Bhaktas* lead a life of love for their Lord. What they experience can't be grasped apart from what they do, or more appropriately said - how they live. This makes some philosophers of religion draw the conclusion that love for God is only an attitude towards life and world— a way of life or a specific policy of behaviour. God as such is not a reality in their view but only an image used to make this particular way of life appealing and acceptable to the members of a religious community. In the opinion of these thinkers God does not exist apart from the religious way of life. So to understand this way of life is to understand a policy of behaviour and not a statement about an independently existing realty. To take God as an independently existing real person is a misunderstanding, in their view, because, they think, the *bhaktas'* intension in making statements about God is, primarily, not to report about the existence of such an independently existing person but to express their of such an independently existing person but to express their complete obedience and reverence to an image of God.

In a way above view is correct since no *bhakta* ever gives any overt statement that the God of his love is a real person *also*. Through parables some moral is conveyed but we all know that the characters of parables are merely fictional and don't exist in physical world. Similarly the *Bhaktas'* statements that by the benevolence of God's they got peace, contentment, enormous joy and so on seem to underline the importance of a life of tranquility, contentment and inner joy. It is not necessary at all to accept the reality of God to receive this message of this way of life. However, this view could be considered to be correct if at all the *bhaktas* also admit that while so many good things they say in praise of God, they do not implicitly mean to endorse the reality of God. The *bhaktas* understand what a parable is and they themselves often make use of parables to convey some morals but it is obvious that while talking about God they never mean to use 'God' as a subject of a parable to propagate a way of life only. While Meera or Surdas talk about Krishna, or Tulsidas talks about Rama they don't only mean that that there is a particular way of life that they adopt and approve it for others. For Meera *Kṛṣṇa* is a real person whom she loves as her husband and for Tulsidas also Rama is undoubtedly a real person whom he adores as his master. An implicit assertion about the real existence of Lord is made by each and every sentence that the *bhaktas* make about their Lord.

The misunderstanding about the *bhaktas* assertion is due to mistaking the level of their truth claim. *Bhaktas* do make truth claims about the God of their love: all the assertions about God of love implicitly contain truth-claims that God is a real person but these are assertions primarily about an emotional experience which is a human experience. The emotional experience is different from sense experience. Truth claims are generally made about the objects of sense experience. Utterances about an object of one's emotion are deemed to be a sort of spontaneous verbal behaviour and it is believed that their essential function is not state anything about the reality of the object. While it is true that different sorts of sentences perform different kinds of function in language and conflating one function of a particular type of sentence for sentences (which are used for giving vent to some emotion) can *never* perform the function of an assertive sentence (which is used for describing a fact), is a wrong assumption. In a sentence like- 'What a great sacrifice Gandhi Ji made for the nation!'— respect is shown primarily for Gandhi Ji but at the same time implicitly it is firmly admitted that such a person did exist. It is clear from such usages that in some exclamatory sentences an implicit statement about the reality of the object of emotion is undoubtedly present. The *bhaktas'* utterances about their Lord also contain emotional overtones but it would be a mistake to think that through these utterances the *bhaktas* don't mean to assert about the reality of the object of their love (i.e. their Lord). Even as expressions of emotional experience such utterances are deeper than all other emotional experiences.

The utterances made by the *bhaktas* describe the actual encounter with that Supreme Person who is the embodiment of all the highest qualities that human beings could understand. Naturally a plain statement is not only badly inadequate but also inappropriate. The *bhaktas* can't help using the language of complete reverence because they state about their actual experience of the object of complete reverence. One can never understand the truth-claims contained in these utterances unless one gets some familiarity with the world of that level of experience.

Any truth-claim about the objects of a world of thought or experience, which is higher or deeper than the world of sense experience, can be vindicated only in that world and it is necessary to get some familiarity with that world to understand them as truth-claim at all. An objective way to ascertain the truth of falsity of a claim presupposes a division at any point of time in any specific world of discourse where certain claims are accepted to be unproblematic. The possibility of an intelligible (not necessarily rational) way to relate the problematic claims to the unproblematic one so that their truth or falsity could be ascertained varies in nature in various worlds of discourse. The unproblematic truth-claims also vary in respect to worlds of discourse. Although it is generally accepted that the unproblematically accepted truth is not a matter of proof, they are considered not to be beyond the question of truth or falsity. The unproblematically accepted truths are regarded

The unproblematically accepted truths are regarded to be *truths* after all. Had the unproblematic truth-claims not been regarded as genuine statements of truth-value assignments they would not been accepted to be true. But they are accepted to be true. The truth of the objectsof direct sense perception can't be supported by any other truths. The colour of an object is directly known to us with our eyes. It is unproblematically accepted. Nevertheless we say that it is true that this object is red (or of a particular colour). In light of this (or these) unproblematically accepted truth alone other truth-claims of a world of discourse are settled. The question of truth of problematic claims regarding certain other items of that world could be answered only in accordance with it. It is important to note that every world of discourse, even if it is not directly concerned with the question of truth or falsity, implicitly but necessarily presupposes a truth relation among the statements (implicit or explicit) about its various entities. In the *bhakta's* world also such implicit truth-claims are made through the assertions of the glory of the God of their love, about the bliss felt in His proximity etc. In this world the implicit truth- claim about the reality of The Lord of love is accepted unproblematic since He is present in the direct experience of *bhaktas* as the sole object of his love. Any other truth-claim in this world is judged with respect to its relation to this unproblematic claim. If accepting any incident relates to this unproblematic claim then assertion about it is worth considering as true or false if the assertions accord with it then it is judged to be true; otherwise — false. Since the *bhakta* gets the unproblematic truth- claim about the Lord through the emotional experience of *bhakti* so practically it means that the assertions about all and only those incidents which effect (favourably / unfavourably) the *bhakta's* love for Lord qualify to be truth-claims, and those claims that promote the love for the Lord are judged to be true. This could be taken as a basic understanding while talking about the truth-claims in relation to any *bhakta's* experience.

In simple words it can be said that the *bhaktas* dwell or partake in a world of emotional experience that is known as *bhakti*. The world of *bhakti* is an independent world in almost the similar senses of the world of sense experience. The objects and events of the world of sense experience are not made by human imagination. They exist independent of human will. Humans could perceive them as they are given to their senses. Similarly the world of *bhakti* also is an independent world. because no one can produce this sublime emotion on one's sweet will. Imagining about a form of God as described in any tradition itself is a very difficult task. But a *bhakta* is not satisfied only by imagining a picture of his Lord. He, first of all, wants *to feel* an attraction for his Lord in his heart. Emergence of this feeling of attraction in his heart is not causally connected to any of the *bhakta's* action. A *bhakta* can't cause this feeling to emerge. He does all sorts of things instructed in the tradition and can only eagerly wait for the emergence of this attraction. All his descriptions about his Lord's grace is *felt* by him only when he experiences this attraction. He does not imagine about it. Only by imagining he can't experience it; and when he experiences it, he experience only that which is given in his experience. A direct or indirect presence of the dear Lord is felt by the *bhaktas* in this experience. As no one can perceive anything other than what is given in sense experience, similarly no *bhakta* can experience anything about his Lord except for what is given in his emotional experience. Hence there is objectivity in the *bhqkta's* statement about his experience of his love for the Lord. He states only what he experiences. So what he states is the truth of experience. As such it is an unproblematically accepted truth However, this truth could be seen as truth only by those people who understand the world of *bhakta's* experience.

In order to understand the truth content of the *bhakta's* statement a minimal willingness to accept the objectivity of the world of *bhakti* is needed on the part of the person. If one has already decided not to accept the objectivity of any other world except the world of sense experience then it is impossible for one to understand the objective status of the world of *bhakti.* Such people would either rigidly dismiss the assertions of the *bhaktas* as sheer nonsense or at the best, showing charity, may grant a sort of emotive or prescriptive meaning to them. But, as it is stated earlier, this is mistake to do so since by so doing one fails to understand what the *bhaktas* understand by *bhakti.*

The people, who are unwilling to admit the objective status of the world of *bhakta's* experience, above explanation regarding the truth content of the *bhaktas'* utterances about Lord could interpret that it is an elliptical way to say that the *bhaktas* only want to underline the importance of those incidents of life that promote their *bhakti.* This interpretation is wrong if it is intended to support the view that no truth-claims are implicitly (but necessarily) present in *bhakta's* assertions about the Lord of their love. A *bhakta* is not a logician and ordinarily he avoids philosophical debate regarding his dear Lord. It is, however, obvious that he can't accept at all that the Lord of his love is an imaginary, mythological character. No *bhakta* could ever admit that he is playing a game of imagination, or what he experiences is just an illusion. Hence, in order to understand what a *bhakta* means in his assertions about his Lord, it is important to see that a truth-claim is implicitly present in his assertions and this is an essential part of their (these assertions') meaning Any attempt to eliminate this implicit truth-claim is to mutilate his assertions and not to understand them.

It is true that *bhaktas'* assertions present the problem of truth-claim if one tries to understand them from the world of sense experience. In above discussion it is made clear that truth-claims pre-suppose a world of experience and it would be an illegitimate demand to prove all truth-claims in the world of sense experience only. However, it can be shown that in the world of sense experience the assertions of the *bhaktas* can never be proved to be conclusively false. By finding that these assertions do not refer to any entity that can be an object of sense experience does not amount to falsify theses assertions. What the *bahktas* say can be ridiculed, despised and even condemned but can't be proved false. In order to prove that the *bhaktas'* assertions are conclusively false we need an argument of the following form:

All that is real is the object of sense experience.

Nothing that the *bhaktas* experience in *bhakti* is an object of sense experience.

Therefore nothing that the *bhaktas* experience in *bhakti* is real.

The argument is formally (it is the *CAMESTRES* mood of Second figure of Aristotle Categorical Syllogism) correct. But its conclusion (Whatever the *bhaktas* experience is not real.) can be accepted to be practically true only if the major premise (All that is real is the object of sense experience) of this argument is established to be true empirically. But it seems practically impossible One reason is very simple but strong. Our use of the term 'real' is not confined to the objects of sense experience. Although the theoretically postulated entities of Particle Physics also are not the objects of sense experience but it could be argued that we can define them operationally and those operations are performed in sense experience. But the beauty of an art work, the melody of music, the effect of etc. are the objects of experience and in that sense they are all real although none of them are the objects of sense experience in the sense the colour of a flower or the sound of the rumbling of clouds are. Beauty of an art-work lies in the work objectively and despite the fact that the work as an artifact lies in physical space and time art itself is not occupy physical space. The effect of poetry is not spatial or temporal either. We don't (and can't) say that the beauty of an art work is just the beholders ' imagination, or that the effect of poetry is the production of the listener's own projection. To say that an art work is beautiful is to make a true statement and similarly to say that a poem is powerful is also to make a true statement. *Bhaktas*' experience of God as the object of their emotional experience is real and truth claims made by them implicitly.

It is to be noted that the *bhaktas*' emotional experience of love is not at all a matter of doubt and in view of the fact that no emotion arises without presence of an actual situation as its source, the belief in the reality of God as the very source of *bhakti* becomes stronger. *Bhaktas'* emotion of *bhakti* manifests in all their behaviours. It is not difficult to decide if a person is actually in love or merely pretending about it. Even if at times it becomes practically almost impossible to decide that, it is not impossible to do so in principle since the very conceptual division assumes the possibility to do so at a conceptual level. From the genuineness of the *bhaktas*' love for their Lord it can be definitely concluded that there must be a real source of it. Even if the situation for the arousal of *bhakti* is doubted as a virtual reality, its actually presence as a source of its arousal is necessary. God is not merely the object of the *bhaktas*' love but also He is the very source of it. *Bhaktas* have various reasons to hold that their Lord of love help them constantly in arousing *bhakti* in them, support in deepening this experience and nurture them meticulously so that it could become a permanent way of life for the *bhaktas.* The reality of God as the source of *bhakti* may be shown to be doubtful by the agnostic and atheists but as it is stated in above discussion, there is no conclusive evidence to dismiss its reality. Hence only the personal choice can be held responsible for the decision and the ensuing consequences to accept or reject the reality of God as the source of *bhakti.* By deciding to reject it one can take the credit of avoiding unnecessary superstitions but then, the scope of unfolding of a new dimension of human life is dismissed. On the other hand, by deciding to accept the possibility of its reality not only a new world of human experience begins to unfold but also provides ground to judge this problematic truth claim and to come to a definite conclusion. So the reasons for the *bhaktas*' belief that the Lord of their love is a real person is worth considering. There is no good reason for their summery rejection. Such attempts could be regarded as dogmatic and irrational too. Such attempts, despite all rational moves, blatantly betrays about the hostility of the persons towards the *bhaktas* and religion is general.

After a preliminary clarification regarding certain intellectual objection in the way of understanding *bhakti* from *bhkatas'* stand point we can turn to have a look at some of the reasons, which we can help us understand why the *bhaktas* so confidently hold that the Lord of their love is a real person. These reasons are not explicitly advanced in support of their implicit truth-claim: they don't feel like doing that since their emotional experience never motivates them to do so. However, while talking about their experience to others they very often mention about these and others also, Especially those who are close to them, understand these reasons in their proper perspective. It, is, therefore, worth considering in order to understand *bhakti* from *bhaktas'* stand point.

Reasons for Believing That The Lord of *Bhakta's* Love is a Real Person

(*a*) *Bhaktas* experience the real independent person-hood of the Lord in the emotional state of *bhakti* and also know it clearly that this can't be an illusion. They feel that the existence of the Lord is not dependent on their emotional experience of *bhakti* rather their experience is dependent on the independent reality of the Lord. Their emotional encounter with Lord is enough for them to believe in the independent existence of Lord. However, apart from this emotional experience the *bhaktas* find at the ordinary level of sense experience that their prayers are heard and responded favourably. Not only in the mythologies but also in real life the *bhaktas* of past and present disclose that their prayers offered to their beloved Lord were responded at times so miraculously that they can't overlook those experiences as a matter of chance only.

In philosophical discussion such incidents are not regarded as proof of any sort. But for all those who are in the proximity of the *bhakta's* life such incidents serve as a sort of weak proof since the persons, who are not *bhaktas* but take their reports seriously, find that these are true. Such people, who choose to judge the *bhaktas'* report not with the attitude of doubt but with a willingness to find its truth can see that the reported events do actually point to an independent higher will-power functioning in their (*bhaktas'*) life.

Above reason to believe in the independent real personhood of God may apparantly resemble the Argument from Miracles but it is not that. Above stated reason is not to support the view that miracles do really happen and they prove the existence of God as a supra natural will power. *Bhaktas'* belief that their dear Lord hears and responds to their prayers favourably is the natural outcome of their vision of God's will underlying the laws of nature operating behind every worldly events. In *bhaktas'* view miracles, which are deemed as aberration from the normal course of natural law, are not proofs for God's existence rather the presence of such laws in nature instead of total chaos is the greatest miracle that pre-supposes the presence of a supra natural intelligence and limitless will-power. 'Why is there law in nature instead of chaos?'— is a question which may not be of any interest for most of us. Most of us can find no reason to ask such a question. But it can't be dismissed as a meaningless question since the possibility of total chaos or the dominance of chaos over a small constellation of order can never be completely ruled out as logically impossible. There is no logical absurdity involved in imagining that most of the events could have been happening at random Water would not have boiled at 100 degree Celsius or on one occasion it would have boiled with just little heat and on another it would have not boiled at all or would have boiled only after too much of heating etc. are the state of affairs that never happen but can be envisaged without difficulty. The logical possibility to envisage a purely chaotic situation of universe shows that it could have been a reality. The rein of natural law that enables the causal reproduction of an event is a necessity for any meaningful human action —physical or mental. The fact that this could have been a possibility but it is not the actual state of things – makes the above question a meaningful question. Natural law itself can't be an answer of this question. Nature, on observation, can disclose its laws to us but it remains mute on our curiosity regarding why should there be any law in nature at all. If chaos could have been there instead of laws why and how these laws came into being? As a possible reply to this question the hypothesis of the presence of a supra-natural intelligent power of will is not an absurd or irrational imagination. Thus a *bhakta's* vision that the will of their dear Lord is operating behind every event needs to be seen in the right perspective. Given the understanding that the will of Lord is operating behind all the big or small happenings it becomes intelligible that anything that happens favourably in the life if the *bhaktas*–within the framework of natural laws or without it, happens since the Lord wills so. From this perspective the possibility of favourable response to *bhaktas*' prayers remain no more problematic. In fact, from this perspective, an altogether different scenario emerges before us. Fulfillment of *bhaktas'* prayers is not a miracle (since if it is a miracle then every other event occurring under natural laws also is a miracle) but the *bhaktas'* feeling to pray for any thing is a way of God to appraise him of the truth that everything happens due to Divine will. From this point of view the fulfillment of a prayer is a God's grace in two senses—(i) an overt sense that it happened in an extra-ordinary way, and (ii) a deeper sense that by making the *bhaktas* pray for something God appraises him of the presence of His will in every event. Seen from (ii) every event is a miracle since the laws-like connection between events, being contingent in nature, can not operate if the Lord's will does not constantly support them. From this stand-point every thing is a miracle. This understanding itself is, for the *bhaktas,* a boon of his Lord. since it fills his heart with the divine feeling of gratitude for everything and turns his attention towards divinity operating all around .him. For a *bhakta* favourable responses to his prayers is a miracle not only in the sense that of fulfillment of some desire but also in the more important sense that the arousal of the intension in the *bhakta's* heart to pray to Lord is itself consequence of Lord's will. This understanding makes the *bhaktas* immediately aware of the functioning of divine will in his heart. This awareness of the divine presence in his heart is more than a miracle for the *bhaktas* that overwhelms him completely. This immediate awareness of the divine presence in praying even for any mundane thing gives him reason to strongly hold that his Lord is a real person, not merely his projection.

(*b*) A very important reason to acknowledge the real personhood of God that is valued by the *bhaktas* and also by others (who look at the *bhaktas'* life without an attitude of doubt) is to see that God is not only the object of *bhakti* but also the very source of it. *Bhakti* – the sublime emotional relation with the Lord is so ecstatic that it becomes immensely valuable for the *bhaktas. Bhakti* , for the *bhaktas,* itself is one of the greatest divine gifts. The sublimity and ecstasy is a matter of direct experience of the *bhakta*s and that they can't think of attributing it to a chance caused by material forces. No one else except the *bhaktas* and some of the persons willing to understand *bhakti* know it better that there is no physical and even psychic method or technique to producc *bhakti* in anyone's heart. Except for Lord's will nothing can be acknowledged as the reason for the presence of *bhakti* in any human heart and nothing else can be acknowledged as the source of *bhakti* except Lord Himself.

It is not difficult at all to understand that the Lord—the object of *bhakti,* is its source also if we remind ourselves that *bhakti* is essentially the emotion of love. A person's beloved – his object of love is the very source of arousal of his emotion (of love). In *bhakti* the situation is somewhat different since the *bhaktas'* Lord is not physically present before them to arouse in them the emotion of love by His extraordinary attributes and charm. *Bhaktas* have with them an image of Lord only. By keeping this image in the mind they make constant efforts in the form of chanting His holy name, remembering His glorious deeds etc. to arouse love for the Lord in their hearts. These efforts are merely the ways to create a situation conducive to ignite the fire of love in their hearts. They are not the source of it. The moment a *bhakta* feels an emotional attraction for the image of Lord he finds himself emotionally connected to the Lord Himself. He finds himself in the emotional proximity of his dear Lord. When the image of the Lord begins to act as a real person and does not remain an image at all then alone the love for Lord is aroused. An image of Lord in itself can't arouse love for the Lord. Its transmutation into a real person in a *bhakta's* experience alone arouses love for the Lord. There is no method to bring about this transmutation. But this happens in every serious *bhakta's* life and even an ordinary person, who is only at the initial stage of journey of *bhakti,* understands that this change can and does take place indeed in all *bhaktas'* life. Hence the fact that *bhaktas* do indeed feel enormous emotional attraction for their dear Lord makes it an acceptable reason to hold that the Lord – not as an image but as real person is the source of it.

The problem remains—What does the phrase 'transmutation of the image of Lord into actual person' mean? Is it to be treated as a plain factual statement or is it only another way of saying that the *bhaktas* fall in love with an image? From a *bhakta's* point if view, who has already achieved the deep and stable emotional relation with his Lord, the image was never an image but it was Lord Himself in limited form. From the point of view of those, who have got the taste of the emotional relation with the Lord but has not gained stability in it, this transmutation is a reality but unintelligible since one can see the image from this world only and can see the Lord as a real person from that world (world of *bhakti*) only. There is no way to look at the image of Lord from an in-between position since experientially there is no such position at all. It can be only thought of but can't be actually experienced. Since the question arises when the situation is looked at from this world so the transmutation can be accepted as a real phenomenon. But, since the answer of this question (in the sense of its dissolution) is found when the situation is looked at from that world only, it can be acknowledged that Lord Himself manifests in a limited for in the image. We can have answers relative to the perspectives only.

In view of our purpose of understanding *bhakti* from a *bhakta's* standpoint, the latter answer is acceptable.

Above reasons and many more, related to the biography of different *bhaktas,* about which they talk to others serve (for others) as some sort of weak proof for the real person-hood of the Lord. The belief that the Lord of *bhaktas'* love is a real person can be accepted on its face value as a truth-claim that is made on the basis of and verified in the immediate experience in the world of *bhakti* and to understand this (that it is a truth-claim that is made on the basis of *bhaktas'* immediate experience) makes it intelligible as a truth-claim in this world of ordinary experience also.

Bhaktas' experience is essentially an ecstatic experience. The object and content of this experience is not a matter of verification primarily but a matter of overwhelming joy. But the joy he feels is actual, it is neither his dream not illusion. As such his experience itself is an actual experience is taking place in this space and time and is a matter of sense experience for others. To an extent this experience can be compared to the ecstatic experience of beauty.

. The ecstatic experience of beauty of nature that overwhelms the person also confirms the truth that beauty <u>is</u> there in nature. The person is not fancying or dreaming about it: it actually is over there in nature. The beauty of an art-object is, in the same way, present in the art object and experiencing it as beautiful is the proof that it (beauty) <u>is</u> in that. The experience of beauty alone is the proof that beauty is there and this is a confirming experience that leaves no room for doubt. The object that is beautiful may not be a real object in the sense that it might not be placed in space and time but its beauty is a reality if it is beautiful. An imaginary object also may be beautiful.

It is important to note that the beauty of an imaginary object and that of an object placed somewhere in external space and time both are real. The reality of an object and the reality of beauty are not one and the same thing. Presence of abstract qualities (in any object) is a real state of affairs, a fact, and it is not affected by the presence or absence of an object (to which it is attributed) in the world of sense experience. This is an important philosophical question and deserves serious attention. The question of reality of beauty can be seen as a case of philosophical problem regarding the nature of abstract quality in general. It should be clear that the aim of this discussion is not to prove that beauty exists independent of an object. Present discussion is directed to underline the importance of a rather simple (or a trivial) point that the reality of an object in external space is not a necessary condition for its being really beautiful. This question directly concerns present discussion especially from the point of view of understanding the *bhaktas'* love for the Lord since love in general and love for the Lord (His ineffable glory and beauty of His deeds and form) in particular are instances of ecstatic experience that resemble the ecstatic experience of beauty. The joy felt by the a person in seeing a beautiful object is a matter of ecstatic experience for him but his experience manifests through his behaviours and is a matter of ordinary perception and understanding for others. Others can understand from his behaviours that the person is enjoying what he is seeing. Similarly others can also understand, and do understand, that a *bhakta* is greatly enjoying his *bhakti* for his dear Lord. It was explained in above discussion that there is an implicit truth-claim contained in *bhaktas*' emotional assertion about their dear Lord. A similar truth-claim is implicitly present in the assertions of aesthetic experiences also. A person, who undergoes an aesthetic experience, asserts about the beauty of the object of his experience and does not intend to state primarily about the reality of the object. But, now, it is not difficult to see that a truth-claim is implicitly but necessarily contained in it. A person who undergoes this experience does not explicit say that a beautiful object is really present before him, he only talks about its beauty in detail, but this talk loses its empirical import if it is deemed to be empty of such an implicit truth-claim. When a person talks about the beauty of an object does not intend to say that he is imagining that it is beautiful. To imagine an object as beautiful and to see it beautiful are two different sorts of assertions and the difference is not a matter of privileged access to the person only. Anyone can and does understand this difference. This difference lies in the implicit truth-claim that is present in the latter but lacks in the former. Since aesthetic experience is regarded as an experience that is more commonly available to people, in comparison to the ecstatic experience of *bhakti*, an attempt to understand the latter in the light of the former may be of some help.

The Question of Truth Claims Regarding Beauty

As a first response to the question of truth-claims of beauty of an object one might doubt about the meaningfulness of the question itself. It can be said that the question can be asked meaningfully about the existence of beautiful object but the question about the existence of beauty itself makes no sense. Ordinarily the assertions regarding the beauty of any object is deemed either as an exclamation or as an evaluation according to certain standards. These assertions are not accepted as factual statements primarily since they are supposedly made not to describe an object or report a matter of fact about it but to express what one feels about an object. To say that the flower is red and to say that it is beautiful, are to make two different sorts of assertions. The former is a description or a report whereas the latter is regarded as a way of expressing the delight felt on seeing it. However in the latter a truth-claim that *beauty is there in the flower*, is contained implicitly as an essential part of the intension of the speaker. To make it clear that the speaker indeed has an implicit intension to make a truth-claim about the presence of beauty in the flower one can ask him if he only means to disclose his feeling of joy that he gets on looking the flower and does not intend to say that there is beauty *out thoro in the flower*. It is obvious that the speaker can never agree with this sort of interpretation of his assertion about the beauty of the flower. No person, ordinarily, will admit that when he talks about the beauty of an object he only means to express his feeling of joy and does not mean to say about a quality that is present in the object

The question of existence of beauty is not related to the existence of the object. The flower he is seeing may be an illusion but even then seeing beauty in it is not his illusion. Irrespective of the knowledge of actual epistemic status of the flower the person's assertion that the flower is beautiful presupposes that beauty is in the flower (and not in the imagination of the person). Beauty is not a property of the flower in the sense its colour and its fragrance are. However, when someone says that the flower is beautiful he ascribes beauty to the flower but his ascription is not an arbitrary subjective imposition. It is not a matter of his choice. He can't choose to see it beautiful. He just looks at the flower and finds that it is beautiful. He finds beauty in it and does not impose *it* on it

Beauty is found or felt in an object by a person—is a fact. This indicates clearly about the objective status of beauty. Whether its objectivity is due to its objective status as a felt quality like other qualities found in an object or is it due to its appreciation according to certain rules, which people internalize in course of their upbringing in their culture, is a matter of philosophical debate. Whatever the case be, it is indubitable that a person, who says that an object is beautiful, feels that beauty *is out there in the object* and not in his mind. Even if it is admitted that it is a matter of appreciation by the person and the ground for this he learns through his cultural upbringing, it can't be denied that this training can't generate beauty in an object of appreciation. In other words it can be said that even if beauty is present in an object one would fail to *see it as beautiful* without an internal training for aesthetic appreciate of things, and if one is given the training then one would be able *to see* the same object beautiful in which he missed it earlier. By this internal training a person does not feel that he judges an object as beautiful since he begins to imagine beauty in it and does not judge another object as beautiful since no such imagination starts in him on seeing that. By the training of taste a person only *discovers* that he can see beauty in those objects where he was missing it earlier. Altogether it means that in stating about the beauty of an object a person does implicitly hold that it is true that the object is beautiful. A truth-claim implicitly present in aesthetic judgment, therefore, could neither be dismissed completely nor could it be ignored. It is implicit but it forms an essential part of the meaning of aesthetic judgment. Had it not been the case a meaningful agreement or disagreement regarding the beauty of an object would not have been possible. A person who perceives beauty in some object is one who has entered into a world of higher order human experience and many more person's like him could enter this world and perceive the beauty of the object. There is nothing private about it that only one person can see and understand and others can't do[1].

In cases of those works of art in which much refined taste is needed to appreciate its beauty it appears that only a privileged few are enjoying it but that is not true. Some works of art are highly abstract in nature and such training is needed to appreciate its beauty that it becomes out of reach of common folk. But its going beyond the reach of common folk is due to subjective differences in persons' interests, attitudes, priorities and many other factors. It is not true that the beauty of some works of art is accessible to only one or only a few persons. Philosophically speaking, if beauty of an art-object is accessible to one then it is, in principle, accessible to all.

Assertions of a lover (about whom he love) also could be considered as an exclamation of the joy that a person feels in the proximity of, or even remembering, the person whom he loves that contain implicitly a truth-claim within it. A person who loves someone understands that he gets great joy in the presence of his beloved and this is what he wants to say when he says something good about her. However, in saying all those things he also says implicitly but definitely that he *finds* certain qualities in his beloved that give him joy and attract him towards her. He does not intend to say that he *projects* those qualities in the beloved and can't agree with someone's opinion that he is under the influence of some hallucination. What a lover says about his beloved is what he actually feels about her and anyone else also can understand it without any doubt that the lover's assertions are not exaggeration regarding his beloved but an honest report about what he actually feels. Any other person, if he has also loved someone, can understand that it would be wrong if the lover does not say things he is saying and says something which could appear to be more rational. A lover usually says that he would die without his beloved. It would sound bizarre if he says instead that *he would feel very uncomfortable in the absence of his beloved but he would actually feel no physical discomfort* Neither his feeling nor the actual state of affair would be intelligible with such extraordinary statements although realistically only this much can be said about the lover.

In *bhakti* also a person simply and honestly says what he feels about the beloved Lord. He does not deliberately exaggerate. He is simply overwhelmed by the emotion of love for the Lord so he says that he is overwhelmed. Whatever he says is his honest feeling and, in fact he could not say so much as he wants to. If he would try to look more rational by saying some thing less emotional then he would be telling lies only and become an object of ridicule in his own eyes and before them also who understand his feelings. The way a *bhakta* says about his relation with his beloved Lord is *the* normal way of saying of what he actually feels and an attempt to put that in a more rational way would prove be to abnormal only. The real intension of a *bhakta's* expression is captured only if we accept that by saying all beautiful things about his beloved Lord he is simply and honestly saying that those beautiful attributes he finds *in* Lord, with Whom he is in direct contact in the emotional experience of *bhakti.* Like beauty, and very much like love, *bhakti* also is an experience in which a person *finds* himself and does not merely imagine arbitrarily. Even if the person keeps on imagining the form of Lord as a matter of spiritual practice he aspires for that stage in which the image of Lord will remain before him without his effort. Reaching the experience of *bhakti* through practicing *bhakti* is the sole goal of every *bhakta* and he knows it well that his practice is not the cause through which the experience can be produced. Experience of *bhakti* is not within the control of the *bhakta.* As seeing beauty in an object is an experience and can't be produced by merely imagining about it, or being in love is an experience that can't be produced by imagining about it, *bhakti* also is an experience and can't be produced by mere imagining about it. The implicit truth claim regarding the beauty of an object is a relevant claim and its relevance lies in understanding that one can lie about the beauty of an object. A person is only lying if he does not *actually see* (i.e. experience) beauty in an object but declares that it is beautiful. A person is only lying that he loves some one unless he *actually feels* so about that person. Similarly a person only lies that he loves his Lord unless he has *actually experienced bhakti.*

In above discussion an attempt is made to make it clear that there are some other human experiences also in which an implicit truth claim is essentially involved although that claim can be validated within the world of that experience and not in sense experience. However, *bhakti*, as it is said in the beginning, is love.

So to understand it more fully we must try to understand the nature of beauty that the lover sees in his of beloved. This is an important task in view of the fact that some serious misgiving is prevalent regarding it. In view of the fact that certain English locutions like 'making love' equates certain aspects of love with sex it becomes serious and urgent to set right our misgiving regarding it. That investigation will form the content of another chapter.

In the light of above discussion we can now form an understanding of *bhakt* as a state of emotional experience of the *bhaktas* who express their ecstasy in saying all those things in the praise of their beloved Lord that a human being can say at all, but by doing so they implicitly make a definite truth-claim also that the object of this experience— his Lord, is a real person. The reality of the Lord is not to be compared to the reality of a person's existence in space and time. The reality of Lord as a real person is to be seen as the reality of a person's beloved in respect to his/her (beloved's) extra-ordinary features that attracts and bind the lover with the beloved. The lover *sees* his beloved as the possessor of certain attractive (attractive for him) qualities. In love the lover experiences these qualities in his beloved but they are not found by others in his beloved in a plain sense experience. Despite the fact that others don't find those extra-ordinary qualities in a person's beloved the lover can't be blamed either for exaggeration or for lying. In fact, the lover perceives in his beloved a person whom no other persons perceive since they are not undergoing that experience, i.e. they are not in love with her. It is not subjective or personal because if anyone else will be in love then he will also *find* those qualities. But the most important point is that it is not at all necessary for any one to fall in love with each and every person to understand that what his lover says about him/her is something that he (the lover) actually *finds* in him/her since he is in love. What good things a lover says about his beloved are quite expected from him since he is in love. This wide agreed upon expectation about the assertions of the lover clearly indicates about the objective regularity in his behaviour brought about by the experience of love. But we hardly ever try to understand that what he says is what he actually *sees* or *finds* and not imagines. We think that he is projecting all those good qualities in the beloved and making exaggeration. So we think that it is devoid of truth-content and overlook it. This aspect of the experience of love that a person in love *finds* those qualities in his beloved and does not project them is never given due consideration.

In love a person sees some qualities in the beloved that can be seen in his beloved in love only. Even if some one sees (i.e. perceives in sense experiences) special quality in a person's beloved he does not see in it what the lover sees. The difference is not a difference of seeing and imagining but that of seeing it at the level of sense experience and seeing at the level of aesthetic experience. One can see that two parts of a figure are equal but may not see the symmetry in it. It is also possible that someone discovers symmetry in a figure that is ordinarily not seen as symmetrical because the two parts of it may not be visibly equal. If the equality of the parts is visualized under certain specific conditions only then the symmetry also can be seen under that condition only. Suppose a coloured picture is developed on a black and white photographic plate then the certain features of it will not be visible to us if they are depicted with colour contrast. We can again discover those hidden features if we see it through the appropriate colour filter. A lover's seeing beauty in his beloved and seeing beauty in the work of art – both are the instances of *seeing* or discovering (not imagining) but the latter is the seeing of beauty under a condition (a sort of filter) without which it can't be seen. That condition is love. Love is an objective (not subjective) condition that enables one to see some specific beautiful qualities in the beloved. The lover does not project these qualities in his beloved ; he could just discover it because he in love.

It is not the case with the love of men and women. Any love relation essentially has this feature. A mother feels something in her child that gives her great joy that she can't find seeing even more beautiful child than her own. This is a truth about all love-relation that a person feels something in the person whom he loves that attracts him and gives him joy in his presence, in his contact and even in remembering him. He does not project anything on him: he just feels that. In fact this feeling of joy that a person gets in the presence and contact of some particular individual is the essence that creates the relational bond of love (if both the persons have this feeling then the love relation becomes mutual but remains unidirectional if only one person has this feeling). Love relation perishes with the disappearance of this feeling. When this feeling of joy in the presence of the beloved disappears then he/she remains no more dear and complaints begin to crop up from both sides. Love relations, usually, ends in this manner. Had it been possible to generate this feeling by some method, it could have saved the love relations. But it is not within the person's control completely.

If both the persons –the lover and the beloved are of high understanding then the relation can be saved by mutual understanding. But then it turns into a relation of understanding and it lacks the warmth or ecstasy of love relation. It, then, remains no more a love relation. The joy or the warmth that love gives to a relation is somewhat a sublime gift. No amount of imagination of an individual can ensure generation of this warmth/ joy. Through imagination one can project some quality in an individual but to behave in accordance with this imagination would possible for the person (who is imagining) only if he constantly force his imagination to interpret that individual's inconsistent behaviours also in that light. But in so doing he will never feel that that quality is present in that individual rather his constrained imagination will remind him constantly that he does not *feel* it.

Imagination of a quality in an individual would not remain a constant constraint for the person only If that quality is already present in that individual, or that individual developed it in him in course of that person's efforts to imagine it in him. But in either case it becomes a really present quality and remains no more imaginary. The relation between imagining a quality in an individual and its actual presence in him needs a limited elaboration at this point.

Let us suppose that a person imagines a quality in an individual but that is not present in him. In this case in order to keep his imagination alive he will have to reinforce his imagination again and again. Especially in the situations where his imagination comes in direct conflict with reality he will have to exert additional power of reason also to present an interpretation that can defuse tension between reality and imagination. This case is case where the person who is imagining will have to face constant tensions.

In another case where the person imagines a quality in a person and that is really present in it although he is ignorant of its presence, will be a matter of delight for him since he will soon realize that he has a made a discovery or that he is proved to be true. There will be no stress for him in this case.

In the third case, if a person has not imagined the presence of a quality in a person then either he will be startled to discover it on some occasion, if it is present in that person, or he will never come to know about it.

However, above possible consequences presuppose implicitly that the quality under discussion is directly observable to the person who imagines its presence in another person. If the quality is not directly given in the sense experience, but requires from the person to educate himself to reach a higher/deeper level of imagination then these consequences would be noticed on that level only. Beauty of an artwork can be seen by any ordinary person if it is a realistic art. But to *see* beauty in an abstract painting requires some cultivation of taste to raise the person's level of imagination. By rising a height of imagination one can *see* that a painting *is* beautiful. This cultivation does not mean that the person learns to imagine something as beautiful that is not so. It is to imagining beauty in an art-object, which is actually beautiful, to see it so. These are two different situations and the difference is clearly marked in the difference of the person's feeling of stress or its absence respectively. Cultivation of taste is only a way to prepare oneself to see beauty.

A *bhakta*, through the acts of worship, prepares him/herself to enter into the experience of *bhakti* and sees that his Lord is an actual embodiment of grace and unbound majesty and infinite power. If his Lord of love were not actually a person having so many of the attributes of which the *bhaktas* talk about he would have felt a burden – a stress all the time. But no *bhaktas* ever undergo any stress in *bhakti.* On the contrary they feel unfathomable ecstasy. In *bhakti* he feels the presence of his Lord of love as the condensation and constellation of enormous grace, unbound majesty and unlimited power that fills his heart with enormous joy. This is a mark of the fact that he is *experiencing* these attributes in his Lord and *not imagining* about them. As it is explained in the above discussion a lover sees certain beautiful qualities in his beloved because he is in love. This is mistaken to be a subjective state that makes the lover project those qualities in the beloved. This is wrong. Love is the objective condition that enables a person to discover these qualities that can't be discovered without it. If the qualities were not actually present in the beloved and the lover would have been exerting his power of imagination to impose them on the beloved's personality. But it is a matter of a clear distinction by the lover and very largely by others (by closely examining the spontaneous responses of the lover) too. The lover can know and does know if he is imposing a quality on his beloved or only seeing it in her. Others also can decide about it. So it is necessary to come out of the general misgiving that the pretty things that a lover states about his beloved is only his subjective imposition. While it is true that lovers may subjectively impose so many things in his beloved and make exaggerations, it does not belie the fact that they do *see* certain qualities in the beloved, which others can't see, only because they are in love.

Bhaktas, the lovers of Lord, do *see* their Lord as the embodiment of innumerable high qualities because they are in love with Him. Anyone in love with Him also could *see* him as the condensation and constellation of these and many more qualities. It is all due to their *bhakti* and this statement should not be mistaken for a subjective imposition on the part of the *bhaktas.* It clearly means that anyone whofulfills the objective condition of *bhakti* can and does see Lord as a real person as an abode of all these high qualities.

A preliminary background is prepared in this chapter to understand *bhakti* from the standpoint of a *bhakta.* With this background we can now proceed to understand the subtlety of human love and then – the holiness of divine love. But before that it would be more fruitful to underline the reason or reasons for the difference between the *bhaktas'* understanding of *bhakti* and a non-*bhktas'* understanding of the same. That is the subject matter of the next chapter.

References

1. Sutra—2, Narad Bhakti Sutra
2. Immanuel Kant also, in his *Critique of Judgment*, expresses similar view and acknowledges that aesthetic concepts are, in a sense, objective since the feeling of pleasure and pain have a universal appeal.

4

Bhakti–a Transformation of Doer into an Instrument of Lord

Kṛṣṇa! The realization that the *bhakti bhâva* and the *bhakti rasa* are divine gifts begins to transform the life of the *bhakta* in a radical way. He makes his heart more and more receptive to receive this divine gift as much as possible. Either he suspends rest of his worldly activities and devotes maximum time to remain absorbed in remembering the name and the image of the Lord to experience the joy of *bhakti* or he tries to do the same while doing all his worldly duties. Whatever life-style he chooses for himself he only wants to keep on enjoying the *bhakti rasa.* Outwardly he may or may not remain a doer but inwardly he becomes a receptor only. He makes his body and mind instruments in and through which the ecstatic experience of *bhakti* could manifest and make him overjoyed. A *bhakta* transforms himself into an instrument in the hand of his dear Lord. Every form of *bhakti*— any emotional relation with the Lord— brings about this radical transformation. If a *bhakta* puts himself as a servant in relation to his Lord then he does all his duties in the world not as an active decision maker but only as an obedient servant who is ordered to do so. He does not attach himself with the result of the action and offers it at the feet of his Lord at the end. If he succeeds then he does not take its credit and if he fails then also he most humbly submits it before the Lord He gets the pure joy of obeying his master in whatsoever he does. This is an actual joy and not merely an idea of it. Ordinarily a person does any work with the motivation of getting favourable result since it gives him physical and/or psychic pleasure. A *bhakta's* motivation also is favourable result but this favourable result is to remain placed in the blissful contact with his Lord while doing any work. As it is said earlier it is an actual motivation for the *bhakta* to do any work so he does not do or at least want to avoid all that in doing which his contact with his Lord is severed or weakened. This results into his attitude to his actions which now his does only with indifference. This is a direct consequence of his experience of *bhakti bhâva* and *bhakti rasa* as divine gifts. *Bhakts*, thus, do all or most of the works but don't remain the doer since they don't take any interest in doing those deeds. They are (and should be) held responsible for their actions and for all practical worldly purposes passing judgment on their action accordingly is not wrong either. However, to understand their position it is necessary to realize that they don't take themselves as the doer of any action and only want to enjoy the feeling that his Lord has kept them in His graceful contact. The *bhaktas* only want to enjoy the experience that Lord is giving them the joy (i.e. Lord is doing something to them and they are the object of His actions). The feeling of becoming the instrument of Lord's acts is the only desire of the *bhaktas* that takes away from them the attitude of doer completely.

Bhaktas don't do any *sâdhanâ* for achieving the state of non-doer (i.e. ego-less-ness) but it is very naturally attained by them as a direct consequence of their desire to enjoy the state of becoming an object of the Lord's acts. It is not quite inappropriate to cast a quick look at the possibility of any method of achieving ego-less-ness. It seems logically impossible that a person decides to do any action to drop his ego and becomes successful in his aim because the very act of deciding and pursuing a course of action is impossible without a doer (an ego). The *bhaktas* don't have any such aim at all. They don't want *moksha* either. They only want to enjoy the love of their Lord by becoming the object of His acts of grace showering on him. This desire very naturally results into the no-doer attitude of the *bhaktas* without their conscious effort or knowledge.

Whether it be 'servant-master' relationship or any other form of relationship in which a *bhakta* finds himself emotionally connected to his Lord, he (the *bhakta*) becomes the non-doer of actions. If the *bhakta* finds himself placed in relationship of friend or father/mother of Lord even then he wants only to do that which could give him the joy of remain engrossed in that emotional relation and despite all his actions he remains a non-doer.

The non-doer attitude blossoms in the *bhaktas*' life with any form of relation with Lord but in relation to Lord's beloved this feeling (of being an instrument) becomes overtly and most intensely clear. In *bhakti* tradition in India this is called *Madhurâ Bhakti*. It is that form of *bhakti* for the Lord in which a person offers himself to the Lord as His beloved and desires intensely that the Lord would kindly reciprocate to his love at all levels of his being— physical and psychic also, as a lover does to his beloved. Radha and all her friend gopis of Vrindavan, who loved Sri Krishna as their lover, are the ideal of this form of *bhakti*. In different ages this form of *bhakti* was practiced by some *bhaktas*. Meera in the north of India and Andal in the south are the paradigms of *Madhurâ Bhakti*. However, it is not only for women. In the ensuing discussion it will become clear that it has nothing to do with the gender of the person in the biological sense. It only involves the typical feminine attitude with which a woman offers herself to her husband or beloved. Since in a conjugal relation female is ordinarily supposed to be a partner who basically and mostly helps her male partner to do all what he wants to do with her in love and this is what the *bhaktas* are supposed to do in order to become a mere instrument in the hand of the Lord, this form of *bhakti* requires the development of this feminine disposition in the *bhaktas*. Men can (and indeed do) go on this path of *bhakti* by developing this disposition in them in their emotional relation to their Lord. Some people begin to lead life overtly also as a woman but essentially it is necessary for the *bhakta* of this path to drop his disposition to respond like a male in relation to his Lord.

Madhurâ Bhakti

In *Vaiṣņvism Mdhurā bhakti* is given the highest position and revered by all Krishna-*bhaktas*. This is the path of loving the Lord

Lord as one's lover and offer oneself to Him as His beloved. It is the path of reducing oneself to a mere object of Lord's love. It is not passivity at all. It is to act–to live a life of a maiden who very eagerly desires to get a response of love from her lover. To drop one's physical-social identity and to transform oneself into a being who thinks, speak and acts to get the response of Lord's love only and to have no other desire at all–is the essence of *Madhurâ bhakti.* To have no desire for the world and to seek eagerly a response of affection from the Lord is present in every form of *bhakti bhâva* for the Lord but to offer oneself as His beloved to get the uninhibited love-response is the specialty of this form of *bhakti bhâva.*These love-responses cover the *bhakta's* entire being. Some of the expected love-responses have reference to the *bhakta's* body, which, he feels, is feminine, but it is not taken as a physical sensual act. Two reasons are behind it—first, this is a very special *bhâva* of love, and second, the *bhakta* is not merely in a state of *bhâva* – he is well in a state of enjoying its *rasa.* So much is said about *Madhurâ Bhakti* from the literary perspectives. This is such an enchanting theme that engaged hundreds of poets in all ages and it still gives mesmerizing effect to their subject. Not much psychological effort is made to understand it. In philosophical discussion also it is very much neglected because anything emotional is, ordinarily, deemed as a sort of weakness or hindrance to attain truth. In order to understand *bhakti* it is necessary to understand the non-doer attitude of the *bhaktas* and without understanding *Madhurâ Bhakti* the actual depth and power of this attitude can't be assessed. A close look at it, therefore, is much needed.

Madhura Bhakti bhâva is apparently an emotion of love that a woman feels for her lover. The form and intensity of the power (of attraction) of this emotion is the same as in case of ordinary emotion of love of a woman but because of its depth it becomes very different. As it is said in Chapter- I, ordinary love also is a spiritual force of attraction—it is neither physical nor merely psychic. It degenerates into physical and personal relation and disappears. This so happens because ordinary experience of love does not bring with it the awareness that it is attractive unto itself. People in love do so much for each other since they get great joy in so doing but hardly ever notice that it is the beauty and ecstasy of love independent of the beauty of the beloved and of the joy of proximity with him/her. Persons in love ordinarily mistake it for the physical attraction of the persons whom they love. Although in *Bhakti* this does not happen since Lord is not physically present before the *bhaktas* and the beauty of Lord is seen in the beauty manifesting in *bhakti* but it may also happen with some people who get lost in the joy of singing devotional songs for Lord but don't become aware of the fact that *bhakti* itself is an extremely beautiful an experience. The beauty of Lord manifests only in the experince of *bhakti.* To feel that *bhakti* itself is a beautiful gift of Lord and to feel gratitude for it makes the love for Lord a divine experience— makes it *bhakti.* If it does not happen then one can get the joy of singing devotional songs and can experience calm in chanting His name but despite a touch of divinity in them these experiences of joy and calm don't rise above the ordinary level of joy of music and the calm of relaxation from the stress of duties.

As it is discussed earlier, even ordinary love relation with ordinary persons acquires divinity and becomes close to *bhakti* if awareness of the spirituality of this experience is achieved. *Bhakti,* therefore, is a very special type of human emotion and can't be experienced if physicality dominates in a person's life. The *bhâva* of *bhakti* can't dwell in a person's heart if sensuality enters into his mind. If a person's mind tends to make Lord into an object of sensuous pleasure it does not remains *bhakti* at all. In Narada Bhakti Sutra it is said that forgetting Lord's godliness reduces the love for Lord to an illicit relation[1] It is this essential nature of *bhakti* due to which in *Madhurâ Bhakti* a person stands as the beloved of Lord and invites Him to play with his entire being but does not involve himself in sensuality. Although the *bhakta* offfers his entire being to the Lord including his body and mind but desired responses at these level are governed and dominate by the spiritual aspiration to enjoy the pure spiritual beauty of Lord's love.

The second reason due to which *bhakti* can't be sensuality is the fact that it is not merely a *bhâva* but essentially it is a *rasa.* It is important to note that *bhakti,* in fact, is primarily and essentially a *rasa.* It would not be wrong to say that it *rasa* first and *bhâva* latter. Or, in other words, we can say that it is a very special *bhâva* that is felt only if it becomes a *rasa.* If one does not have the taste of love for Lord then there is no reason for its arousal and being operational in one's life. *Bhakti* is different from ordinary love because bodily urge generates a feeling of attraction for another person and love can serve as a condition to enter into a bodily or some sort of physical contact with another person. Although ordinary human love also is pure spiritual force of attraction but it becomes an occasion for falling into physical contact. Pure bodily urge can force the persons to enter into bodily relation even without the presence of love between two persons but love also becomes an occasion for that since the person usually does not take note of distinction between two sorts of attraction. Love for the beloved is accepted (socially and personally too) as a sort of pre-condition to make love (i.e. to have physical contact) with her/him. If two lovers enter into a physical contact they take it as an offshoot of expression of their love that they distinctly feel as a psychic attraction. It is not the case that the lovers don't feel the difference between physical and psychic attraction but under the intense effect of the physical attraction they forget this difference for a while. Love that is a force of pure psychic attraction is deep but mild in intensity in comparison to physical attraction. Hence two persons, who get attracted to each other due to psychic attraction of love, fall in physical attraction and their psychic attraction to each other becomes only a pretext for it. However, this can't happen in love with the Lord.

Bhakti can't serve as a condition of a physical contact with Lord. Although the *bhakta* eagerly desires for the most intimate relation with Lord this does not include a sensual relation. Even in *Madhura bhâva* it is not allowed although lot of reference to physical relation is found in the poetry of the *bhaktas* of *Madhur bhâva.* It is worth noting that it is not a taboo. It is only a warning to not conflate the pure spiritual force of attraction with any physical attraction or demands since it is then missed altogether. If the person is not aware of the spirituality of *bhakti* then he has not yet experienced its essence. To experience the bliss of it is to understand its spirituality since it is the bliss of rising completely above the mundane and entering into a realm of pure sublime *bhâva.* Even without having the experience of *bhakti* as a fully developed *rasa* (i.e. without having an explicitly clear taste of this emotion) one feels the spirituality of this emotional force of attraction. An ordinary person, who feels joy only while singing devotional songs but does not enjoy it with awareness, also feels clearly that he is passing through an experience that is different from the joy gained from any other physical means. Although such persons by themselves and by others also are called 'God-intoxicated', they themselves and others know that it is only a figure of speech and it is an intoxication of very different kind if at all it is intoxication. So, even in the most ordinary level of *bhakti* a person has some taste of it and can't pass through it purely mechanically (as it is possible to fall in some one's love without being a little aware of the spirituality of the force of this attraction). Love in the case of ordinary humans may remain only an emotion – a *bhâva, bhakti* can never remain a *bhâ*va only. It is a '*rasa bhâva'* (not *rasâbhâva*) —if we can say so, to distinguish it from all other emotions that human beings pass through without having their taste. Ordinary human love also is a higher cognitive emotion according to modern psychologists and *bhakti,* if we follow that way of classification, is still a higher or the highest type. But its position is not only due to its depth and over all effect on the person: it is the dimensional difference that gives it a very special place in human life.

Most emotions in humans and animals are generated by survival instinct to arouse favourable and unfavourable responses to different situations faced by the animals. Higher cognitive emotions in humans are not directly related to that instinct but indirectly they are also related to the same since almost all cognitive and intellectual enterprises help in widening and heightening its (survival instinct's) range. Scientific endeavour can be easily seen to be related to it but art, craft and cultural and religious activities also can be shown to be related to it in depth. Religious life and especially emotions arising in this life are deeply related to person's concern about the relation of life with its end –i.e. death. Obviously it is out and out a human concern and that also is of a very high order. Every one knows that every body will die some day but most of us remain forgetful about our own death. Any ordinary fear about our money or position makes us restless but death, which is so certain, does not become the reason of the concern of most of us unless it comes in the form of specific fatal disease or something like death punishment. When it comes in such forms then it usually arouses the emotion of fear only, makes the person extremely tense and motivates him to escape it by all possible means at any cost. Normally it is a state of panic. But religion helps a person to feel this concern with most seriousness and urgency and to prepare for it in a calm and composed manner. Generally this preparation takes the form of arousing the emotion of complete surrender before God Who is beyond death. Some how or the other a religious fellow tries to develop an intimate emotional relation with God to transcend the fear of death. This is not necessarily the emotion of love. It may be an emotion of awe for the deity so that in response His favour can be won and the believer can find himself placed in a secured position against the fear of death.

Development of an emotional relation with God places a person beyond the fear of death. An emotional relation with God emancipates the person form this fear and in this way it is deeply related to human survival instinct. However, this instinct remains hidden and operates in human life the way a need to learn science and art or literature operates. Neither science nor art and literature are needs of humans in the sense food, water and shelter are. Yet we concede that an urge for these things are linked deeply with their beings and are necessary for their existence as human beings. Religious belief in general and *bhakti* in particular also are linked to human existence in similar manner but they are linked to human existence at the deepest level. This manifest through human beings' aspiration to know the unseen and unknown that is beyond sense experience. An unknown attraction that still operates in them despite knowledge of all the sophisticated theories of science gives almost all humans motivation for that in the form of a taste for that. Potentially this taste is found in almost all humans. Education, environment and personal conditions help in the growth of this taste to the level of active choice of the person. In *bhaktas'* life this taste grows as an emotional attraction for their dear Lord and operates very clearly as a driving force. This motivation can't be produced in anyone if it is potentially not present in him as taste for some sort of emotional contact with the unknown object of faith. This taste is already given to almost all. In the *bhaktas'* perception this is a *divine gift* since it could not have been achieved by human efforts if it were not *given* to them. Acceptance of *bhakti* as a divine gift underlines two facts; first, it is a gift and not a product of human effort and second, it is divine and not just humanly. Acceptance of *bhakti* as divine gift manifests practically in his internal and/or external behaviour as an instrument in the hand of his Lord. In *Madhurâ Bhakti* this becomes very clearly visible.

Bhakti, a complete and unconditional surrender at the feet of the Lord becomes possible only if a person already has a taste for it—only if he gets *rasa* in it. This *rasa* is spoiled if it is overpowered by sensuality. It is a necessary condition to experience *bhakti* as a *rasa* that all manifestations of love for the Lord be completely under the domination of the force of pure spiritual attraction for the Lord. In simple words- the *rasa* of *bhakti* can't be experienced if sensuality dominates in a person's life. So it is clear that despite apparent sensuality in the *Madhurâ bhakti* for the Lord there is no sensuality in it. It is not wrong to say that *bhakti* and sensuality can never go together. *Bhakti* lifts the person to the highiest level of his being—the level of pure spirituality. Sensuality pulls down and ties him to the lowest level of his being—the level of physicality There is nothing wrong in physicality as such if it does not comes in way to a person's movement to the upper levels of his being. To remain confined to only the lowest level of one's being is a clear morbidity. To remain confined to the spiritual level only is not morbidity but definitely it is also lop-sidedness. There are two ways to overcome this lop-sidedness. One, bringing the spiritual level of one's being under the control of physical level and two, doing the opposite, i.e. bringing physical level under the control of spiritual level. A materialist tries to do the former (whether he succeeds in so doing is a different matte) and a spiritualist either tries to remain confined to the level of pure spirituality (success in this also is doubtful) or he does the latter. *Madhurâ Bhakti* is the path of spirituality in which physicality is used in its fullness but under the full control of one's spiritual level of being.

In *Madhura Bhakti* for the Lord the person achieves that intimacy with Lord in which he does not allow even his gender to become a hindrance to avail Lord's favourable response. A lover, in the love-play, actively plays with the body of his beloved to express his love, and the feeling of being touched or used by the lover becomes a matter of intense joy for the beloved. The *bhakta* of *Madhurâ bhakti* belies his gender identity in placing himself in relation to Lord as a *sakhi* (friend) of His beloved Râdhâ and enjoys the uninhibited emotional proximity with Him. This is the '*Râgânugâ* form of *Madhurâ Bhakti*' that means to become the follower of those girlfriends of the Lord who loved Him[1]. This is differentiated from '*Râgâtmikâ* form of *Madhurâ Bhakti*' in which a person feels that she/he herself/himself is a *gopi* or a beloved of Lord and tries to avail Lords love directly. Meera, who loved Lord *Kŗşņa*! as her husband, was on the path of *Râgâtmikâ Madhurâ bhakti*. Both these forms of *Madhura Bhakti* need to be dealt with meticulously in the light of above discussion regarding the specific relation between the spiritual and physical levels of the *bhakta's* being.

Râgânugâ form of *Madhurâ Bhakti*

In *Râgânugâ bhakti* the *bhakta* tries to envisage himself/herself as a close friend of Râdhâ. The *bhakta* (even if a male) assumes himself to be a *sakhi* of Râdhâ. It is not necessary for him to show it overtly in his behaviours (although in some sects of this *sâdhanâ bhaktas* actually do that), it is necessary to inwardly feel so. He tries to imagine of the situations of love of Râdhâ-*Kŗşņa*! in which he plays some role to bring them closer or to help them in their love-play. All the apparently erotic references to their love, as described tastefully in Sri Madbhâgvat, are imagined by him and assuming that he also is a part of this divine love-play gets himself completely absorbed in that situation. This joy of sharing the joy of love of Lord through Râdhâ makes him aware more and more of the intense joy of the internal world of the divine love-play and the physical surrounding is dropped far below. It is an imagination of the *bhakta* that he is participating in the divine love-play but the joy he gets is not imaginary— it is real. It is not a thought of the *bhakta* that he is getting intense joy, it is his actual experience. It can be said that he is getting a joy of imagination, that it is a result of auto- suggestion. In a way this objection is valid, but only if we accept that whatever is not happening in outer physical space is not real at all. To do so is to misunderstand *bhakta's* view of *bhakti*. In the last chapter this objection was met with and it would be only a repetition to answer to it. But we should remind ourselves that this sort of divine imagination itself is a great divine gift and not a sole product of human effort, and as such it is not merely an imagination but a higher realm of reality for the *bhaktas*. In fact every ordinary person, only if he does not deliberately choose to stick to some sort of material realism, can easily understand that to enter into this sort of vivid imagination that can produce so powerful emotional effect is extremely difficult. But the fact that this is not only difficult but impossible for human effort – can be realized if we take into consideration some of the following factors that are necessary for its production but none of which are in human control:—

(a) To produce the desire to imagine about divine love (For a common man who has no inclination towards religion in general and in *bhakti* in particular to imagine such thing is either ridiculous, nonsense or useless. There is no direct way to generate the desire in a person to do so. Indirect ways are also ways of creating favourable circumstances. That a person will have such an imagination is always a matter of chance.),

(b) to get enjoyment in this imagined situation (Even if somehow the person prepares himself to imagine such a situation of divine love he himself can't produce joy in having this. It can happen only per chance or with the Lord's grace —as the *bhaktas* claim),

(c) to continue in this situation and to be aware of it for a considerable period of time to have its taste (Awareness of this situation is availed just by reminding oneself to be aware but to remind oneself itself is a matter of chance or again Lord's grace—either it happens by itself or there is no way to produce or make it happen if it does not happen), and finally

(d) to lead a *Râgânugâ bhakti*-centered life —all these are beyond human control. No one can achieve all these by remaining mentally tied to the material world of sense experience. It could be possible since the world of *bhakti* exists independently of the material world. A *bhakta* through the acts of *bhakti* gets transported to the world of *bhakti* where all these happen naturally. The reality of the life-world of

bhakti is given in the experience of *bhakti.* The Lord is the centre of this life-world and His reality can't be denied without completely denying the undeniable reality of *bhakti.* Not only the dwellers of this life-world (i.e. *bhaktas*) but also any one who is close to them can understand this truth. To understand *bhakti* from *bhakta's* standpoint it is necessary to not forget that although the *bhaktas* imagine the beautiful form and features of his dear Lord he uses his imagination only to go beyond the boundaries of material world of sense experience and to enter into a deeper level of reality of human experience.

In the *Râgânugâ bhakti* the *bhakta* feels the presence of the Lord. As a *sakhi* of Râdhâ the *bhakta* also comes in direct contact with Sri Krishna. However, the *bhakta* maintains a distance with Him in view of his position of a servant. He never tries to acquire the position of Lord's beloved. He aspires for his share of Lord's favourable response merely as Râdhâ'*s sakhi*—a friend or a servant. He never tries to become equal to Lord's divine beloved Râdhâ. He only aspires that Lord should give him a blissful smile or a graceful patting etc. When the *bhakta's* attention is drawn by the immensely deep joy arising out of the internal perception that he actually gets all the favourable responses in abundance from the Lord then he remains no more conscious of the mundane world around him — he is thrown into the *bhâva samâdhi* (emotional trance). He becomes almost completely insensitive towards all that happens to his body and in his physical surrounding. The *bhakta* is shifted to the lived-world of Vrindâvana. A *bhakta* of *Râgânugâ Madurâ Bhakti* aspires for this very blissful contact with his Lord. He desires for nothing except for this and wants to remain lost in this experience if he achieves it. This is an experience of eternal present or timelessnerss. A glimpse of it is availed by all worldly lovers,who in the ecstasy of their union (not necessarily physical) want to remain immersed in the ineffable joy of union and desire that the moment should freeze for ever. Human love gives a glimpse of what eternal present or timelessness means but it can't place the lover into eternity: it passes out and the lovers have to part with it. Only a memory is left in their hearts and that also fades with the passage of time. On the other hand, a union with Lord in *bhakti* becomes a way of the *bhaktas'* life. A *bhakta,* who has got the experience that his dear Lord has actively responded to his love, transforms into a living specimen of a unique Divine response like Meera. Worldly life is either meaningless for her or it is only an extension of the inner world of *bhakti* in which she finds herself in the close proximity of Krishna. There is no separation from Krishna in that world. Even if Krishna is invisible for her for a while she feels His presence in the experience of His absence. Meera is an specimen of the *Râgâtmikâ* form of *Madhurâ Bhakti.*A *bhakta* of *Râgânugâ Madhurâ Bhati* also attain the same eternal union with Lord since it is substantively the same. The relationship and the content of the experience only varies in style. A *bhakta* of *Râgânugâ bhakti* experiences Lord's direct responses of his love as a *sakhii* of Radha but it unites him with his dear Lord directly since the response of the Lord is made directly to him. It may be for Radha and may be for her also. Even if the responses are for Radha and not directly for him, he becomes the first and direct object of that divine response

As it is stated in above paragraph, from an ordinary person's standpoint it all seems to be a play of powerful autosuggestion. Autosuggestion generates a hypnotic sleep. But a *bhakta's* effort to imagine the situation of love of Radha-Krishna and to imaginatively place himself in an active role of Radha's *sakhi* is not intended to generate sleep at all. On the contrary, his imagination only enables him to consciously enter into a deeper level of an actually possible world of human experience from where the reality of this physical world is dimmed. This world becomes non-existent for him till he remains absorbed in this emotional trance. No stimuli of this world disturb him at all. He may even be killed in this state and he will remain unperturbed. Death really disappears for him. It is all due to the immense depth of the emotion of love for the Lord that absorbs *bhakta's* consciousness completely in Lord's feet and his identity as a physical body is left far behind. Death occurs to his body and he remains engrossed in the feet of beloved Lord without being least affected by this event. This can't ever happen just by rationally thinking about the unreality of the world or about the existence of Lord. It is the actual experience of *bhakti* that is emotional in nature but has a clear cognitive content also that manifests in the *bhaktas*' full awareness of the state of his experience. One can imagine the intense erotic joy of love affair of a loving couple. They forget everything in this joy. But they have to fall back to ordinary mundane world since ordinarily their joy of love degenerates into a sensual joy that comes to an end. A *bhakta,* who enters into the *Râgânugâ Bhakti* with Lord, also enjoy a deep erotic sort of joy but it never degenerates into a sensual joy and never comes to an end. A *bhakta,* therefore, enters into the *Bhâva Samâdhi* from where he fears not to fall back. He comes back to ordinary plane only with a clear instruction from Lord and his old physical identity does not bind (not even touch) him at all but he deliberately uses it for serving Lord's purpose to spread the message of *bhakti.* A *bhakta* does not desire for anything except his Lord's love and it is easy to understand in case of a *bhakta* of *Râgânugâ* form of *Madhurâ Bhakti.* It is quite intelligible that one who has got a taste of an erotic-sort-of-love for Lord wants to live and die in it only. He wants nothing except his beloved Lord or more precisely — Lord's love. Indeed these two statements are not two—they have the same experiential meaning. The Lord of love is not independent of or different from His love so far as the actual experience is concerned. Epistemically Lord is independent and different from the *bhakta's* love since He is the source and object of it. But a *bhakta* comes in contact of his beloved Lord only by having the awareness of the *rasa* of *bhakti.* Lord is, experientially, the very content of the *rasa* of *bhakti.* So to say that Lord and His love are one and the same is a true statement of the *bhakta's* experience. To take it as an expression of the *bhakta's* overwhelming joy devoid of truth content is to mistake his experience and his intension both. No doubt the *bhakta* is overjoyed in having the taste of *bhakti* but it is the joy of having the taste of this experience of the close proximity of his dear Lord. So what the *bhakta* states is a true statement about his experience. A *bhakta* who enjoys the taste of *bhakti* enters into a world of human experience that is not real *at the same level* as the world of sense experience is but it is *as much real as* (or more real) the latter is.

Râgâtmikâ form of Madhurâ Bhakti

It is that form of love for Lord in which the *bhakta* enters into a direct conjugal-sort-of- love with Him. Radha's love and the love of all the queens of *Kṛṣṇa!*, who are deemed mythological characters, come in this category. In modern times Meerâ's love also comes in the same category. She loved the Lord as her husband.

The *bhakta* who follows the path of *Râgâtmikâ* form of *Madhurâ Bhakti* offers herself/himself to Lord as His beloved or wife. No inhibitions are allowed to come in the path of getting a favoured response of Lord. But this is such a depth of love where even the most sensual responses drop all the physical reference. This seems impossible since sensual desires are conceived only with reference to their connection to the body. To talk about a sensual desire without any reference to body appears to be a blatant contradiction. But since no such description is found in Meera's poetry although for her *Kṛṣṇa!* was her husband – a relation where sensuality is permitted and dominates, it becomes necessary to re-examine the nature of sensuality.

Sex desire is found in almost all animals. Reproduction is a biological phenomenon and the organic urge to mate with opposite sex partner is quite natural. But observation of most of the developed animals' behaviour before mating and in course of that does not give any indication that they get a similar pleasure as the humans do. It appears from these observations that they feel a sort of organic pressure and sexual intercourse with opposite sex-partner helps in releasing this pressure. No indication of joy is received rather in some animals it seems to be peculiar sort of painful phenomenon especially for the female. Sex is a periodic phenomenon in most animals and after or before that they don't feel any urge for entering into sex relation. In humans the situation is very different. For humans sex is not merely an organic urge. Humans get the most intense joy in entering into sex relation with the opposite sex partner. It is primarily a desire to have this intense joy that motivate them to enter into sexual intercourse more and more and they hardly ever miss an opportunity to have it subject to limitations of social morality. Very often they even transgress the social limits and commit heinous crimes like rape to satiate this burning desire for pleasure. These observations suggest contrasting the phenomenon of sex in humans with the same in animals. For animals it is essentially and primarily an organic urge. For humans it is essentially organic urge but primarily a desire for pleasure. It is not wrong to say that most people for most of the time in their lives would not like to enter into sex if they had not got intense pleasure in it. The desire for this pleasure is psychological (although related to body) and not a desire to get a relief of any organic pressure. If we identify sensuality with this desire of bodily-pleasure seeking and the urge to get relief from an organic pressure then we can admit that human beings undergo both the experiences simultaneously and, ordinarily, they are not felt as two. But they are distinguishable not only conceptually but experientially too. It is not to say that they can be experienced as two separate phenomena. It only means that anyone, with some reflective awareness, can distinguish them sharply (psychological desire for pleasure tends to extend the duration of experience and the organic desire to get relief from the pressure tends to finish it soon). An actual possibility to have this sensual pleasure in the most elongated manner, or without finishing it, is admitted in Tantrâs and practiced by the followers of that path as an intermediary stage on the journey of self-realization. In this path, the joy is the focus of attention, but it is done by sexually exciting the body more and more. This is not the path of *Madhurâ Bhakti.* But in view of the above stated distinction it is also possible (at least it can be thought) that a person has full attention on the joy and forgets the body completely. It is said that some higher order of creations e.g. — the *devtas* enjoys all sorts of sensuous and sensual pleasures without any physical body. It is imagined that they enjoy the taste of delicious food and drink, smell of fine fragrance and all other pleasant sensation in a subtle way since have a subtle body but don't face the fatigue or other negative consequences that is inevitable in physical body. In the *Râgâtmikâ* form of *Maldhura Bhakti* also the *bhakta,* who takes herself/himself as Lord's beloved or wife, enjoys an intimate relation with Lord with all the nuances of personal contact without any reference to physical body. Full attention of the *bhakta*, absorbed in enjoying the *rasa* of *bhakti*, makes him forget her/his physical body completely. A person, who is interested in the *rasa*-the taste of food, uses his tongue as a means only and does not remain particularly conscious about the sensation of the contact between the tongue and the food. Putting any food on the tongue gives two types of sensation—a sensation of touch of the food and the taste of the same. If we touch the eatable from our hand or any other part of the body then we will have the sensation of its touch. Tongue also gets the sensation of the touch of the eatable but that overlooked or neutralized almost completely due to the sensation of its taste since that is the main function of this organ. One can use one's tongue to have the sensation of touch of a thing (eatable or non-eatable) along with having its taste. Since tongue is the organ mainly to have taste, the sensation of touch can be had with it with additional awareness only otherwise it is overlooked in normal condition. Similarly when the *bhakta* enjoys the taste of *bhakti* its manifestation on bodily level does not remain in the focus of his attention –it is overlooked. Although this explanation is analogical this actually happens in the life the *bhakta*.

Another and perhaps the most important aspect of *Râgâtmikâ* form of *Madhurâ Bhakti* is the predominance of the strong spiritual attraction of love that makes even the sensual desires and their satisfaction a beautiful phenomenon and sublime experience. Crude bodily references remain no more the focus of attention – they become only a means of another aspect of the manifestation of pure spirituality of *bhakti.* In fact, anything, even the crudest kind of physical response, gets transformed if it is touched with the tremendous powerful spiritual attraction of *bhakti.* Under the dominance of the immensely deep attraction of spiritual love for the Lord the sensual desires take a beautiful form. There is no doubt that the intimate bodily relation remains a bodily relation but it is neither physical bodily relation (since the Lord is not physically present or we can say He has no physical body) nor is it felt by the *bhakta* as a physical bodily relation. The allegory that is envisaged about the *devtâ's* sensual pleasure with a subtle body becomes almost a matter of real experience of *bhakta* of *Râgâtmikâ Bhakti.* What does this actually mean in experiential terms? A clarification is very much needed here.

The very first point that is to be taken note of is that 'experiential' does not mean sense experiential only in this discussion. Any thing is experiential if any human being experiences it at any level of his being and its veracity is to be decided in the world of that experience (illusory experiences are those which don't form an independent world of their own). *Bhakta's* have an independent world of experience. What he experiences in this world he understands them too. He understands any happening of this world in course of experiencing it. Since it is a human experience any one else also can *understand* it too without necessarily experiencing what the *bhaktas.*experience. Hence a *bhakta's* experience of a transformed bodily response in a situation that is ordinarily deemed as in extremely erotic is quite an intelligible phenomenon for every human being. Everyone, who wants to understand the *bhaktas*' transformed experience, can understand that a *bhakta's* reference to the physical sort of contact with Lord is a contact that does not pull his attention towards the sensual pleasure of bodily contact but directs it towards the pure beauty that manifests in such contacts. Any one can understand that the *bhaktas* experiences pure beauty manifesting in all that. The actual vivid content of this beauty can't be captured without undergoing the experience but to understand that it is an experience of pure beauty of the gracious response of Lord for the immensely deep love of the *bhakta* is enough to acknowledge it as a right understanding of *bhaktas'* experience.

With the touch of divine even the most sensual act transforms into a beautiful act. This is a plain and many times heard statement. There is nothing unintelligible or strange in it. This ideal sounding statement is generally taken to be a theoretical statement. For the *bhaktas* (especially the *bhaktas* of *Râgâtmikâ* or *Râgânugâ bhakti*) it is not theoretical but an experientially true statement. They experience its truth in the emotional proximity with their Lord. A non-*bhakta* also can understand it since there is no logical impossibility involved in accepting that in the apparently sensual acts of physical contact with Lord the *bhaktas* experience divine beauty. It may be taken as a logical impossibility only if it any particular physical contact necessarily implies a desire for sensual pleasure but this is not so. We can envisage many situations in which a physical contact is just accidental or forced on a person. In such situation the question of sensual desire does not arise at all. Even in those situations where physical contact is not forced on but made willingly, it dose not imply that the person desires for sensual pleasure. One can make such a contact as an experiment to check whether the sensual desire is necessarily aroused just by physical contact. All these possibilities pre-empt the doubt about its logical impossibility. So far as the apprehension about its empirical impossibility is concerned we can admit that in a particular environment it is almost impossible for any normal healthy man and woman to resist the desire of sensual pleasure. However, this normal condition does not pre-empt the possibility that a person can resist this desire and/or keep his attention fixed on something else. Hence it is not empirically impossible either. The intelligibility of the *bhaktas'* experience for a non-*bhaktai*, therefore, can't be denied on any ground. There is no reason to think either that it is merely an ideal dream and an actual experience of this sort is just impossible, or that this is an experience that only *bhaktas* can understand it.

The *Râgânugâ* and *Râgâtmikâ* forms of *Madhurâ Bhakti* are only two forms of it; they should not be regarded as two stages – lower and upper. A *bhakta* of the former is not inferior to the latter. One, who assumes the role of Râdhâ's *sakhi* and loves Lord *Kṛṣṇa*! in that way, leads a life that is centered on the Lord and the mundane world in its mundane form disappears completely from one's psyche. The physical world exists for such a *bhakta* only as an extension of the world of Lord's grace. Such a *bhakta* is not at all bound to the world. He is centered within himself and enjoys the bliss of Lord' s love. A *bhakta* of *Râgâtmikâ* path also gets complete liberation from mundane world and enjoys supreme bliss of Lord's love n her/his complete self-centered life. So far as the degree of freedom from the limitations of relation is concerned there is no good reason to place the former as inferior to the latter. We should not forget that when a person assumes a role of Râdhâ's *sakhi* he is placing himself in relation to the beloved Lord only through his deep love since through the image of Râdhâ, which personifies a specific form of deepest love for the Lord, the *bhakta* directly avails His love. To be Râdhâ's *sakhi* is to place oneself in that specific relation to Lord that even Râdhâ can't replace. To be in the proximity of Lord without being His direct beloved is a very special form of love that can be envisaged as rich as Râdhâ's love could be.

To understand *Râgâtmikâ* or *Râgânugâ Bhakti* is to understand a very special condition of the *bhakta's* mind. In any form of *bhakti* the *bahkta* develops an emotional relation with the image of the Lord and begins to live in the world of this fully conscious emotional experience. If the *bahkta's* experience develops without any impediments then he is completely shifted to this world of experience and the world of sense experience in itself becomes irrelevant and exists only as a part of manifestation of that world. Lord—the centre of that world becomes the complete controller of his whole being – his thought, feelings and action *Bhaktas'* relation to his Lord is not a projected relation. Given the uni-dimensionality of thought such a relation with the image of Lord can't be developed by keeping oneself only conceptually involved the image. A complete involvement with image could be availed only in an emotional relation with it since that alone integrates all the aspects of a person's being). It is felt that various sorts of personal relations bring about this integration to various degrees. The relationship of brotherhood is deemed to be closer than the relationship of father-son, friendship is deemed to be closer than brotherhood and the relationship of lover-beloved or that of husband–wife is deemed to be the closest of all others relations. This is the relation that integrates a person's being completely in respect to the object of relation. That is why it is believed that in *Râgânugâ* and *Râgâtmikâ* forms of *bhakti* the *bhakta* enters into the fully conscious experience of the highest degree of emotional involvement with the Lord and it brings him most easily in full control of the Lord. The enormous emotional joy that the *bhakta* gets in developing this relation with his dear Lord makes him forget completely the entire world around him and he is shifted completely to the fully conscious experiential world of his dear Lord's utmost proximity.

In *Madhra bhakti* the *bhakta* enters into the most intimate emotional relation with the Lord. It is regarded as *the* most intimate emotional relation due to the above-explained reason. No bit of the *bhakta's* being is left untouched by the love of the Lord in this form of *bhakti.* But as we saw the physical level of its manifestation gets transformed in such a way that the desire of bodily satisfaction, in ordinary sense, disappears completely. Given this fact about *Madhura bhakti* it is functionally not much different from other forms of emotional relation with the Lord such as the *Dâsya bhâva* or *Putra bhâva* etc. Relational form and emotional content varies in these forms but in these forms also entire being of the *bhakta* – his consciousness with his life-force is shifted to the pure spiritual level. Hanumana is the ideal of *Dâsya bhakti.* It is obvious that the relational form and emotional content of this form is very different from that of Radha or Meera. But so far as the quantum of dedication is concerned both are on absolute position.

Certain emotional relation with the Lord, due to their typical form, is deemed to be an obstacle to complete dedication. A person may love his dear Lord as his/her son. Complete absorption in this emotion also brings about the radical change in that person's life but fatherly/motherly care and concern that is natural in it comes in way of dissolving his/her identity in the Lord's love. That is why it is regarded in *Bhakti* tradition that in some relational forms one can never get complete dissolution of one's being in the Lord's feet. In other words one can have the full taste of the experience of love by forgetting one's identity completely. If one is additionally conscious of one's identity then taste of love is missed (since the attention is focused on one's identity and adequate attention is not given to the taste). The situation of *Râgânugâ* and *Râgâtmikâ* forms of *Madhurâ bhakti makes* the person forget his identity. But in some other relation e.g. 'father/mother-hood' a person can have the full taste of love for the Lord in every situation since he/she may feel that some of his dear *Son's* (Lord's) responses are hazardous to Him (to the Lord). Naturally, in such conditions, his attention would be drawn to the safety of his *Son* and the taste of love will be missed. So it is assumed in *Bhakti* tradition that full taste of *bhakti* can't be had in certain relations. However, if a complete dissolution of one's identity is possible in *Dâsya bhâva*—that means, if it is possible to have full taste of *bhakti* in *Dâsya bhâva* then it becomes questionable as to why the same can't happen in *Pitâ/Mâtâ bhâva* since it is possible to develop an emotional relation with the Lord as one's son without missing the taste of his *bhakti* for Him. This point needs elaboration.

Dâsya and Other *Bhâvas* of *Bhakti*

In *Dâsya bhâva* a person can get complete dissolution of his identity at the Lord's feet. He feels that he will be blessed if every bit of his being gets used in the service of his dear Lord. This feeling is different from the feeling of a beloved who gets ineffable joy in being played on or used by his/her dear Lord. A fully dedicated servant also finds great joy in serving his dear master–the Lord but certainly it is different from the former in content. The difference is generally marked by the expected bodily response of a lover in this situation. But it is to be noted that the expected bodily responses could be identified as intentions to respond in a certain manner before they actually manifest on the body. Actual bodily manifestation of any response is not necessary. It is discussed earlier that gross bodily responses are felt as pleasure but this feeing is purely psychic since the joy of the *bhakta* lies in the perception of pure sublime beauty of the divine response. One can attend to the psychic feeling and keep the bodily responses under the dominance of this feeling. For such a person the psychic joy is the end and he does not desire to go beyond this. His identification of a feeling of joy in *Dâsya bhâva* and its differentiation from that of *Madhura bhâva* is not based on bodily responses either directly or indirectly. So at this level *Dâsya bhâva* could be identified as different from the *Madhura bhâva* but no reason remains to place the latter as higher in comparison to the former. This difference holds at the initial level of the *sâdhnâ* of these different *bhâvas*. After the *bhaktas* of theses two forms of *bhakti* are steadily placed in their desired *bhâvas* they may find reasons to praise each other *bhâva* but can't find reason to accept that in *Dâsya bhâva* all the dimensions of a person's being are not affected.

It is assumed that in *Mâtri/Pitri bhâva* the *bhakta* can't remain aware of the taste of his *bhava* because his care for his dear Son (the Lord) draws his comlete attention to certain external factors that he feels as dangerous and the awareness of the taste of his *bhâva* lost. It is believed here that a mother/father is necessarily disturbed even on the thought of any harm of her/ his child. In this assumption an implicit assumption regarding the possibility of some harm to the Lord is involved. But it not impossible to think that a *bhakta* of this *bhâva* can not be disturbed by any such thought since he may believe that no harm can touch his Son. Despite the fact that a mothers/fathers are emotionally weak for their child this weakness varies in degree depending on their image of their child that is affected by the age, strength, position and several other factors. For a grown up and strong child the mother doesn't have that much of worry as she could have for her young age and weak child. A mother becomes excessively worried if she sees a mouse around her child but she does not have any worry at all if the same mouse or a bigger one runs around her grown up child. In view of these factors we can envisage a mother who is not worried about her child against most common dangers of life since she is confident of her child's strength and believes that he would come out safely from them. Such a mother/father would not be disturbed with the sight of an imminent danger on her/his child rather she/he would enjoy the whole episode of her/his child's victory over it. This thought experiment helps in envisaging an actual possibility of the state of *Mâtri/Pitri bhâva* of *Râgânugâ bhakti* in which the *bhakta* is not disturbed by a seemingly disturbing situation and keeps on enjoying tastefully her/his Son's responses in those situations too.

The above stated possibility is open to debate and the reason of above thought experiment is to bring it notice that it is it is not a closed issue. Although traditionally it is believed that in the *Mâtri/ Pitri bhâva* complete dissolution of the *bhakta's* ego is not possible, it is not necessary to stick to the traditional belief on this issue. In this *bhâva* also the *bhakta's* ego can dissolve completely and the taste of *bhakti* can be enjoyed without any disturbance.

To understand that the immense depth of the emotion of *Madhura bhâva* (and other *bhavas also*) of *Râgânugâ* or *Râgâtmikâ bhakti* places the *bhakta* in such a relation with the Lord that makes the world of emotional relation with the Lord as the only worth living world and the reality of the physical world is belied — is only a partial understanding of *bhakti.* It can't be called a complete understanding of a *bhakta's* understanding (of *bhakti*). One also has to understand the mutual exclusive relation between the world of *bhakti* and the physical world not as the worlds of the same levels but the latter being inclusive of the former. In other words, the world of *bhakti* has to be acknowledged as a world of higher order of experience and the physical world —that of a lower order. When the *bhakta* is shifted to the world of *bhakti* the physical world does not disappear completely for him. *Bhaktas*' awareness of the reality of the world of *bhakti* does not necessarily result in the perception of the unreality of the physical world It becomes less important for him and does not remain in his focus of his attention, It becomes secondary and insignificant. Only those aspects of the mundane physical world remain within the span of the *bhakta's* attention which accord with his experience of *bhakti*. *Bhaktas* also, at times, call this world *mâyâ* but they don't mean thereby its unreality. For the *bhaktas mâyâ* is the power of Lord that deludes people by generating attachment for mundane things and make them tied to the physical world. This *mâyâ* is an excessively strong force, which makes everyone succumb to its pressure unless one has surrendered oneself at the feet of Lord.

The world of *bhakti* as a *rasa* is a world of fully conscious experience. As such there is no good reason to doubt the reality of this world. This point is discussed at various occasions in different contexts. The world of sense experience also is a world of conscious experience. The reality of this world is the most agreed on matter and hardly ever doubted. The relation between these two real worlds, therefore, warrants explanation. After this explanation the reason of a non-*bhakta's* misunderstanding regarding the *bhakta's* understanding of *bhakti* will become completely clear. But that will form the content of the next chapter.

At the end of this chapter it is now clear that in and through *bhakti* a *bhakta* experiences with full awareness the pure spiritual joy of love in its highest intensity. He/she just enjoys it by getting himself /herself reduced to a mere object of this divine love. Reducing oneself to an object is almost impossible since no one desires to be so. Only in love, one desires to be object of love of the person whom one loves. The joy of lover lies in *being loved* and not merely in loving. Hence here this reduction becomes easy and natural. In sensual love affairs one desires most sincerely to become an object of the lover's love-play. In this form of love the experiences being an object of the fulfillment of the lover's desires gets manifested most intensely and vividly at all levels of his being—

psychic and physical too. In both the forms of *Madhurâ Bhakti*, therefore, it becomes natural for a *bhakta* to desire most intensely to become an object of dear Lord's love-play. A non-*Bhakta,* who thinks that the Lord of the *bhaktas* is their own imagined entity and wants to understand this experience without giving the status of real person, misunderstand it badly since that amounts to emptying this experience of its experiential content. To take this experience in this way is to believe that the *bhaktas* want to become an object of the object of their own imagination. One can have a pure physical pleasure from this kind of imagination but the joy of pure love of *Madhrâ Bhakti,* in which bodily manifestations of love remain in complete spiritual orientation and not enjoyed at the physical level at all, can't be experienced. To assume that this experience as a sort of day-dream also is another misunderstanding since the *bhaktas* achieve this stage only by having full awareness of the experience—by having the *rasa* of it. To understand this experience in the right way it is necessary accept the reality of the world of the *bhaskta'* experience where the status of the Lord is indubitable since He is the very centre of that world.

Bhakti is the world of human experience where one does not like to remain a doer anymore. He only wants to enjoy all that his dear Lord does to him. This loss of agency –the dropping of door-ship, which is regarded as the essence of *bhakti*, is given to the *bhaktas* in the most natural way in the *Madhurâ Bhâva* of *Râgânugâ* and *Râgâtmikâ Bhakti* It is traditionally accepted that in other *bhâvas* of *Râgânugâ Bhakti* also this transformation takes place in various degrees but it is not unintelligible to accept that in these forms also absolute dissolution of ego takes place. In the light of the above discussion the traditional view regarding the supremacy of *Râgâtmikâ* and *Râgânugâ bhakti* is not an acceptable position. We can understand its uniqueness and difference but in other forms of *bhakti* also some uniqueness of the relational feature and its details are present.

As the gist of the chapter it can be stated that becoming an instrument in the hand of the Lord is the aim and essence of all forms of *bhakti. Bhakti* is for the sake of complete dissolution of doer ship. In all other paths of spiritual discipline also this aim acquires central place. In *bhakti* this aim acquires a central place but not aspired to be achieved directly. It is achieved as a necessary consequence of love for the Lord. The *bhakta* feels blessed for the ecstatic experience of *bhakti* that he finds is a gift of his Lord. Enthused by this divine gift he wants to offer himself completely at the feet of the Lord so that the divine responses of his dear Lord could suffuse his being completely.

Reference

1. Substantively *'Râgâtmikâ* and *'Râgânugâ' Madhurâ Bhakti* are the same. However, the former is seen as the form in which Radha and Gopis offered their love to Sri Krishan and the latter is the form that is adopted by the followers of the former with a sense of reverence for Radha and Gopis and placing oneself much below them. Authors of this theme make this division and it has a scholarly significance for understanding *bhakti,* See, *(Hindi) Bhkati Rasâmrita Sindhu, p—16-17, ed.*—Dr. Nagendra and Dr. Vijayendra Snataka, Pub.by Hindi Dept. Delhi University,1963.

5

How a *Bhakta* Looks at the World

Kṛṣṇa! We live our life in this world at various levels. Grossly at least three levels can be enumerated as physical, psychic and above psychic –a big part of which forms the spiritual level. We live at all these levels of our life and are familiar with their objects and events by a direct acquaintance. There is no need to describe them and there is no point in describing them either. There is no need to describe them since we all have acquaintance with them and there is no point in so doing since no one can understand what they are if one really does not have an acquaintance with them. However, there is no problem in understanding all of them because even if one prefers to pass more time in one of the three, or leads life of control over the two by any one of these levels one understands the two independently. A materialist, for example, may hold that there is no spiritual level and the psychic level is reducible to the physical but he knows well what he denies and what he reduces to physical. An idealist may think differently. The claims made about the other levels of life from one specific level are not necessarily false. From within that level theses claims are definitely true. A counter-claim made by a person placed in another level of life is also true within that level. However, there is no way to compare these claims from a place apart from these three dimensions since there is no such place of human life. This is not a serious problem for an objective understanding of these different truth-claims because from within one level one can understand whether there would be any corresponding event of any event of one level on another level, and if yes then what it would be like.

Human understanding is not tied to any one level although it is deemed to be a phenomenon of the psychic level. We can understand the natural laws operating on material objects although we are not that. Truth of law-like beaviour of material bodies could be very objectively tested at the material level and grasped by human mind that is not at the material level. Due to self-reflexivity of conscious phenomena psychic level is also intelligible to us and the unconscious phenomena can be grasped by postulating theory about that. These theories also could be tested objectively to some extant by observing human behaviour. Phenomena of beyond psychic level could not be grasped by a direct self- reflexivity since we are not aware of them in our present level of being. We can postulate theories about them but these theories can't be tested even in the weak sense since present level of human behaviour can't verify them. We can understand these phenomena by understanding how those people understand it to whom it is a matter of direct self-awareness. If any human individual undergoes is any experience then it s intelligible to him. It is unintelligible that a person experiences something but can't understand it. If one experiences it one also understands it. And if something is intelligible to one then it is, in principle, intelligible to all. Hence if any human *bhakta* has experienced the pure spiritual joy of *bhakti* then what he understands about his experience is available to all.

When something happens at the psychic level then something happens at the neural level also as its analogue. Some of the psychic happenings manifest at the physical level also but not all such events get manifested at that level. A method of grasping any psychic event by reducing it to its physical manifestation is not correct. The greatest demerit of this method lies in its irrational dismissal of all those psychic events as non-existent for which no behavioural analogue is immediately available. In fact there is no need to take recourse to the method of reduction to understand any phenomenon of psychic and above-psychic level.

Every psychic phenomenon that a person experiences with awareness, grasps it, in course of experiencing. And the way he grasps it others also understans it in the same way.

The most important question that appears to be puzzling is –how can a person understand an experience of someone else that he himself has never undergone? This question is answered in previous chapters. It is explained that it is not necessary for every individual to pass through an experience in order to understand it. If any one human individual has undergone an experience then every other individual, who himself has not experienced it or cannot experience it, can also understand it. It is not merely a comment on our use of the term 'understanding' but it is a description of the actual state of affair regarding the phenomenon of understanding. A man can never experience labour pain but he can and *does* understand it. Not only labour pain but any one else's pain we can never experience either but we *do* understand that some one is in pain if he/she is in pain. At times we also doubt that some one is merely pretending and not actually suffer from pain. But this (the doubt) only presuppose that there is an actual suffering from pain The doubt about the pretension of pain is intelligible only if we first know that there is an experience called pain, then we reflect on it and find that some one can show in his behaviour that he is experiencing pain although he does not experience it. The presence of doubt does not preclude the possibility of understanding other's pain. Every case of other's declaration about his/her pain does not necessarily result into a failure to understand what he/she experiences.

The genuine question of not understanding of an experience could arise only if it is an experience of an individual who himself fails to understand what he experienced. But in that case he will not call it as an experience. He may have a very hazy or mixed up sort of experience but he *understands* that it is 'hazy' or 'mixed up sort'. Is it possible to have an experience about which a person can't *understand that it was an experience*? The answer is negative. Seen from this way it becomes clear that experience without understanding is unintelligible. The scope of intelligibility is much wider than that of experiencibility. All that is intelligible is not necessarily experiencible but everything experiencible is intelligible.

That is why a *bhakta's* experience is intelligible to any non-*bhakta* . A *bhakta's* experience is purely spiritual. Although it brings about a change in his life completely but neither every part of it manifests at the physical level nor on the neural level. The deep silence that results from the full dissolution of the *bhakta's* identity in his Lord can't be registered at neural level but it is true that he consciously undergoes this experience. Others do not experience what he experiences but others can understand *what he is feeling like.*

Immanuel Kant said that there are only twelve categories of (human) understanding and no one can understand anything beyond them That is why he assumed that ontology is worthless since we can't know the things as they themselves are, And we can't know the knower self because self can't be made an object of knowledge. For him self is a necessary presupposition for explaining knowledge.

It is true that self can't be made an object of knowledge but that is not sufficient reason to conclude that self can never be known. Self as pure consciousness can be known in every ordinary experience only if the attention is withdrawn from the object and directed to the event of experiencing. It is possible for the knower to do this and it is not very difficult either. Just by will to shift attention from the object to the experience itself does this. Choice-less awareness is an actual experience and this is the very being of self as pure consciousness. A person, who has never experienced the choice-less state can at one experience it and understand it. But even if he does not undergo this experience he can understand that it is a state of awareness (he could distinguish it from unawareness), in which the attention is not focused on an object (he could understand what does this mean) but it is directed to the event of experiencing (he could understand where the attention is focused). Although the choice-less awareness of a person reflects in his berhaviour also distinctly but it is not the behaviour alone that is the basis of his understanding. It is on the basis of the assumption that if he feels like this then he would behaviourly respond in such and such manner, and that others also behaviourally respond in the same manner if they feel like that he conclude that possibly the person who is showing such behavioural responses is feeling what he himself feels. Behaviour is made the way to reach the feeling of the person always on the basis of the assumption that from certain feelings some specific set of behaviours follow and not the other way round. Everyone understands a feeling directly without mediation of the ensuing behavioural responses. So, in fact behaviours are not included in the process of understanding. They are only a way to guess other's feeling and the feeling is grasped directly. In the light of this insight we can now understand what a *bhakta,* who enjoys the taste of *bhakti,* understands about this world.

This World as The *Bhakta* Looks at It

Except for the period in which the *bhakta* remains lost completely in the ecstasy of Lord's love this world of space and time exists for the *bhaktas* as much as it exists for any one else. However, it does not exist for him the way it exists for others. People ordinarily live in the world that is a construction of their own. Human world is basically a social world and not primarily a natural world. Plants and animals live in the natural world but human beings, each individual of which is a self-conscious being live in a world where social construction replace or suffuse natural reality and known as social reality. Instinctual demands functions in human world very largely through the relational web in which a person finds him safe and secure. The basic instinct to survive which is supported by nature in animal and plants is supported by human community through the control of natural resources via social laws and injunctions. Except for certain crude organic needs human beings express their desires and get their satisfaction only in and through this complex web of personal and inter personal relations of various types and various levels of priority. His desires and interests direct and colour his perception. He looks at the world not as the world in itself is but as he *wants* to look at it. The world in which we ordinarily live is a world of construction. This is a truth that every common man knows. Despite the acceptance of this sort of subjectivism we believe that we all live in an objectively given world of sense experience because we have an agreeable way to point to the external objects of spatio-temporal events. Ordinarily like a naïve realist we think that the basis of this agreed on way of reference is due to the existence of the objects in a public space. But most of us don't see that this naïve belief itself is a belief that is accepted not by verification. Since I can't see a thing as what others see my belief that others also see the same thing remains always an unverified belief. So far as the perception is concerned every individual perceives any object through his perceptual mechanism, which is different in different individuals. I can see an object and others also can see the same. My perception is my perception since it occurs in my mind as an individual psychic episode. Other's perception also occurs in every other person's mind as his or her own individual psychic episodes. There is no way to compare these psychic episodes because they can't be brought to public space and there is no way to directly enter into someone's mind. Yet, when I see an object and talk to some other person about it, who is also perceiving it, I believe he is also seeing the same object and seeing it as I see it. We have no strong reason to hold this belief as true. However, this belief is not irrational completely because we have no positive reason to believe that it is not so. In all the responses that others make on my querry regarding an object I find no reason to doubt that the other person is not seeing that object towards which I am pointing or is not seeing those features in it which I am referring to. We do not unnecessarily doubt about other person's perception and the common practice of not doubting other's perception without any reason gives others and me also the reason to hold that we are seeing the same object and finding almost the same features in it. We all accept that others also see the thing the same as I see it as a matter of doxastic practice.

It is our naïve realistic approach to the world due to which it appears to us world of purely given realities. We saw that it is not true. Much of the world we live in is either a psychological or socio psychological construct. This is a conceptual realization of a deeper truth about our experiential world. Although this does not ordinarily come to our experiential level but it is not impossible Mere reflection can't put anyone at that level. One could *see* this truth if only one is set free from the compulsions of the deeper desires that make one *see* the world of human construction as absolutely real. A *bhakta* in the love of his Lord becomes easily free from these compulsions and can *see* this world of human construction as a construction. The illusion about its being absolutely real disappears. A new face of this world appears before him. To have a look at that is not only interesting but illuminating too. Only by having an understanding of that face of the world that the *bhakta* beholds one can understand an important aspect of the *bhakta's* understanding of *bhakti.* So, in order to understand *bhakti* from a *bhakta's* stand point, it becomes necessary to understand how he looks at this world. A *bhakta* in his love for his dear Lord experiences that Lord's will operates latently behind everything—every happening in this world. This does not mean to say, as it is ordinarily thought, that the *bhaktas* view is against the natural law.

Natural events big or small take place as if there is an independent domain of Laws of Nature. But a *bhakta* can *see* the contingent nature of these laws. He can see that there is no logical compulsion behind natural laws. Every material body attracts another body in proportion to its mass –is a law. But there is no answer to the question as to why is it so? Must it be so? Can't we think of something else? In the light of our modern rational attitude towards the events of the world we are tempted to answer in negative or reply that such questions are nonsense. This is not so. There is no rational compulsion to give a negative reply to the above questions and to hold that such questions are nonsense does not actually prove them nonsense either.

The answer to the above questions is positive. There is no logical compulsion behind natural laws. This answer, then, leaves room equally for an explanation by chance and by teleology. One can hold that natural laws started operating in the world as a matter of accident. In other word they are what they are because physical events started happening the way they happen. If it were otherwise then that would have been the law of the nature. So it is a matter of chance or accident. A religious believer on the other hand can say that the natural laws operate the way they operate because it is God's will. The fact that it could have been otherwise gives the believer a reason to ascribe it to the will of the Supreme Creator. It is important to note in this regard that both the parties are correct in their position since they have reason for holding what they do. Neither of them is more rational than the other. However, it would be irrational to declare that the other as irrational. A *bhakta* prefers the teleological explanation because he finds that the conscious will of the Supreme Person –of his dear Lord is operating behind these laws. He takes the natural laws as the manifestation of Lord's will. This points needs elaboration.

A *bhakta* looks at the world as nature (*Prakrit*) and world human construction (*Samsâra*). Nature is the sum total of natural objects and also it is the natural law according to which these objects exist and act and react. In the terminology of Spinoza the former is *Natura Naturata* and the latter -*Natura Naturance*. A *bhakta* finds that his beloved Lord has manifested Himself in both the forms. As the manifestation of His will operating in the form of natural laws material things come into being and behave in a fixed manner. Had Lord not willed to bring material world into being it would not have been present before us. Material world, being material in nature, can't by itself come into being from the state of its non-existence. In this sense nature or natural world is the pure manifestation of Lord's will. There is nothing artificial in it. Artificiality or pollution is that which comes not from natural process. Following the laws of nature, therefore, is to follow Lord's will.

Human world or *samsâra* is not a product of pure natural process. It is a compound effect of human aspiration working on nature. When laws of nature approve human will a desire is fulfilled and when these laws disapprove it then it is frustrated. Human world emerges from the multi-tiered scaffolding of human will. A *bhakta*, who can *see* Lord's will operating behind every event, can *see* where it is not operating either. Going against natural laws does not necessarily mean to go against Lord's will. If an individual wills to avail Lord's love then to some extant he has to go against his natural tendencies that he has got from nature. Such an effort is not unnatural or anti-nature: it is super-natural or trans-natural. This is a very important distinction to understand *bhakti*. A *bhakta* keeps himself away from sensual pleasures although it is a natural tendency of human being. Denying this tendency is to go against nature but if it is denied to lead life of bliss of *bhakti* then it is not against nature, it is an attempt to transform nature.

In fact a *bhakta* does not intend to stand against nature, which, he knows, is functioning completely by his Lord's will. He can see the intervention of human desires in the natural realm and wants only to remove it to make room for *bhakti.* This is to be elaborated in various stages of the development of *bhakti.* At first, the face of the world is being outlined as the *bhakta* of highest position (the *bhakta* completely lost in enjoying the taste of his love for his Lord.) sees it.

Bhakta's **View of Natural Laws**

Bhakta's only duty and only pleasure is to remain lost in enjoying the taste of love for his Lord. He feels that this is *the* duty of everyone, not only his. One, who does not make effort in this direction, only wastes his valuable time. He can also *see* that anyone who does not have love for the God and undertakes any task to for his so called noble cause (not for any selfish motive), in fact, does it for a very deep selfish motive. Till the false feeling of doer-ship remains in anyone's heart even the noblest of acts are done by the person only for a selfish motive that 'I am doing it'. Doer-ship can't disappear without realizing that God's will is supporting and sustaining each and ever action but this realization comes only with *bhakti.* The *bhakta* finds that nothing is being done in this world by any individual without Lord's will. So if any one thinks that he is doing something, great or small, without at least admitting the presence of God's will in it then he is only on a deep ego trip. *So* for a *bhakta* this human world of great deeds is very largely a world of deep ego assertions.

In love for God one loves to do all sorts of daily routine work with the realization that in all these his dear Lord's general will power is operating He feels hat his dear Lord's will is operating as laws of nature in his breaths, in his heart beats in the systematic function of all his organs and the natural urge to do all the routine works also is a manifestation of His will only. A *bhakta* uses his body as an instrument and does a work for getting the joy of being supported by dear Lord. He does not launch any special project unless he is directly instructed by his Lord A *bhakta* gets such instructions only in a clear way by Lord Himself. This s his general attitude towards his body

Given the realization that in every deed only Lord's will is operating, a *bahkta* never takes words of those persons on its face value who don't admit the presence of Lord's will in everything.

He only directly apprehends the motive and intension of such people. It is easy for any one to understand that, in general, such persons only want to assert their deep-rooted ego sense. A *bhakta,* however, does not take it as a conclusion of his discursive understanding. For him it is a direct awareness/apprehension of other's intensions and motives reflecting in his attitude sharply as different from the attitude of the *bhakta.* A *bhakta* can *see* this difference immediately. It is not to say that what the *bhakta* sees does not presuppose the general belief that egoism of doer-ship functions behind every action. But a *bhakta's* vision is not based on this general conceptual understanding. Looking at the facial expressions and implicit tone of the person a *bhakta* comes to *know* wherefrom the person's action is coming. Every one can't directly *see* it but everyone can understand that a *bhakta* can *see* it and can also understand the nature of this difference. A non-*bhakta* can understand that a *bhakta sees* that one who does some work with the implicit but dominant feeling of doer-ship is both an ignorant and pitiable fellow since he is under the influence of a false belief and he misses too much for it. The feeling of doer-ship present in anyone is a matter of sorrow for the *bhakta* and not a matter of either competition or condemnation or hostility. For a non- *bhakta* other's ego is a matter of competition or hostility. Other's ego is acceptable to anyone only if the other person does not assert his ego before him. But other's ego is not that for a *bhakta.* It is only the veil of his dear Lord's *mâyâ* due to which a person fails to see the truth that he is not a doer at all and misses Lord's grace that, he sees, is operating every moment in his life.

Nature, for a *bhakta,* is a manifestation of his Lord's specific will. Laws operating in nature are not logically necessary. There is no contradiction involved in thinking of any alternative law of nature in any sphere. The question why this law instead of its alternative law operates in nature – is a genuine question for *bhaktas* and for everyone who is not committed to materialism. Even for a materialist this is not a meaningless question in the literal sense. It is empirically impossible for him since he wants to define every natural kind word in terms of given natural law. But it only sows that a natural kind word must be defined with reference to *some* (*or the other*) law but does not show that it can be defined *only* with reference to the given law Changes in scientific definition of terms make this point clear that some property was deemed to be defining property of a term but later some other property was accepted as defining and the earlier one was dropped. The classification of whale is well known. It was defined as fish in early stage of development of biology and later it was defined as mammal. It shows that alternative law of nature is not unintelligible. As it was discussed earlier the presence of a law in nature can be regarded as a matter of chance and we can think of a law only because ourselves as rational beings are the product of laws. However, the possibility of envisaging alternative law make the question *why this law instead of its alternative*—a meaningful question. Its meaning is independent of its actual empirical knowledge in the sense that we need not *know the specific law operating* to understand it *as law.*

Apart from the fact that the intelligibility of alternative laws of nature makes the question *why this law instead of its alternative* – meaningful, *bhakta's* experience makes it a simple meaningful question that can be answered with reference to his dear Lord's will. As it was stated in above discussion, in *bhakta's* view, Lord's general will for the emergence of the world manifests in the laws of nature.

Laws of nature operate not only in material world but also in the functioning of human psyche. It is important to understand this realm of the functioning of natural laws since here *bhakta's* vision becomes easily accessible to everyone and it helps in understanding his views regarding this world more concretely. If we understand it then we can see why a *bhakta* says what he say about nature and human world.

Bhakta's View of The Laws Pertaining to Psychic Functions

Human mind functions in an orderly manner. All the mental activities take place in a systematic way and various activities co-ordinate with each other. Lack of systematic functioning of these activities gives rise to psychic infirmity or illness and loss of co-ordination results into psychic disorder. Central and peripheral nervous systems are generally held to be the basis of this systematic functioning and co-ordination. There is no answer to the question— *why do certain neural structures or properties produce psychic order?* For a materialist it is a meaningless question but, on the same line of argument that was discussed in above paragraph, it is clear that it is not a meaningless question at all. But apart from that formal defence the systematic function of one's own mental activities beyond one's knowledge and control arouses a sense of wonder not merely in the *bhakta* but even in the minds of most non-*bhaktas.* I call it my metal state, my mental activities etc. but I don't know how they function and what makes them function in the systematic way they do. Can my brain be the co-ordinator of all these complex activities? In a way –yes. All mental activities are related to neural functioning. So in a way these activities are under the control of neural functions that governed by the physical laws operating on electro-chemical impulses. But the central question—how can a physical event recognize a mental phenomenon so that it can relate itself with that in a consistent manner. Even if it is admitted that these neural functions produce related mental activities, the detail content of mental activities that give them their specific characteristic can't be accounted for by these neural functions. It is every body's common experience that thoughts come to one's mind from within but one does not produce them. Emotions are deemed to be closely related to instincts that are biological in nature; but higher emotions can't be accounted for in that way satisfactorily. The view that consciousness, reflecting on a subject matter, discloses its inherent properties that manifest as thoughts or ideas, and higher emotions emerge not for the instinctual reason of survival but dawn on us from our higher nature —seems to be more plausible and acceptable.

A *bhakta* can see that a person engaged in thinking about anything is interested only in the content of it but never cares to enquire where from it comes. Every time a person thinks something a thought in a vague manner or in a clear manner as an idea comes before his mind's eyes. He applies it to the concrete objects to see how far it accords with them and see its relation to other accepted ideas to understand if it accords with them. If it corresponds with the concrete object (or situation) and also accords with earlier established ideas then it is accepted to be a knowledge-promoter otherwise remains merely an imagination. Ideas and imagination are not different from one another in their essence. Some ideas are knowledge-promoter and some are not but in order to have either we have to think. To imagine we have to think and to reflect on anything also we have to think. Thinking itself only produces images and the further functions of its connection with reality and with other accepted ides make it a knowledge-promoting idea (or merely an idea). An idea is given importance since it promotes knowledge and an imagination is not given that much importance since it does not do so. However, we hardly ever care to investigate the origin of either.

We know that ideas come to our mind. An idea is identified at a particular point of time. It has a beginning in the history of human knowledge. A period can be referred to before which it was absent. This history is in a way a racial history since one race can trace the beginning of an idea in its own history. However, the same idea could have emerged in some other race's history earlier. So we can't say when an idea appeared in man's history for the very first time. A history of ideas itself (independent of history of human races) is something practically impossible. That does not amount to saying that history of ideas is reducible to the history of the knowledge of a race. That is very different sort of controversial claim. A pure history of ideas seems practically impossible since we don't exactly draw a line that we can as *the beginning* of an idea. Logically it is not impossible but practically it is so.

Despite admitting that an idea dawns on a man's mind at a particular point of time in a certain period we want to avoid the question wherefrom the ideas come. There are several fashionable pretexts of avoiding this question but they are merely fashionable pretexts— not genuine reasons to stop asking us about it. A *bhakta* finds it pertinent to ask this question. He has a clear answer to it so he can reasonably ask about it. Since any one can understand what a *bhakta* holds hence not only they but others also can reasonably raise this question. Wherefrom the thoughts come? It is important to hear and understand the *bhakta's* answer to this question.

In *bhakta's* vision every thought comes from the random wandering of consciousness. Consciousness, unless composed in self-conscious state, illumines that layer of anything with which it comes in contact. A simple sense perception is the state of illumination of a material object's apparent form with which consciousness comes in contact with the related sense organs. When some reflection on various aspects of matter raises certain questions that can't be answered within this perceptual knowledge then a search for its *deeper* nature begins. Various ideas are tried as tentative candidates of that and eventually one is reached at its true nature. Although this process is more or less mechanical the fundamental intuition regarding the connection between and among ideas are directly apprehended by consciousness. At times these intuitively grasped connection also seem to present certain questions. Further corrective reflection is done for that and again consciousness revels the relation between various ideas working underneath. A *bhakta's* eyes remain always and only on the intuitive functions of consciousness. Hence changing truth-claims does not bewilder him. He knows firmly that all knowledge of the world is produced either by the contact of an object, or by an idea or by intuitive content with consciousness. Knowledge emerges in consciousness and seen as the person's knowledge. Knowledge is not something material: it is of the form either of the content of memory or of a direct awareness. In either case it is a modification of consciousness and not material. A *bhakta* looks at knowledge from the side of consciousness and not from the side of its content. So he can *see* that all knowledge, in order to become knowledge, is dependent on Lord's will. For a *bhakta* we can know things in their real form only because the dear Lord has granted us that capability and enables us for that. It is not a trivial truism. Animals also have the capability to know about the world for their survival. But their knowledge is used somewhat subconsciously and they can't understand it as knowledge. Apart from that they can't recognize their knowledge as an important tool to control and shape the environment in their own ways. It is a great boon given to human beings that they have the capability not merely to know but also they have the capacity to recognize knowledge as knowledge and to use it in their own interest. For an atheist it is a matter of hance. He has no satisfactory answer for why it is so. A *bhakta sees* that it is all a great boon and this boon is not possible without the boon-giver–his dear Lord. To see a boon in all these is almost experientially equivalent to seeing the hand of the Lord in it. In fact to see a boon is itself a boon of Lord. There is no scarcity of good things happening in life but we are so engrossed in our selfish ends that it becomes impossible for us to see them in their pure given-ness. We can accept only those things as good that are profitable for us. To set us free from our own made imprisonments Lord's grace is absolutely necessary. We within our selfish way of perceiving things think of Lord also in relation to our profits. Only the *bhaktas,* who are gifted with b*hakti,* can see that the blessing of the Lord is always available to everyone. Given this clear vision a *bhakta* can see that one who attains knowledge in any sphere (except for spiritual knowledge) does get only half truth since one misses an important aspect of it. Every time one gets knowledge one comes to know what is truth but fails to notice the divine will that ultimately makes it true. The relation of ideas, which is proved to be a valid knowledge-claim, emerges from within the person's consciousness and the realization of the methodology of its validation also emerges from the same source but the knower does not care to notice it. Since he does not do so he can't see the necessary connection between the piece of knowledge-claim and consciousness that is its matrix. Ignoring it without any good reason he makes the knowledge-claim as a claim completely independent of consciousness. This makes his claim a half-truth. This is not the case with any one special field of knowledge. In all knowledge, especially that which is called scientific knowledge, this sort of half-truths are accepted without hesitation and boasted as objective knowledge.

A *Bhakta's* View of (Scientific) Knowledge

It is necessary to note that in above paragraph the claim of objectivity of knowledge as independent of consciousness is criticized as half-truth. Objectivity of mind-independent knowledge-claim is not criticized there. These are two different things altogether although it is materialist bias to identify the two. Any knowledge-claim, in order to be called genuine knowledge claim, has to become mind-independent but it should not be consciousness-independent. No knowledge-claim can be consciousness-independent. As such no knowledge-claim can be independent of the Lord's will. An ordinary person looks at knowledge as its content since that of great use for him. A *bhakta,* on the other hand, looks at it as its content and also as a very special event that takes place in human mind. He *sees* that knowledge as its content as well as an event takes place always and only due to the Lord's will. But apart from these he could also *see* that the consciousness, from where knowledge emerges, is not separate from the Lord.

Knowledge is not merely knowledge for people. At the personal level knowledge becomes a matter of pride and at the community level it becomes power to control the less knowledgeable. This is a direct consequence of accepting knowledge as dangerous half-truth –as truth-claims detached from its relation to Lord's will. A non-*bhakta* ignores it and does not find it necessary to take note of it even if reminded of this essential relation. A *bhakta* sees it as the most important part of knowledge. For him to know that the proposition 'P' –'Earth has the power to attract material bodies'— is true is to know that it is true along with the truth that it is Lord's creative will (that manifests in the laws that gives rise to the formation and its orderly behaviour of the earth). This part is the most important and fundamental part of the knowledge of earth's gravitation for a *bhakta*. For him to know the law of gravitation is to realize how Lord's will is operating in this sphere. In fact Newton was discovering the laws of mechanics as '*Celestial Mechanism'*. He was strong theist and felt that the laws of nature could be grasped rationally since God has made these laws. God is not a whimsical dictator who infringes his own laws for the satisfaction of his will. Newton was interested primarily to know the divine law according to which entire universe functions in a systematic way and that motivated him to study the laws of nature as a careful and sincere student of nature. He wanted to know what nature tells. He was against hypothesis formation which is now accepted as a necessary step of scientific enquiry. For him making hypothesis is to impose one's own ideas on nature. That amounts to not to listen what nature tells us but to force it to conform to our options for it. Newton was a strong God-believer: he was a *bhakta.* A *bhakta* can't accept the laws of nature as purely material since he *sees* that it is not so. For him it is amazingly irrational to accept that all the laws of nature are operating just per chance. To see divine will behind them is the most natural response to them. *Bhaktas* accept the most natural response.

For a *bhakta* knowledge acquired by human beings is, in fact, not a pure quest for truth. It is more a passion to over power others-personally and politically. The attitude to acquire knowledge, for a *bhakta,* therefore, is generally a matter of ego-trip. The motivation to acquire knowledge itself is prompted from Lord's will. The desire to get knowledge and the possibility of its attainment is a boon to human beings. In the early stage of acquiring of knowledge this is clearly felt by the people who feel the motivation in this direction. Newton and others proceeded in the direction of search for knowledge with the strong belief that God has made this world to function in a perfectly orderly manner and it is possible for human beings to know that. But with the passage of time and with the accumulation of bulk of knowledge people begin to understand its use to dominate the lesser knowledgeable. The quest for knowledge, then, becomes a search for device to compete with others and to win. Hence a *bhakta* does not approve the life dedicated to the search for knowledge. This is, ordinarily, deemed to be his irrationality and attributed to his faith in his Lord. But his disapproval is due to the attitude of accepting only the half–truth as scientifically or rationally important. Detached from Lord's will that has allowed and enabled humans to know the truth acquired as the objective truth-claim is false and irrational for a *bhakta.* Science, in its present form, therefore, is not acceptable to the heart of a *bhakta.*

Bhaktas' concern is the human attitude towards any action with which people do it. If some action—physical or mental, can't be done without an implicit arrogance based objectivity then he can't ever approve it. The truth that every action is performed only with the primal and ultimate support of Lord's will —needs to be explicitly accepted according to *bhaktas.* The kind of knowledge that denies this fundamental truth is not worth pursuing. This does not necessarily amounts to the denial of scientific knowledge at all. The truth that scientific knowledge is a boon given by Lord is to be accepted as the primal basis of it. Everything else in scientific knowledge will remain almost the same but it would be a qualitatively different knowledge in many important respects. The most important sense in which it is different is the fact that the causal explanation is accepted with a clear and explicit feeling that Lord's will is operating behind them. Materiality is not replaced by spirituality but it is overtly supported by the latter.

A *Bhakta* Lives in The World With Others As An Ignorant Person

A *bhakta* lives in a world where he finds himself completely isolated. Hel finds that hardly anyone understands his love for the Lord and although the people themselves lead a life of utter ignorance they blame him to be ignorant, over-emotional and superstitious. He finds it advantageous from the point of view of his relation to his dear Lord since this condition helps him easily withdraw from the world and spend more time in the raptness of Lord's *bhakti.* However, he also find, at times, that the feeling of freedom that every ordinary person enjoys is the most dangerous gift of Lord because it hardly ever takes them towards Lord but keeps them away from Him almost for the whole life. Most people use this freedom for ignoring the truth that Lord's will is the pervasive basis of every happening and keep themselves deliberately deluded. It is a painful situation for a *bhakta* and it is but natural for him that he does not like to be an active part of this world of arrogance and ignorance. For him this is the world created by Lord's will so that exercising the given freedom one can come in dear Lord's contact. Knowledge, wealth and every other possessions are given in abundance to all by the will of the Lord without any discrimination. One who goes on the path of Lord's *bhakti* finds all these in abundance without any effort. But the lust for worldly possessions and scientific knowledge makes these boons extra-ordinarily difficult for every body and also deprives people form the most valuable thing in this world i.e.- Lord's *bhakti.* A *bhakta* never chooses the latter. He chooses only Lord's *bhakti* and every other possessions are less valuable to him. After all the most valuable thing —Lord's *bhakti* is with him and everything is valuable only to the extant it helps attaining it or co-ordinate with it.

How A *Bhakta* Solves His Problems of The World

A *bhakta* has a single solution to all the problems that arise before him. He puts it before his dear Lord and leaves it to Him for its solution. In fact, for a *bhakta,* who is completely absorbed in the taste of love for his Lord, no problem arises at all. In such a *bhakta's* knowledge, whatever happens occurs due to the will of Lord, and as such it is for the good of all: it is not a problem. But for a *bhakta*, who has not yet attained the state of constant absorption in the taste of Lord's love, problems arise and disturb him also. But he knows how to handle them effectively. He just leaves it for the Lord to do with it whatever He wants to do. He knows that his Lord teaches him and helps him to reach Him through all the events of the world. He tries to decipher the encoded lessons in a problematic situation, learns them and rises one step higher than his earlier stage. His love for his Lord gives him a straight direction to do that (i.e.- to decipher the lesson) successfully. In this process of learning his *bhakti* becomes deeper and deeper and takes him in the direction of complete absorption only n the taste of Lord's *bhakti.*

The *bhakta's* effort to solve his problem by leaving it to the will of Lord solves it not only in the sense that he detaches him from the problematic situation. The *bhakta* and others too find that his problem is actually solved in a strange way, which he had not even thought of earlier. This is the experience of the *bhaktas* that Lord solves their problem in that way and to that extant that they had never expected. Lord's proclamation in *Bhagvadgita* that He carries the burden of *yoga* and *kshema* of all who take refuge in Him[1], is the common experience of all the *bhaktas*. The belief in miracles is the outcome of this perception. The belief that Lord changes the laws in favour of his dear *bhaktas* is never regarded as the belief in the irrational and shallow character who can be flattered by his praise. It is the belief that Lord does not need to take recourse to the causal path to produce what He wills to produce. Laws themselves are the manifestations of his will so His will to help and reward his dear *bhakts* gets easily accommodated in the system of prevailing Laws just because Lord wills. Such interference in the system of laws do not create anarchy since Lord does not want that. Prevailing system of laws remain operating as usual without being disturbed by Lord's special will since Lord wants to that. Prevailing system of laws of nature manifests Lord's general will and on this backdrop the instances of His grace over His *bhakta* that expresses his special will shines out distinctly.

The gist of this chapter can be presented as follows:

A *bhakta* lives in the world and looks at its events occurring with and around him as fundamentally activated by the will of his dear Lord. Seeing His will operating behind everything he accepts them as His *prasâd.* Even the Scientific Knowledge is a boon given by his Lord because he *sees* that the laws that are discovered by science is ordained by the Lord and its knowledge is also given by Him. He does not oppose science as such but opposes the ignorant arrogant anti-spiritual attitude associate with it. He does not get involved in worldly affairs since he is completely involved or lost in the *bhakti* of his Lord. However, he does not support the ontological view of the unreality of this world because he knows that it is in and through this world that his dear Lord's will operates and helps the people to reach Him.

However, the important question of the *bhakta's* response to the pain-giving nature of this world is not yet considered specifically. Everyone could accept this world as Lord's boon only if enormous sufferings were not present in it. Apart from the cases where suffering is caused by a single or group of human beings there are cases of natural calamities and destruction that can't be ascribed to human agency. *Bhaktas'* response to this question needs to be discussed in its fullness. This would form the subject matter of the next chapter. A general answer to this question can be given in terms of this world's privation (or deprivation of itself) from the presence of the dear Lord. It needs elaboration.

Reference

1. 22/9/ Bhagvadgita.

6

The World is a Boon Only with Lord's Presence in it

Kṛṣṇa! This world, according to the *bhaktas,* is his dear Lord's creation. As such it is beautiful and full of all that is needed to fulfill everyone's need and to take everyone near the dear Lord. This is the experience of every *bhakta.* Everything becomes beautiful with Lord's presence. In fact beauty itself is beautiful since it is Lord's attribute. The *bhakta* feels the presence of his Lord in his heart and in the world too. The non-*bhaktas* have no experience of Lord's presence in their life. Physical and psychic enjoyments alone make this world attractive for them and they naturally want to enjoy those at the maximum and try to keep away the sufferings as much as possible. They want to avoid or defeat the particular instance of suffering that come in their life but despite a deep desire in the heart that alas, there were no suffering at all, they never actually believe that it is possible. They think that their sufferings are due to physical conditions that can be avoided or removed in particular cases but can't be eliminated as such. They hardly ever think about the reason of sufferings as such. From the *bhaktas'* standpoint suffering is the absence of the dear Lord. Not feel His presence is the greatest suffering and. to feel the presence of Lord is the source of all enjoyment in all conditions

Suffering is usually divided into two categories in view of their cause— Moral and natural. Moral suffering is that which is inflicted upon human beings due to other human beings or by him/ herself. Human free will is held to be responsible for it. It is argued that human beings are made free to choose among various alternatives to decide a particular course of action. They can willingly create situations for other's suffering indirectly or even directly they can hurt others physically by the power of their muscle power. By being morally unfair towards others (or even to themselves) the suffering is generated. This is Moral evil or moral suffering. Natural evil or suffering, however, is caused not by humans but by nature. Epidemic, Sunami, flood etc. are instances of destructions or annihilation caused by nature. How nature, which is creation and creative power of Lord, can bring so much of suffering to men? This is a question before the *bhaktas*. The *bhaktas* have more than one answer to this question and each answer helps in understanding *Bhakti* from different aspects.

Natural Calamities are Present in The World with The Lord's Will

Nature is the creative power of Lord. It is just like Mother for all animate beings. As Lord's creative power it is not separate or independent of Lord. No ill-will can be attributed to Lord's will. How can Lord think of hurting his creation? But it is a fact that human life, health and human world suffer a great deal with natural calamities. Un-surmountable losses are incurred by earth quakes, cloud burst and other events of natural destructions. Although these can't be ascribed to Lord's but they can't be taken as Lord's helplessness. For almighty dear Lord it is not difficult to make this world free from such evils. But their presence is a proof that Lord does not want that. It is therefore necessary to admit that if evil is present in this world its present with the will of Lord. But this does not amount to ascribing ill-will to Lord either. Lord gives a definite and clear message to the humans through the events which hurt him irreparably. This is not a strike from Lord's position. In Lord's heart pure love is present and from that pure love He chooses to awaken human beings form their dream of mortality so that they can realize their immortality. To awaken the He does something to them that could prove to be disturbing for their dream. Natural calamities are such events chosen by the Lord to destroy the sleep of attachment (*moha nidrâ*). A rational understanding about Lord's purpose is not sufficient to understand the *bhakta's* standpoint. It is necessary to understand it existentially. A purely rational explanation does not indeed answer the question. Rather it generates several other questions. But the *bhaktas* understand it existentially. An existential understanding is not opposed to conceptual understanding; it the former involves the latter. However, in pure conceptual understanding (or understanding it only at the pure conceptual level) raises many other questions that are relevant at that level. If, on the other hand, understanding develops existentially then so many conceptual doubts loose their practical significance. This understanding brings about an actual solution. This solution is not a clearing of doubts at the rational level but it is a dynamic force that motivates the *bhakta* to accept the world without attachment.

Nature Does Not Always Allow Reason to Predict and Prepare for Its Future Course

Reason has the capacity to understand the laws of Nature and to predict its future course. Nature seems to co-operate with humans and enables him also to know its mechanism of operation. On the ground of this knowledge man can predict about future happenings and to some extant those predictions turn out to be true also. But the enormous expansion and complexity of nature, both at the micro and macro levels, make it impossible for human reason at any point of time to take into account all factors of an event. As such a future plan envisaged by man to control the future course of nature or at least prepare for a safety against its harmful effect can never be completely ruled out despite all possible precautions. The bulk of human ignorance, at any point of time, is enormously bigger than the bulk of knowledge and any ignorance may lead to devastation. In view of this all-pervasive truth the idea and enthusiasm to reign over nature seems to be childish. But it is generally appreciated under the implicit assumption that there is a possibility of success. This belief is strengthened by the great successes achieved by science and technology. In the intoxication of these successes people forget or like to forget the infinite power of nature. The fact that the infinite power of nature does not always care for man's plans and safety provisions prove that it is not meant for that. For a *bhakta*, who sees Lord's will in the power and functioning of nature, believes that his Lord does not want to make man the absolute conqueror of nature. Had He wanted that He would have made him that. But despite all the earnest efforts man could never succeed in so doing. This, for the *bhaktas,* is a sure sign that his Lord wants something else. Through the forces of nature Lord wants to give a clear message to human beings that this world is not their permanent abode and they can't make the forces of nature their loyal servant. This is a hint for them to turn their attention towards Him and find permanent abode in His grace. Lord is not a despot and does not want to deprive human beings from their freedom. So the Lord gives them enormous opportunities to willingly come to His holy feet. The life of a man is a series of opportunities to realize the truth that this world is not his permanent abode and to find it at the Lord's feet. Since forces of nature give this message only implicitly and one can interpret this situation in an entirely different way (in an agnostic way) Lord reveals Himself before the humans in an unequivocal manner so that they could accept His grace if they like to. If people normally don't withdraw from the world and don't accept Lord's grace then it is only because they just don't want to do so. Lord can't be held responsible for this. Attempts of the agnostic thinkers to show that ultimate responsibility of people's attitude lies with the Lord, is practically irrelevant and ridiculous, and conceptually untenable. Worthlessness of some such agnostic attempts would be discussed in the following paragraphs.

Worthlessness of The Rational Argument That Omnipotent God Could Have Given His Intended Message Without Mediation of Evil

Some agnostics are of the view that God could have given His intended message or lesson to human beings without bringing in evil in the world since He is believed to be omnipotent. To take recourse to a particular means to reach an end is necessary for a person of limited capacity. For God, Who is believed to be almighty, such dependence on means to reach a desired is not necessary. God is believed to have created the world out of sheer will. Laws of Nature, as discussed above, operate according to His will. Such an omnipotent God could have taught the intended lesson to human beings directly. To give so much of suffering to humans to teach that this world is not their permanent abode seems to be a lame excuse to defend the belief in God.

Conceptually the argument seems to be sound and formidable too. In fact the argument is sound *only* conceptually. It is of no use either in the actual life of a *bhakta* or in the theoretical framework that stands as the backdrop of his life. It is irrelevant and prompted from the misunderstanding regarding the relation between religious way of life and religious rationality. A religious person is not an irrational person. He leads life according to his reason but his reason travels on that path that is lighted by *bhakti.* His practical reason is for deciding practical issues in the light of *bhakti* and theoretical reason is for constructing a conceptual framework for his practical decisions in the light of *bhakti.* Any other use of reason is irrelevant for a *bhakta.* Above stated argument against God's omnipotence is an irrelevant argument for a *bhakta.*

For a *bhakta* the argument that God could have done otherwise is merely a logical possibility but empirically impossible from the standpoint of the limited reason of man. If the instances of natural calamities were not present in the world then the human beings could not have got the shock that they get from them. If all such instances of natural destruction were absent then how could have the human beings got the pain that they get from these instances? Having the feeling of suffering without any actual cause for suffering is somewhat a preposterous thought. Any omnipotent God can do that but at least from our present normal understanding of normal man such people could not be called normal. A normal man is one who feels pain when some cause for it is present before him.

The agnostic, however, may argue that an omnipotent God could have given an attitude of disinterestedness to all humans so that they could not have ever thought of this world as their permanent abode. But from the point of view of the *bhaktas* God did not want to give this lesson to humans. The lesson that God wanted to give to humans was not to be tempted by worldly possessions, powers and relations despite feeling all the temptations that it presents before them. Human beings would not have been able to feel the temptations of the world if they had been made disinterested towards it. The message that God wanted to give to humans could not have been conveyed to them.

The agnostics could argue that an omnipotent God could convey the message to humans to remain disinterested in the world despite feeling its temptations by making his vision clear and his will strong enough. But if it were so then there was nothing for the humans to learn (since everything was already given). Then there is no point in the idea of a *teaching* a lesson.

By creating or allowing situations of natural destruction to be present in the world Lord gives opportunities to humans to learn the lesson of dispassionate living and to emancipate themselves from the shackles of materiality that they have made by the passionate way of life. Without this learning the growth of human conscious from the stage of psycho-somatic identity to the higher and *real* identity of pure consciousness is not possible.

Agnostic could further ask as to why God could not make a world where some lessons, at least this lesson, could have been taught to the humans directly. The folly of this question becomes clear by understanding its practical import. This question is, in fact, the question about why God has left human consciousness at a lower level, why He did not just made consciousness in every individual fully developed. But this question is practically worthless since it amounts to asking about why God has made room for the growth of consciousness.

The presence of evil in any form, in fact, is a situation that is present. Had it not been present something else would have been present. Let us suppose that God could have made human beings, who had been able to grow without actually passing through physical suffering. How does it ensure that such humans were free from all sorts of suffering? How does it ensure that there could be mental suffering for such humans? The susceptibility to various sorts of sufferings can't be ruled out completely from the nature of human consciousness. If human beings have the consciousness then the possibility of suffering is inextricably connected to it. Consciousness, if it is consciousness at all, then its freedom of choice can't be determined in advance. As such the possibility of its choice that could bring suffering, can't be precluded either. All rational arguments fail to take note of this point. These arguments try to highlight that the logical possibility of creation of an evil-free world was within the power of an all-powerful God but undermine completely the logical contradiction involved in accepting the free nature of human with God's intervention to use this freedom. The argument becomes worthless, at the logical level, because of its logical inconsistency. At the practical level, it becomes worthless because of its failure to take note that if the laws of nature were not compulsive in their reign then they could not have been accepted as laws at all.

Consideration to The Existential Shape of The Problem

The problem of evil as the question of human suffering takes an existential shape and becomes powerful not only rationally but practically too.

Suffering, especially acute suffering, usually make people complain against the situation. Such situations neither enable nor help them see that this could be taken as a situation of learning. One can take it as a situation of learning only if one is mentally calm but the acuteness of pain, especially physical pain, takes away from him his calm. To preach someone else not to take his pain seriously, when he is completely under its influence, is to ridicule his pain and not to help him at all. When someone is in pain then he normally wants to get rid of it first and can't think to make the situation a learning-situation. Although, from a logical point of view, he can think of that and act according to that decision also and it is not practically impossible either. But this normally does not happen. To do so requires a realization of overpowering grip of pain. But when someone feels the overpowered by his pain then, naturally, it appears to be impossible to him. The key to accept the situation as a situation of overpowering pain (being overpowered by pain) or as a situation of overpowering the pain is factually one and the same. The difference between them, however, is absolute. The difference lies not in the factual structure of the situation but in the attitude of the person to that situation. A person may blame God for creating such a painful situation but a *bhakta* may find it as a situation that not only facilitate but is necessary for realizing in actuality that he has overpowered the suffering. It is also necessary for *seeing* that natural forces by themselves can't beget such an attitude. Such an attitude necessarily presupposes the divine will behind it. Lord's grace manifests directly in the growth of this attitude. For a *bhakta* a new meaning comes to fore. He realizes that only through the grace of his dear Lord he has got this attitude, otherwise there were many possibilities for developing an opposite attitude. And through this attitude only he could see that his Lord's grace has put him beyond the grip of pains and suffering. What a great achievement is this can't be realized without taking into consideration the unbearable-ness of the experience of suffering. Although all of us have passed through suffering but the experiential unbearable-ness of suffering can't be captured in thinking about it. As such liberation from suffering also, at the level of thought, can be understood only as concept. Its experiential element is lost in thinking about it. Consequently the actual value of a *bhakta'.s* feeling of gratitude for his Lord also remains merely a thought in which the bliss is lost and it can't result into a change in attitude that is centrally important for bringing about a change in actual situation from the experiential aspect. An actual feeling of gratitude for the Lord draws the attention of the person from the pangs of suffering. Thus the pain is lost by the *bhakta* in the love of his Lord although the factual conditions may remain the same. A *bhakta's* condition may appear to a common man as a situation of extreme suffering since all objective factors are present in which any common person suffers a great deal but despite having a full sense of his condition objectively surrounding him a *bhakta* is not at all moved or disturbed and remains lost in the bliss of the proximity of his Lord. Pain can't touch the *bhakta* who has lost himself in Lord.

This happens in our daily life also. If someone is so completely engaged in some work that his attention totally absorbed in it then he does not get moved if a small pain is occurs to him. But this depends on the intensity of the pain. An excruciating pain may cause disturbance or even force upon the person to withdraw from the work. It is all a matter of degree of intensity of pain in ordinary experience. A *bhakta's* absorption in his dear Lord is a matter of qualitative difference. When a *bahkta's* attention is drawn towards his Lord it is not focused on any physical object. It is drawn towards and fully absorbed in the very beauty of *bhakti.* In the light of discussions of previous chapters it is clear that the Lord of a *bhakta* is *in* the *bhakti.* A *bhakta's* Lord is not a person out there but He is experienced as condensed form of the pure and infinite beauty, majesty, power and divinity of *bhakti* itself. Hence the absorption in Lord for a *bhakta* is an absorption of his attention in the very content of his own emotional experience. Once it happens then no events occurring in the surrounding can disturb him since this is the necessary condition for achieving this sate of absorption. Conditions of suffering also, therefore, can't disturb him at all

Pain or Un-Easy-ness is a Sort of Privation But It Manifests Always as Positive

In above discussion it is important to note that the presence of the factual condition (or set of conditions) that is felt as pain is necessary for feeling of relief and consequent gratitude. If there were no pain relief from pain would never have been felt by anyone. But the presence of pain is not for making the experience of relief from it possible. It would be preposterous and cruel too if in schemes of the *bhakta's* dear Lord pain were provided *only* to make the relief of pain experientially possible. For a *bhakta* the conditions of pains are allowed to make the realization possible that involvement of person's attention in body and/or mind is *the only* cause of pain and this is due to the reason that the person's attention is not involved in the love of Lord. Pain is, in general, a feeling of uneasiness. Uneasiness is the lack of easiness, i.e. the state of at ease. But this lack or absence expresses itself in a positive feeling. Pain, of any sort, is always a positive pressing feeling that an ordinary person can't normally ignore. Even a smallest pain at once draws a person's attention. Person's attention is drawn to a pain almost in the same manner as wind is drawn to a place of vacuum. In the presence of hundreds of other positive stimuli a small pain becomes dominant. All other stimuli recede in the background and pain acquires the front stage.

For a *bhakta* it results only when the person's attention is not involved in Lord's love. There is only one thing worth attending—

Lord Himself. To think of Lord's forms and attributes, remembering His glorious deeds, are the only things that actual deserves attention. Everything else is just secondary or unimportant. To be completely involved in Lord is to be involved in the content of the in one's experience of *bhakti*—an involvement in one's own being. So the involvement of a person's attention in Lord is be at the state of perfect at ease. To go away from Lord is to fall from the state of ease. This is uneasiness or pain. To retain the state of at ease is the state of no pain. In *bhakti* one retains the state of at ease. By getting himself lost in the *bhakti* of his Lord a *bhakta* drops all the factors that take him away from the state of at ease.

The Positive Occurrence of Un-Easy-Ness is a Defense Mechanism

For a *bhakta* the positive feeling of pain is an indirect but clear message from the Lord to the person that either the external conditions or his own mistaken identity is putting away from Him—from his own real self. As every message of Lord is grace for the *bhakta* this also is a grace for him. However, this is somewhat special because if the state of absence would not have been felt positively and strongly then it would not have been felt at all. It would have been just lost. This definitely had caused devastation since need to make effort to remove that absence and to restore the state of ease could not have arisen. Unattended that absence would have made permanent damage to the person's life (imagine a person's finger is cut by a knife and he does not feel any pain then he would die due to constant bleeding). It is due to its occurrence in a positive feeling–in the form of a demand to get rid of it that motivates a person to find a way (to get rid of it). The way can be found at a particular level or at the most general level.

A particular solution to a specific pain is found by us all. We all make efforts to come out of the situations of pain or try to remove the present conditions that cause it. Persons like the *bhaktas* are endowed with the vision to see the deepest reason –the most general reason of pain as the distancing from Lord and try to restore the broken link with the Lord to have a permanent and real solution to all the actual and possible pains. *Bhaktas* could understand that it is his dear Lord's mechanism to save the valuable life by restoring the state of at ease at the particular level and to find a way to its permanent solution also. So the *bhaktas* see a special grace in it.

The *bhaktas'* vision that a special grace of Lord is present in pain shows the worthlessness of the agnostic's demand for absence of pain in the world created by the benevolent God. Despite the analytical rigor of reason the agnostics fail to see that pain is not for pain's sake. Pain is not allowed by the Lord to make people's life miserable or to teach harsh lesson to them who forget Him. It is a privation – an absence of normal state of ease that has been made to manifest always as a positive feeling by the will of the most benevolent Lord to help everyone save his life even if he never remembers Him. Physical or psychic pain motivates a person to find a way out of it. Everyone wants to get rid of his present pain and most people find a way out for the present pain only. They get an earthly remedy for that. Had there been no pain in human life people would not have done anything to fulfill the vital demand of the organism in course of restoring the state of at ease and the organism could have perished any moment. The agnostics, due to their bias, could not (or do not want) to see this so important reason behind the presence of pain in human life. This failure (or this irrational rigidity) makes their argument of the presence of pain as a support of atheism worthless. An existential consideration to the nature and function of pain in human life does not prompt anyone to declare God's cruelty and to dismiss theism. It, rather, gives him a new understanding about human life in which he could clearly see (if he is not irrationally rigid) a supra-natural benevolent hand working behind ever instance of physical and psychic pains. Very few persons, like the *bhaktas*, with the grace of Lord, could see that although dear Lord has devised the mechanism of pain to save the precious human life, He (Lord) has left it completely on the person's will to find its real and permanent remedy by taking refuge at His feet. To restore the forgotten link with Lord is the real and permanent remedy for it but Lord has done nothing that could be called coercion. He has not imposed upon the people to necessarily remember their link with Him (Lord). Dear Lord has only left the scope open to everyone that he can remember and try to restore link with Him, if he so likes, but has made no compulsion for anyone to do so.

Agnostics see God's cruelty in the presence of the situations of human suffering especially in the form of physical and psychic pains. Is it rationally necessary to look at the world in this way from a theistic assumption? The answer is obvious— no. One can rationally look at the world with the belief in God, the way a *bhakta* looks at it and finds a special grace of his Lord I the presence of human pains. If an alternative rational outlook is possible both logically and practically then to adopt the agnostic's outlook is only the agnostic's own choice and not a necessary rational implication. Although a *bhakta* is usually accused of being intoxicated in his Lord's love in seeing God's grace in pains and his constant appeal that he is only stating a matter of fact is ignored completely. If the arguments of both the agnostic as well as the *bhaktas* are judged impartially then it would be clear that the former also fails to prove a rational point if the latter fails in so doing. An agnostic argues for the cruelty of God not because it is rationally necessary to hold that argument but only because he *wants* to buy it. If a *bhakta*, on the other hand, wants to buy an argument for his dear Lord's special grace in the situations of pain then this is also his own choice and instead of deriding against him we should learn to congratulate him for this because he uses reason to link himself to the divine.

Common Inclination towards Agnosticism is Disproportionate and Irrational

It is quite appropriate to congratulate the *bhaktas* for their deep vision. However, even if we don't congratulate a *bhakta*, it is rationally necessary to see for ourselves and also to help an agnostic see that his argument is the result of his own *non-rational choice* and not a rational necessity. This realization at the intellectual level is of seminal importance but ordinarily we ignore it completely. This situation turns out to be unfortunate due to the fact that the tendency to ignore it is quite disproportionate. Most people ignore the fact that the agnostics use argument against theistic belief due to their non-rational choice to do so. If 50% of the population would have ignored it and the rest would have not then the situation would not have been so dismal. But prevailing situation is a case of disproportionate ignoring of a point of rational and practical importance. If it were not so then normal human life could have remained open to understand and to accept another aspect of human life where there is infinite hope and possibility to turn that into an actuality.. In the prevailing situation this possibility is marred and our motivation to that ignored aspect is left to sheer chance. Rather it would be right to say that all possibilities are made to help us ignore that, and it is almost an accident or just God's will if anyone gets motivated to look for that then. The world of our selfish motives doesn't give us any let up to come out of its hold. It makes all provisions to keep its firm grip over us and even in some situations (like unsurmountable loss) one gets disillusioned by the plans of this selfish world, it produces enough programs to falsely make assurances that everything will be alright very soon. It is due to this terrible hold of the selfish human world that a *bhakta* believes that without Lord's grace one can't come out of it. Human world is not just the given natural world. From the very beginning it is a world that takes shape and functions according to selfish dichotomy of 'mine and thine'. This dichotomy is not in nature. It is not based on any natural urge and man finds himself acting in the world in a way in which this is necessarily presumed but it is not deliberately created by humans either. This is operating in human world before human beings became mature enough to use their faculty of reason. In this sense this tendency is beginning-less—'*Anâdî*'. This force keeps a person attached to some physical objects and some persons and makes him think that they belong to him, that he has some right over them. About the rest of the things and people the person thinks that they don't belong to him and are 'the others'. The functioning of this force is essential to give the human world the shape in which it exists at present and to keep it going the way it is going. So it is a creative and sustaining force. *Bhaktas* call it the '*Maya*' of Lord—His creative power. Under its influence people get attachment not merely with other persons and objects but also with the physical body as an integral part of their identity and pass through pains and pleasures. Suffering can never completely end till the force of attachment with the body is functioning. But no one can ever successfully go beyond the influence of this force with his efforts alone. *Maya* can be overcome only if Lord takes someone in His protection. Only they are the most fortunate persons in the world whom Lord takes in His protection. Only they can get rid of the influence of *Maya*. But that does not make a reason to doubt that Lord is unjust, that He does favour to a few only. This point needs some elaboration.

'*Maya*' is explained in various ways. Although it has a positive and a negative usage, ordinarily it is used in negative sense. In one of its negative sense it stands for God's that power due to which the person falls into an emotional attachment with the object as my possession, my belongings etc. and fails to see its real nature. A world of hallucination is created around the person due to *maya* and he gets so used to it that he can't see the reality beyond it *just because he doesn't want to do so*. Remaining under the influence of this dichotomy of 'mine-thine' is not always pleasant for anyone but one doesn't find any motivation to move out of it. He lives in a world of falsities that are quite obvious but under its influence all his desires are based on and guided by this phony dichotomy. Remaining under its influence one can have no desire to step out of it—one does not want to go beyond it. A person under its influence may be ignorant of the obvious falsity of the world sprung from this dichotomy, but even if understands this falsity as falsity he wants to cling to it and does not want to drop it. Even if a person rationally comes to understand that the boy whom he calls *his* son is not *his* except in the sense of a biological co-incidence his attachment for him would not cease to operate. If he contemplates more then it become clear to him that he has no control over that boy either biologically or psychologically. Occasions come in his life when he witnesses this plain truth in the bitterest way. Despite all this knowledge he can't overcome his attachment with that boy who does not want attachment with him. Knowing well, at least in those moments, that he is a victim of this attachment he feel very bad about his plight but finds himself helpless to overcome it. So it is not merely an ignorance-based lack of will force on the part of the person but is an objective force of that keeps the person stuck to the falsity. Since this force operates through the person's desires he can't understand that it is really an independent force and not his own will. He can't see the truth that whenever he acts with some selfish motive (based on the dichotomy of' mine-thine') he is being used as an instrument by this independent force. Since his will is under the influence of that force it seems to him that he is doing it on his own and more often he fails to notice that an independent force made him to do what he actually did.

Normal earthly human life, in which emotional attachment plays most significant role, would be just impossible if this force does not operate in the disguise of desire for emotional attachment. Functioning of this force at the mass level is a practical necessity to keep the human world going the way it is going. But it is important not to forget the truth that although this force functions through the individual's will it is not within the control of the individual. I can't overcome the force of the desire of attachment by my efforts only. I can destroy the object with which I feel attachment or run away from it but that can't destroy or weaken my feeling of attachment. Such acts can't result into the cessation of the feeling of attachment with that object. May be destroying the object of attachment or distancing from it may make the feeling more intense; I may go crazy for it. There is no direct way to control or regulate this force of attachment. Distancing from the object of attachment may make the person forget it gradually but it can't arrest his feeling of attachment for it, and he will have the same feeing again when it will turn up before him again. There is no way to overcome *maya* by one's own efforts. Grace of Lord is necessary for it.

Maya is not merely the power of ignorance. A person in ignorance does some work motivated by reasons which are not present but he thinks them to be present. After his ignorance is dispelled his behaviour is changed and he may abstain from doing what he was doing earlier. At least he does not feel any motivation to do that. If a person comes to know that what appears to him as a pond of clean water is a mirage indeed then he would not feel a motivation to move towards it. With the knowledge of reality the feeling of temptation to move towards it ceases and the movement stops. *Maya* does not cease to operate in this way. So it is not proper to think that *maya* is a force of ignorance. It operates independent of the person's knowledge or his ignorance. It is not absolutely wrong to say that it works in ignorance but it if we think that it operates *only* through then we don't understand it properly It functions, in many cases, independent of the forces of ignorance and at times, through knowledge too. So the explanation of *maya* as a force of illusion needs to be presented carefully The above analogy of mirage may help in understanding it if it is extended in a right direction.

It is true that a person traveling in a desert will not get tempted to move towards the visible pond if he knows that it s only a mirage. But if he is thirsty then despite the knowledge that what he sees is a mirage he feel motivation to reach it due to the hope that it might not be an illusion but a real pond. Motivated by the hope of quenching of his thirst he may think and argue that although mirages appear to be a pond but a real pond also appears to be a pond just because it really is a pond. Knowledge of the general law in this condition can't directly arrest his motivation. Even if he is given with the definite knowledge about the specific instance that he is witnessing his temptation to reach there doesn't cease to exist. He may forcibly stop himself from moving in that direction but his temptation can't cease to operate. In this condition the reason of motivation is not the ignorance of realty. It is the hope (of quenching of thirst) that motivates the person in this case. This hope is an independent force. It may listen to reason but it might not care to do so at all. Very often people don't loose hope even if all rational possibilities of its fulfillment are denied. The force of *maya* operates in this very manner. In fact hope is a manifestation of *maya*. It does not depend or get affected by the person's knowledge or ignorance. Considerations of good or bad with respect to the person's actions are not of much use here since he is not free to choose either. He may be forced by others or can force himself to choose this or that it is not his free choice.

Free choice is, ordinarily, identified with rational choice. If it is taken to be a matter of definition then there are several ways to define it and rational choice too can be taken as one of the conventionally accepted definition of free choice. Free choice, however, can be seen as a choice that a person takes without any compulsion, in which he does not feel any constraint. In this sense free choice and rational choice are not always identical. One may rationally find that his decision is correct but he if this decision is going to give him physical or psychic pain then he would *feel free* in implementing it. In order to implement such rationally correct decisions one has to nearly crush one's emotions or has to bind them. One can't emotionally remain free in the implementation of such decisions. The decision may prove to be correct on a pragmatic or on an absolute standard of evaluation but that is a different matter altogether. It is clear that such a decision, at least at that moment, does not grant him emotional freedom. So from a different point of view a decision of a person can be regarded to be *free decision* only if it does not disturb his emotional equilibrium. If a person in some situation may find that his own nearest-ones have ditched him and yet he feels attraction towards them then to break all relations with them may be a correct rational decision but it would not be an emotionally free decision since in implementing it he would have to forcibly suppress his emotions. For a peaceful life in future his rational decision may be his only way to come out of his present plight and for this he has to suppress his feelings brutally but this again shows that to feel or not to feel attachment with another person is not within anyone's control. If the other person and the situation respond to his feeling of attachment favourably then one enjoys this attachment a great deal. If, on the other hand, the other person and/or the situation do/does not respond favourably then he suffers for the same attachment a great deal. Feeling attached to a person/an object or not feeling so is not at all within the person's control. In fact the active voice statements like—'I feel attraction for her'. Only states what I feel and not that I actually do anything. The passive voice rendering of this statement-'I am attracted to her', bears its real import without generating any confusion about its being my act. Hence it is clear now that the feeling of attachment is an independent force that operates through the person's will and the person has no control over it. This force implicitly assures the person that it is joy to be in it (attachment). Not always his assurance is fulfilled. But one can't escape the suffering if one tries to oppose it. This independent force makes the person behave in accordance with it or make him suffer. All of us know the pressure of this force working on us through our desires since our life is ordinarily guided by our desires. Although my desire is called '*my*' but I have no control over it (in the sense that I can't stop them from arising in our hearts) rather it controls and forces me to do this or that. The independent force working through my desire is *maya*. *Maya* is not just another name of the force of desires. Realization of an independent force working through desires is the reason to give recognition to *maya* as a supra-human independent force. Since this force has the form of the will force and nature can't have the force of will so the *bhaktas* ascribe it to their Lord. *Maya*, in *bhaktas'* view, is the creative power of his dear Lord that forces humans to lead earthly life. With the grace of Lord alone one can come out of its hold. Through *bhakti* one enables oneself for the Lord's grace achieves a life free from suffering at the Lord's feet. *Bhakti* itself is the grace of Lord, or the beginning of His grace. Although *bhakti* is a divine gift and can't be produced merely by human effort but it is very strange that one can't honestly blame the Lord for favouratism regarding the distribution of this divine gift desire for such an honest complain can arise in anyone's heart only if one has started getting the gift of *bhakti*. So no sooner an honest complaint about the lack of *bhakti* arises in human heart the process of its fulfillment starts. This complaint can arise genuinely only in a *bhakta's* heart. An agnostic of conceptual variety can't genuinely make this complaint just because he has no desire in his heart for it. A *bhakta* can see that his dear Lord's *maya* is operating behind the agnostic's attitude. He (and others who are rationally rigid) can see that the agnostic is happy with his rational argument (which is actually disproportionately irrational) and fails to see what a blissful experience is he missing. An agnostic can't see it just because he does not want to. He enjoys giving arguments against theism and can't see the irrationality and worthlessness of his efforts. It is not within his control not to do so. He, all by himself, just can't stop getting enjoyment in the intellectual project of demolishing theism. He gets great joy in so doing and it is not within his control to stop this feeling to arise in his heart. The force that attaches him to his project operates through his desire to remain attached to it but he can't see that it is not *his desire* but an independent force is *making* him do that. This is *maya* of the Lord, according to the *bhaktas*. This is that form of *maya* that operates through that desire or will of the person about which he is not aware that it is not *his*. It has a practical value. It helps in sustenance of the material level of human life. So it is not a curse. It is also a form of Lord's grace for all those people who have not prepared themselves for a supra-material life.

In the life of *bhaktas* also Lord's *maya* operates but not as force of ignorance but as the emotional force of *bhakti*. It is not at all a force of ignorance. *Bhakti* can't arise in an ignorant person's heart. Above discussion partly brings it to our notice that a person can't genuinely desire for *bhakti* if he enjoys remaining stuck to the earthly objects and projects. Such a desire arises in a person's heart when he becomes aware that all his actions, which he thinks he is doing due to his desire or will are being done by an independent force and he is only *made to do* them. The opposite also is true. When such a desire arises in a person's heart then he can't remain ignorant about the fact that an independent force made him do all that he thought he was doing due to his desire or will. *Bhakti* an emotional attachment with the Lord also is an independent force that operates through his desire to come in direct contact with the Lord and dissolve himself in it. No one can produce this desire in his heart just for the simple reason that no one can produce any desire in one's heart at all. However, it is clear that such a desire has at least two very specialties that no earthly desires have— first, the desire is not oriented to any earthly object or project, and second, the desire here is for the love of the Lord that is an emotional experience itself. Elaboration of these points will be the content of the next chapter. At the end of this chapter it can be said that the presence of suffering in the world that is ordinarily used by the agnostics as an argument against theism is both irrational and practically worthless. Such an argument in its conceptual form is based on the agnostic's pre-occupation for atheism and advanced against theism by irrationally ignoring or hiding that pre-occupation. So it is irrational. When looked at from the existential stand point the fact of human suffering turns out to be defense mechanism for survival and sustenance of human life and the hand of providence is seen behind it that can be overlooked only if one has already decided to ignore that.

The creative power of the Lord –*Maya*, which is independent of the person's desire indeed, operates in the form of *his* (the person's) desire to keep the world of materiality going the way it goes and make people experience the suffering that are inevitable at the level of materiality. But as it is practically necessary for the sustenance of human life and to leave the possibility open for humans to move in the direction of *bhakti* of the Lord. Agnostic's failure to see this point or his decision to ignore it due to his pre-occupation with atheism makes his argument worthless. Agnostic is under the influence of *maya* as anyone else is and contributes to make the business of the material world progress on material lines. Under the influence of *maya* he finds suffering in the world. The *bhakta* also is under the influence of the creative force of the Lord that operates in his heart as the emotion of *bhakti*, enlightens him about the presence of the Lord in his life directly and all around him and enables him see the world worth living due to His presence.

7

Love-the Creative Power of Lord

Kṛiṣṇa! *Bhakti* is an emotion. It is felt primarily by the person as a psychic force that pulls him towards an image of Lord. *Bhakti*–the love for the Lord pulls a person psychologically towards the Lord. But it is not merely psychological in its real nature. It is supra-psychic and it is experienced as such not only by the *bhaktas* of very high level but by ordinary persons also (only if he is not rigid). This point is elaborated to some extant in a previous chapter. At the end of the last chapter it was shown that *bhakti* is the divine will force that operates as the desire to meet and merge with the Lord. Although this emerges in the heart of a *bhakta* and operates as his desire but it is not his: it is completely independent of his psycho-somatic control. As all of us at some situation come to realize that the attraction towards our kith and kin and to our belongings is not within our control and forces us to do things that we don want to all the *bhaktas* realize it from the very beginning that their *bhakti* for the Lord is not within their control –they can neither produce it nor can strengthen or weaken it by their will, and it pulls them towards the Lord independently of their choice and decisions. The difference between the two situations (i.e. the feeling of an ordinary person and that of the *bhaktas*) lies in their subsequent feeling of compulsion and grace respectively. An ordinary person in above stated situation feels helpless and bound to do what he does, but the *bhakta* feels free and delightful (in realizing that *bhakti* is an independently operating divine will force). A *bhakta* in such situations finds that he is under the care and protection of the dear Lord. So he is at ease and happy in all situations.

Bhakti—The Manifestation of Lord's Creative Power in The Purest Form at The Human Level

We can talk about the Lord's creative power in two ways—first, as an ontological assumption to discuss theism and second, as an experience of a real power felt by the *baktas* in their emotional relation with their dear Lord. Our discussion would proceed on the latter.

In his emotional attraction towards the dear Lord the *bhaktas* feel the force that pulls him towards the Lord and he feels the independence of this force also. This is the experience of every ordinary lover too. An ordinary lover feels a pull towards his beloved. He knows very well that he has neither produced nor contributed a bit to make this pull operate. Beyond his control he gets attracted towards his beloved. Irrespective of the form of this love relation the force of attraction operates on the person beyond his thoughts and plans. A mother loves her child and just can't help loving him. If a son also loves his mother then he also can't help loving her. It is due to the independence of this force that a person in love always finds that he is *in the control of* love and not that he controls love. *Bhakti* also is a love relation with the Lord and every *bhakta* feels that he is *in* love with the Lord. He feels the pull towards the Lord. Love is the name of this pulling force.

Love is ordinarily seen as a relation –an emotional relation. This is not a wrong understanding of it but certainly it is not an adequate understanding either. Love is not a relation in itself. A relation between two individuals results from the feeling of this force between them. The relation is the result of love but love itself s not that relation. It is also clear from the fact that no definite relation holds between two individuals if only one individual feels this pull towards the other but the other does not feel the same for the first. When this pull is felt by both then a relation emerges between them that is ordinarily named as 'friendship' or ' love'.

The relational bond is a force of pull that both the individuals feel for each other. The relation survives till this force operates between them. The old relation can be further carried by both or one individuals despite the cessation of the force but then it is merely carrying the corps of the relation: the relation is dead since the vital force of attraction withered away. Love, therefore, is not a relation.

Love is felt (by the person in love) as a psychic attraction. The person feels that the person, whom he is in love with, attracts him. Obviously this not a physical pull like that of magnetism or gravitation. In previous chapters on various occasions it is argued that this pull is supra- psychic in nature. But it is not a matter of argument either for the *bhakta* or for any earthly lover. In this emotion the *bhakta* feels its spirituality from the very beginning. Lovers also, at times, feel the spirituality of this emotional experience. This point is also explained in previous chapters. But given the ambiguity about the meaning of spirituality now it is necessary to elaborate what it means to feel or experience spirituality.

The term 'Spiritual' has several meanings such as –ideal, ethereal, other-worldly, divine, religious etc. All are interconnected but in particular contexts any one is taken to be its central import. In the present discussion 'spirituality' refers to the characteristic feature of the state of experience (or awareness) of the prevailing experience. It would be stylistic to say that it is the experience of an experience. But this stylised way of elaborating its meaning is acceptable only if it does not create a further problem about the very possibility of any such experience. Normally it does so. Hence abstaining from this stylised formulation it is better to elaborate 'spirituality' as the characteristic feature of a normally possible awareness of any kind of normal experience.

Every kind of experience contains within it an implicit awareness of itself (i.e. awareness of the process of experiencing). This awareness remains implicit and operates only implicitly as a part of the process of experiencing. However, it is possible for the person to become explicitly aware of the event of his experience. If something happens before someone's eyes then he sees (have a visual experience of) it. So long as that event is going on before his eyes and till his eyes are open and functioning normally, he keeps seeing it. In this visual experience he, ordinarily, does not remain aware of the event of experiencing that goes on within him. He, however, becomes aware of it if suddenly someone reminds him of this other event. This brings about a shift in his attention. Earlier shis attention was focused on the outside happening that was the object of his experience. Later his attention shifts to the connected-ness of that happening to his awareness. Although this shift makes the outside happening a little blurred it does not immediately throw it out of the span of his attention. His attention is still directed to that happening but now it is focused on the event of its being connected to his awareness.

Given the nature of sense experience the awareness of it disturbs the process of experiencing because sense experience demands exclusive focusing of attention on the outside event. Shifting of attention from the outside happening to the inner event of its being connected to awareness disrupts sense experience. But this shift opens up a completely new dimension of human experience. Although sense experience is disturbed by this shift of attention, there are some varieties of human experience (e.g. Aesthetic experience) that are available to human beings only because they make the attention shift from outside event to the inner event. All such experiences are the forms or modes of spiritual experience. Spirituality –as conceived in above discussion, manifests in these modes of experience.

Love also is a form of human experience in which spirituality manifests with high intensity. The beloved becomes the object of attraction for the lover n love not because some of her physical features or psychic attributes. It is just the other way round. Since the lover feels the attraction of love for the beloved that he discover beauty in her. This point is made sufficiently clear in earlier chapters. But here it is necessary to understand that this attraction is an actual force that operates as a psychic force of attraction. It is really *felt* by the lover to be operating in his life. As stated earlier this force operates through the lover's desire to remain in the presence of the beloved, to keep looking at her and to dissolve his identity in her embrace. This desire is not within the lover's control. This operates as his desire but it is not *his.* No one falls in love as a consequence of rational examination of the features and qualities of his beloved. It does not mean that love is always at the very first sight. One may feel this attraction for anyone after a long duration only but that is not because he rationally decides to love her/him. In longer companionship enough opportunities come in one's life and at some point one may begin to feel this emotional attraction for one's companion. In any case love is not a consequence of a person's active decision. It just *happens* to him – may be at the first sight or after a long companionship. As such it is an independently functioning force that operates as a deep psychic attraction towards the beloved. It is necessary to understand the nature of this force of attraction as a real forc

Love is a Supra-psychic Force

Love is a force but not a material force. This is felt by the lover as a force of psychic pull towards the beloved but it is not a psychological force either if 'psychological' means mental state or mental function of the individual. It is not psychological in the sense of collective mental phenomenon either because it is not confined to any specific community. However, it is not an animal instinct and by no means it can be reduced to any instinct either. On the contrary it is necessary for survival of human race in its 'human-ness' that is typically characterized by the presence of the emotion of love. So, in a way, It is the basis of 'human-survival-instinct' or the survival-instinct for the human race in its 'human-ness'. In order to understand that the nature of love is supra-psychic it is necessary to elaborate why it can't be conceived as merely psychic either in the individualistic sense or in the collective sense.

Any psychic event can be called psychic in the individualistic sense if an adequate theory about the related phenomenon can explain it in terms of the individual' sense experience. The survival instinct, which is assumed to be the most fundamental instinct, is deemed to be functioning behind all the voluntary and involuntary responses of the individual. Emotions of anger, the tendency to be possessive of eatables etc. can be explained adequately in terms of the functioning of the survival instinct. However, any such theory does not remain adequate when it has to explain a person's anger for his opponents who defeat him merely in rational argumentation.

Possessiveness for eatable and perhaps the possessiveness for physical wealth also can be adequately explained in this light but possessiveness for a purely honorific position can't be adequately explained.

Although most behaviourist psychologists don't agree with this view: they think that anger generated due to defeat in rational argumentations also is an extension of response to the extension of the survival instinct (rational survival in the present case) but they don't want to attach any relevance to the question how the physical identity of the individual gets transformed or augmented to a non-physical identity. For them it is sufficient to discover that through cultural upbringing and education the physical is augmented to rational identity. Why should the physical be transformed into a non-physical identity? —is not a scientifically valid question for them. But this is a valid question philosophically. No adequate answer to this question is possible unless it is accepted that the physical identity potentially contains within it a sort of inherent programme or a blue print of its growth as a non-physical identity. The fact that in the psychic growth of man from childhood to the grown up stage this transformation takes place almost with law-like regularity indicates that it is inherent. A contrary case is not difficult to find. But that aberration also is explained on the presupposition that this is the normal transformation. Given this situation it is not completely irrelevant or irrational to raise the question about the transformation of physical instinct of survival into the non-physical instinct if it is not assumed that the former is not barely physical (i.e. it has within it something non-physical).

Anger is a common emotion that is found in animals too. It is clear from above discussion that despite the fact that it is an animal emotion its function in the human race for a purely non-physical reason can't be adequately explained in the individualistic psychological terms. Love is a human emotion that in some of its form becomes completely non-physical and non-psychic. Hence we can't expect to have a psychological explanation of this emotion, at least in some of its specific forms. The experience of the psychic pull towards the beloved that arouses the desire in the lover to get his identity merged in the beloved. Although it brings with it a physical desire of bodily union in the sexual sense, in some of its forms it does not contain even an iota of sexual desire in it. The desire to lose oneself in the being of the beloved is actually felt by the lover with a complete absence of sexual desire. It is impossible to explain it in individualistic psychological terms. This does not mean that a psychological study of such a human experience is not possible but its rigid physicalist assumption does not allow drawing any rational conclusion about the actual nature of it. It is this rigid limitation that forbids many psychologists to accept that there is actually any such human experience at all and makes others accept honestly that within the methodological limits of psychology as a science it can't be explained. Although it is not intelligible within the strict limitation of scientific methodology it is not irrational to talk about it since it actually is a form of human experience and there is no good reason to deny it just because it can't be scientifically explained.

This rare but common human experience can't be explained adequately in terms of community psychology either. Different communities may have different Archetypes that make the members of that community respond in thought and behaviour in the same manner. C.G. Jung has started this branch of Psychology and helped and showed a new way to understand deeper human experience that primarily studies the genesis of religion in human civilization. This path also has its limitations although it liberates the rational study of human psyche from the rigid prejudices regarding scientific methodology. Present discussion about understanding 'love' as a force need not necessarily depend on community psychology since it (love) is not a racial psychic phenomenon. It is found in all human beings and its specific content (i.e. how it feels like) and its overt expressions also are almost the same in all individuals belonging to very different races. Motherly love can be taken as a typical example that is felt as the same and expressed in the same manner by all mothers of all the races. The typical case of love that is under present discussion also is the same for all humans irrespective of their race. Hence to understand the real nature of this form of love community psychology is not adequately helpful.

Love is a typical human emotion that is found to be developed at the level of human species only. A touch of love is seen in some of the behaviours of other species too but does not develop beyond a certain limit. To understand love in its developed form is to understand the development of the psyche of human being as a species which passed through a psychic mutation from the stage of impulse to protect only oneself to the stage of distinct desire to lose one's identity in someone else. This can't be adequately understood either in terms of survival instinct manifested in every individual or as a communitarian archetype to feel and respond in the same way. Love in our present discussion can be understood adequately only as a force that operates through human desire to lose one's identity in someone else. In the light of above discussion it is now clear to a large extent that this study has to go beyond the physical and psychic limitation of the methodology of research.

To understand love in its real nature it is necessary o approach this human phenomenon from side of the person who undergoes this experience. How the first person singular experiences it (i.e. how I experience it) is the only experience in which love is felt directly as a force. This is the only way, therefore, to understand love in its real nature. Whatever a person experiences in this way about love is usually denied cognitive value. A lover's statement is almost despised by most people as statements of a person fallen in a sort of intoxication. Some poetic significance is ascribed to such statements but in so doing its cognitive importance is denied completely. While it is true that a person on love spontaneously uses a language that is almost poetic since he is in a state of emotion but he states basically what he actually feels despite some bits of exaggeration. The tendency to exaggerate also has some sort of cognitive content in it. The cognitive content of what the person in love states and that of his exaggeration can be captured only if his statements are given due cognitive importance. It is not possible so long as we remain captives of irrationally rigid view that only sense experience gives are of cognitive significance. If we think that only a news correspondent or a scientist can give us some new piece of knowledge but a lover or a *bhakta* can't then we are imprisoned in a wrong view. Liberation from this narrowness is necessary to understand the cognitive significance of a person's experience of love.

Every emotional state gives a definite knowledge about what the person in that state feels. Psychologists also accept it. But they take it as a description of the mental state of that person and don't attach any cognitive significance to it. It is believed that a person's statement about what he feels in his sense experience in normal condition gives genuine knowledge of what the case is but his statements about what he feels in normal conditions in an emotional experience does not give any knowledge. This peculiar bias about sense perception is not normally seen as a bias by most of us. But this is a bias and there is no need of any argument to prove that it is so. Arguments are needed only to prove that it is not a bias but a demand of rational methodology of scientific search. This is an endless debate and to enter into it would only prove to be digression from our theme. However, without entering into this debate it will be shown in the ensuing discussion that an alternative science also develops if we don't allow this bias to reign our rational quest. The acceptance of the fact that emotional experience also has some definite cognitive content we only widen the scope of our cognition. It is wrong to think that by so doing we will contaminate the available bulk of our present knowledge. Our attempt to understand the cognitive content of the emotional experience of love would remain either indifferent to what we know through sense experience or it can enrich that: it can't contaminate it. If this attempt seems to disturb the yet available bulk of knowledge even then we should prepare ourselves for a revision in this regard because that is the necessary price that we must pay to buy truth. But this is baseless fear. Scientific knowledge attained as yet is not false. Only the naïve belief that this knowledge is attained pure on the basis of sense experience is false. The cost of accepting the cognitive content of emotional experience and especially of love and *bhakti* is not that high as we think. We don't have to revise our scientific knowledge: we only have to abandon a false belief.

Love is experienced by the person in love directly as a supra-psychic force. It will be a non-starter if we think, as we normally do, that it is merely the illusion of the person. Love is a normal human experience and all of us feel this supra-mundane element present in it. It is belied and belittled by calling it 'romanticism'. But a person in love directly feels it. The very feature of this experience makes him understand that it is very different from all other earthly experiences. In the blissfulness of this experience he forgets the rest of the world. In love a person gets a direct glimpse of spirituality of his being although he can't clearly recognize it as 'spiritual' right then. Vivid realization of it as a spiritual experience comes only later if this experience deepens and becomes stable in its full awareness. But even before that every ordinary person understands very well that it is blissful unto itself; that it is not valuable for anything (physical or psychic) else. A person enjoys this experience for its own sake and unknowingly aspires to sustain it. If for any reason he loses this experience then he bitterly complains primarily against the person with whom he was in love and then with all others although he knows that he has lost nothing except the blissful experience. Loss of love is the greatest loss for a person in love although this loss can't be described in terms of anything material or psychic. The loss of love is the greatest loss for a person because he had experienced nothing-valuable parallel to it.

The pull towards the beloved discloses her several qualities and features before the lover that he identifies as beautiful. Love makes those qualities lovable—i.e. beautiful towards which it draws the attention of the lover. Attraction for beauty is not exactly the same in every respect as the attraction of love. Attraction for beauty also gives joy to the observer and he wants to keep it watching. The desire to get oneself dissolved in it does not necessarily produced by the aesthetic experience. In love (at least in one of its form) this is an essential feeling. A lover not only wants to keep seeing the beauty of the beloved but also wants to get himself completely lost in her. The distinction between the two is not merely a distinction of the intensity of attraction. It is a qualitative distinction too. A person may fall in love with someone who is not beautiful from other people's view. It is not practically possible that a person be in love with someone and does not find her beautiful but it is not necessary that others also are able to find beauty in her. Hence a lover's discovery of beauty in his beloved and the beauty of any object as ordinarily perceived by common people are not exactly the same in all respects. If a beautiful object begins to attract a person in such a way that he also wants to get melt into it the it remains not merely an object of beauty for him but turns into an object of love.

The nature of love as an independent supra- psychic force is felt by many lover from the very beginning. This, however, does not remain very clear to him in the ordinary love. It becomes clearer and clearer only if he grows in love. Love has a definite experiential content and it can be *known* clearly only if the person under this experience is fully aware of it. Ordinarily, in love, the person's attention is drawn completely towards the beloved and he doe not remain aware of the experience itself. People pass through this emotional experience, get some bliss and when it is over then only a memory of that bliss if left with them, and that also fades gradually. People usually don't help in the growth of this experience. This experience is so intoxicatingly blissful that, in fact, they just forget to be aware of it and see it in its vividness. They begin to react almost automatically when they undergo this experience. Hardly anyone becomes aware of the experience itself. To be aware if it and to station oneself in it or to remain in for a considerable length of time is necessary for the growth of any experience and for the growth of the experience of love also it is necessary. A person can educate himself for the importance of this awareness and by disciplining himself he can achieve stability in this awareness. It is somewhat similar to learning the evaluation of art work, especially that of a performative art like music or dance. A good performance casts a spell on the spectator. Ordinary spectator gets enchanted by the performance but the art connoisseur remains aware of this enchantment and tries to find out the subtleties of the performance that create it. A person in love can also achieve this state but this affects his relation with the beloved (since she can easily notice that he is not giving *exclusive* attention to her). This, however, can happen without any difficulty in love with the Lord – in *bhakti*.

In *bhakti* the *bhakta* can and does become aware of the experience of his emotional attraction towards his Lord. This is, in a sense, quite necessary for growing in *bhakti* from the stage of imaginary involvement with an image of Lord to the stage of actual encounter with the Lord. as an objectively real person. As *bhakti* deepens the *bhakta* passes through various stages of inner life and gets different types of joy of freedom. The joy of liberation—from the world of materiality (i.e. shifting to the world of *bhakti*, called—'*Sâlokya*'), from the poverty of limited power and possession (i.e. acquiring higher psychic powers and attaining psychic wealth, called—*Sârsti*), from the imperfection of form (i.e. acquiring perfect beauty in form, called—*Sârupya*), from the separated-ness or distance from the supreme Lord (i.e.coming close to Him, called—*Sâmipya*) and from the disconnected-ness form the supreme Lord (i.e. to come in direct experiential contact with Him, called—*Sâyujya*). Ordinarily these stages are regarded to be developing in a *bhakta's* life in succession but that order is not of much importance. They may come in some different order. The list should not be taken as exhaustive either. There may be very many intermediary stages too. For our discussion the importance of this description lies in the noticing the fact that these high level of refined psychic joys of freedom too are not objective of the *bhaktas. Bhaktas* want neither sensuous pleasure nor do they desire for the joys of all sorts of freedom. He wants his Lord's grace to remain in the close contact with Him and this he gets in and through *bhakti* only. In other words a *bhakta* wants nothing but to remain in *bhakti* for ever. His awareness is completely drawn to this emotional experience itself. This is the highest and the purest state of *bhakti* –the purest form of love. In being placed in it the *bhakta* realizes that the force of attraction that has been pulling him towards his Lord is actually the will-force of his Lord that generates within him that attraction to grace him with the joy of being in His close contact. *Bhakti* –the purest form of love is the manifestation of Lord's will-force. Lord's will-force is His creative power since He creates everything by the sheer power of will. In *bhakti* Lord's creative power is experienced to be manifesting in its purest form. In the close proximity of the Lord the *bhakta* comes to know the purest form of His creative power as love.

In (the purest form of) *bhakti* the *bhakta* realizes the presence of an independently functioning divine power that generates the feeling of love (*bhakti*) in his heart and also generates its sustained awareness in his mind. *Bhakti* is attained in and through the awareness of *bhakti* itself. Self-awareness is necessary for this experience. Hence the spirituality of this experience is clearly given in the very essence of *bhakti*. Spirituality of *bhakti* might not be so clearly manifesting in many of its forms but in the purest form (*Śudhā Bhakti*) it manifests quite clearly not only for the *bhakta* but for anyone else too who is not rigidly opposed to it. A *bhakta* directly feels it in the divinity or piousness of the will of his Lord. But this experience contains in it the awareness of the presence of tremendous power. Lord's will power (that generates *bhakti* in him and also gives its awareness) is experienced by him as a tremendous amount of force that keeps his attention fixed on Lord. This is the most important aspect of *bhakti* for the present discussion. Peace and piousness of spirituality is intellectually intelligible to all. Power of spirituality, not as any esoteric power but as the power of peace, is generally not given recognition in intellectual circle. This is a direct experience of every *bhakta* but is intelligible to the non-*bhaktas* too if they are not irrationally opposed to it. Some elaboration of the conditions of attainment of *bhakti* would make this point clear.

A Tremendous Force Functions in *Bhakti*

It is already pointed out on many occasions in above discussion that *bhakti* can't be generated by any human effort. Its arousal in anyone's heart as a sudden emotional eruption may be taken as a matter of chance. But its sustenance and transformation as a permanent way of life requires a continuous support by several external conditions. Certain external factors can at one point of time may be conducive for the arousal of any emotion but it is not necessary that those conditions will be present always. Even if those conditions are imagined to be always present it is not necessary that they will hep in the sustenance of that emotion. Apart from the organic need-based emotions that prolong for long till needs are satisfied. Other emotions begin to wither away if the conditions prevail for long. Anger becomes weak and eventually lost if the conditions arousing anger prevails. Negative adaptability is a psychological fact. People gradually learn to accept certain adverse conditions and with acceptance the resulting anger disappears. In view of this fact it is clear that no emotion can survive for a longer period even if the conditions that generate them stand as they are. *Bhakti* as an emotion can't survive for long if it were dependent on external conditions. But it is generally known that *bhakti* not only survives in some people for a longer period but turns into a permanent way of life too. This certainly doesn't enable us to logically draw the conclusion that there is an independently existing person having special powers to generate this emotion in us and supports it. But the other side of this situation, which is usually ignored completely, must be taken note of. Logically we can't deduce the conclusion about the existence of any such person but logic can't dismiss any postulation about such a person either. If someone assumes that there is such a person then his postulation can't be logically refuted. The insufficiency of logical grounds to assert anyone's existence does not logically amounts to its logical refutation. Hence the *bhakta's* claim of a direct experience of such a supreme person can't be turned down as illogical either. The *bhakta* will have to furnish evidence or find ways and means to convince them who can't directly see his Lord. That is, however, is a different matter. Anyone who can't be convinced with the *bhakta's* efforts may doubt about his claim but can't declare that it is illogical.

The *bhaktas* directly experience the presence of his dear Lord in and through *bhakti.* This experience in its vividness of content and intensity is so strong that it is impossible for him to deny it. The force of attraction towards the Lord is so strong that he is left completely speechless. In its bliss he just gets so lost that he neither feels any impulse to say anything nor any energy remains left in him to separate himself from the intoxication of this experience and assert anything. Ineffability of this experience is primarily due to the tremendous power with which this experience absorbs the *bhaktas*.

Bhaktas directly experience the tremendous force of love but others also can understand it to some extant if the huge forces of different varieties of disturbing conditions, which this experience dilutes completely, is taken into consideration. In a *bhakta's* personal life such forces act in various ways in course of his growth and diluted by the advent of *bhakti* in his life in a gradual manner or suddenly. Each *bhakta's* biography, if studied carefully, disclose the functioning of *bhakti* in their lives as a very powerful spiritual force but certain general ways of its functioning can be broadly delineated at least in three parts that is being presented as follows.

Bhakti—The Force of Love for The Lord Dilutes The Forces of External Disturbances

Our daily needs and our routine to fulfill them consume the maximum time of our life. The fundamental needs of food, water and shelter make even the animals to run from one place to some far off places. Human needs are not confined to these three needs only. Preservation of wealth and knowledge for the security of one's own and that of the offspring can be regarded as one of the fundamental needs for human life as a rational creature. All these compel every human being to achieve their desired ends. Naturally in this process his attention is drawn completely towards the objects and objectives that are all *out there*. He hardly gets any respite from this run for the survival. Running for the fulfillment of needs and to take rest for a while, when exhausted, to regain energy to run again is the gist of an ordinary normal man's life. So his whole attention is directed always towards outward objects. Since these needs are mostly physical in nature his attention is almost mechanically drawn to external objects and objectives. There is very little scope for his intellect to review this situation and even less scope is left for his will power to choose anything else.

Persons, who are comparatively more constrained by their physical needs, lead their life and finish it almost like automata. They, who are comparatively less constrained and can afford to review and decide to change the situation, are mostly overpowered by lethargy or by the pleasure instincts. Only a few put their will into action to review the situation and to break this mechanical compulsion.

Each person despite all his constraints is free to exercise his willpower to do this. Some do but most don't do this. The exercise of will requires psychic effort. The person has to take pains for it. Not to make any effort to review and not to choose for change does not put the person to any pain. This pain is to be taken not only once. It is not just one time job. It is a continuous process of taking pains. Assertion of personal will force demands its sustenance for a considerable period. Till the effort made by the exercise of will power brings desirable result one has to keep his will force alive. This is an arduous job. Those few persons, who eventually prove to be the lance bearer of any kind of change, have to face this situation. Till their objective is reached they have to strive for it without any reason. They have to keep their hope alive for no good reasons known to them. They have to keep it alive by the power of their sheer will. This is an extremely difficult job. The person has to exert his pure psychic power almost in the same manner as he has to use his pure muscle power in lifting a heavy weight or displacing it. A person, who uses his muscle power to displace or lift a heavy weight, has to apply it on that thing only once but has to keep it applied till it is displaced. With every passing moment his energy dissipates and if it is exhausted completely before the desired displacement is achieved then the effort will be frustrated. The psychic force of will is similar in this respect to the physical force of muscle. There is a difference between the two types of forces with respect to the duration of their dissipation. Physical force normally dissipates very soon but psychic force does take a fairly long time for being completely dissipated. Complete dissipation of muscular force that renders the person literally exhausted for quite some time is a common fact and we are all familiar with it. Complete dissipation of psychic force can't be logically ruled out but is not a common experience. However, hardly ever comes a situation in any one's life when one could find oneself at the complete lack of psychic force to will to do something. One may find oneself too exhausted to put his will into practice but one never finds oneself too exhausted *to will* to do it. One never finds oneself at the complete loss of energy for willing. This is an important difference between muscular (or physical) force and the psychic force of will.

A person, who applies the psychic force of will to withdraw his attention from the objects and objectives of needs, may will to do so but the success or failure of his will can't be assured by his power to will only. Especially in case of biological needs it is almost impossible for any person to successfully put his will force to withdraw his attention from the object of his organic urge. A thirsty person can't withhold himself from searching for water and in this search his attention is necessarily drawn to the thought of water. He can't stop thinking about water just by the exercise of will although he can will to do so.

Withdrawing one's attention from the objects of psychic needs does not seem to be that much difficult as it is in the case of object of physical needs. Psychic needs manifest them in the form of intense desires. Contrasted with physical needs it always appears easy to control any desire. Practically it is not so. Although desires don't lay physical pressure on the person they directly weaken the will of the person if it is directed against it. A person has to struggle with himself a great deal to divert his attention from any desire. If the desire is very intense then it almost kills any will that comes in the way of its fulfillment. So withdrawing attention from desires also is extremely difficult. Even if a person succeeds in some of his attempts to withdraw his attention from the objects of desires he can't always be assured of such a success in future. *Bhakti* is achieved only when the attention of the person is completely fixed on the image of Lord. To fix the attention on the image of Lord is not a worldly desire and a person's will has to collide with all sorts of weak and intense worldly desires who wants to do so. Not one but all desires come in the way of successful exercise of such a will and not merely selfish and immoral desires but good and robust moral ends of human life try to dilute this will. A person's will alone can't survive such an onslaught unless it is internally supported from some independent enormously powerful divine will force. A person attains *bhakti* means that his will (to withdraw his attention and to fix it on his Lord's image) is supported internally by a divine will that has the force to not only neutralize or dilute the distracting forces but also to protect and strengthen it so much that the person is completely relaxed and left without fear. *Bhakti* dawns in a person's life only if this happens. With the direct support of divine will alone a person could attain *bhakti*.

A person's will-force may be strong enough to encounter the force of attraction of all the intense desires. It is neither logically nor practically impossible. One can have such a strong will that one can withdraw one's attention from all the objects of the most intense desires. Gautama The Buddha faced and defeated all such distracting forces by the force of his sheer will before attaining

The Bodhi. The difficult penances practiced by the sages of different ages indicate the practical possibility of the success of person's will force against the forces of distraction. This, however, very rarely happens in human history and does not refute either the existence of an independent divine force of will (that helps the *bhaktas* to dilute the effects of distracting forces) or the highest significance of this force at all. It only shows that divine will operates in these persons' life in and through their personal will. The will to withdraw attention from all the objects of worldly desires itself is a manifestation of divine will. Such a will can't be called an ordinary will to attain any worldly ends. The will to withdraw attention for attaining no other objectives except for knowing what is left after the cessation of all desires is a pure spiritual will. Unless this will starts operating in a person as his will he can't find any relevance for it. The functioning of this will makes the question of relevance of this will irrelevant for him which is otherwise quite relevant for every ordinary normal human being. Moreover, the success of this will definitely shows that such a spiritual will force really exists and it is really enormously powerful. A *bhakta* encounters this will force as the divine will power that functions in his heart as the force of love for his dear Lord. The tremendous attraction for Lord proves its strength by neutralizing all worldly attractions. In ordinary lover also people ignore and demean all other relations. The love for the Lord very easily sets a *bhakta* free from the strong hold of all worldly desires. Love for the Lord is a real force. Had it not been real it could not have set the *bhaktas* really free. The *bhaktas* don't *think* that they are set free from the slavery of desires; they become *actually* free from that. If love for the lord were not a force it could not have neutralized the forces of distraction caused by the objects of desires. If the power of this force were not actually unimaginably enormously strong the forces of distraction would have neutralized it. It is a fact that *bhaktas* get easily free from the hold of desires clearly indicates the functioning of a tremendously powerful spiritual will force in their life.

Bhakti—The Force of Love for The Lord Makes The *Bhakta* Aware of His Experience of Love

A *bhakta* gets liberated easily from the shackles of desires with the help of the force of attraction for the Lord. This force of attraction also enables him to be aware of his extremely valuable experience. The reality of this force is again shown manifesting in the force that directs the *bhaktas'* attention towards the content of his experience and keeps it focused on that for a considerable length of time. In its pure form, as stated in earlier discussions, it is an experience of the emotion of love. Love for the Lord is not an experience of love for a person existing out there. It is an experience of the divinity contained in the experience of love. Lord is a person in the sense of the complete embodiment of pure divinity itself. Hence *bhakti* in its purest form is achieved only when the awareness of the emotional experience is achieved. The *bhakta* has to use his will force to be aware of the fact that the psychic force of attraction is pulling him towards the image of his Lord. Unless some other person instructs him to do so he can't do it by himself since in the experience of love itself there is nothing that can motivate him to do that. Ordinarily the experience of love focuses the lover's attention on the beloved. To be aware of the experience, therefore, a person needs some external agency to get instructed and motivated to do so in the state of utter absorption in the prettiness of the beloved. The experience of love makes the lover so lost in the features and attributes of the beloved that he himself can't remember to be aware of the experience itself. *Bhakti* with the lord also makes the *bhakta* intoxicated in the beauty of that image of the Lord with which he has initially developed an emotional attachment. He gets so involved in this love affair that he forgets everything else. Even this sort of love with the Lord is not possible without the support of the will force of the Lord. But for becoming aware of the experience of love with the Lord a psychic force is necessarily required that can arouse the *bhakta* from his God-intoxication and arouse in him the awareness for his experience. Obviously if any independent will force could do this then that will a miraculous supra-human will. This will force not only have to arouse awareness in the *bhakta* but have to give it sustained support for ever so that it could not fall back. Organising all these and make them realized by the *bhakta* necessarily a divine will force —the will of the Lord is required.

All these could never happen by *bhakta's* imagination since imagination is not required here. A *bhakta* does not have to imagine that he is becoming aware of the content of his experience; he has to *become aware*. The arousal of this awareness can be attributed to mere chance but if the sustenance of this awareness and the occurrence of this chance only in the life of *bhaktas* also are mere chances then we will have to admit the regularity of this peculiar chance. It could be seen as mere chance only if one has resolved not to see in it a divine will force. Any one who has got the love for the Lord finds no reason to doubt that it has happened just by Lord's will. He experiences the force of attraction for the Lord finds that every movement in the direction of Lord needs tremendous amount of force of will which he just does not possess. Hence he finds no reason to doubt that the force that arouses awareness in him and protects it against enormous amount of distracting forces of different varieties is not the force of divine will. Attaining this state of *bhakti* the *bhakta* enjoys a higher order of bliss. This is the bliss of the experience of pure *bhakti*. It is an actual state of several *bhaktas* that clearly manifest in their lives. This state, which is a state of actual experience and not merely an imagination, can't be achieved if the divine will force does not help the *bhakta's* will. While we talk about Pure *Bhakti* (*Śuddha Bhakti*) and hold that it is achieved by the grace of Lord only, we don't ordinarily remain aware of the nature of *bhakti* as a divine force that operates in and through the will of the *bhakta*. Without taking into account its nature as a force emanating from divine will its understanding remains not only incomplete but somewhat fallacious too. If the force- nature of it is not given due consideration then the entire talk appears to be sort of fictitious romantic love affair in which some people get involved. *Bhaktas* don't bother if others misunderstand them and laugh at them. But anyone, who wants to understand it properly, must take into consideration its force- nature. Above discussion is an attempt only to bring to notice this ignored aspect of *bhakti*. In the last part also this aspect is highlighted in the context of the functioning of this force in giving a permanent way of life to the *bhaktas*.

Bhakti – The Force of Love for The Lord Gives A Sustained Support to The Way of Life of The *Bhakta*

The *bhakta* attains the state of direct *darœana* of his dear Lord when he becomes aware of the experience of his love for

Lord. Lord is experienced by him as the embodiment of the divinity comprising all sorts of qualities like beauty, grace, majesty, power, knowledge and so on. Although this is an experience of the content itself and the *bhakta* experiences it not as placed out there in external space and time but it is the very objective ground of this experience also and its manifestation in his experience only shows its independent objective status. A *bhakta* gets the *darśana* of his Lord because He (Lord) manifests Him in his (the *bhakat's*) experience. This statement seems to be metaphysically loaded but it is not so indeed because even if we don't use the word 'Lord' we will have to state that the *bhakta*, in experiencing divinity in the force of attraction for the image of his Lord, realizes the independent status of it (divinity), and to understand its meaning we will have to relate it to the reference given to it by the *bhaktas.* The *bhaktas* don't refer to any metaphysical supposition but points to their experience of the basis of their emotional experience of love for the image of Lord. We can understand it by directly connecting it to the experience of the *bhaktas* or we are bound to misunderstand it. By considering the nature of this experience as an experience of a powerful force (of love) we can understand this point easily and be saved from gross misunderstanding about it.

The tremendously powerful divine (Lord's) force of will is realized in its all pervasiveness by the *bhaktas* in experiencing its operation of sustaining a way of life in which he could remain in constant touch with the Lord. The *bhakta* comes to know that his dear Lord is and has been giving sustained support through His will power to lead a life immersed in *bhakti*[16]. Without a constant support of an independent force that not only keeps the *bhaktas* aware of the experience (of love for the Lord) but also enables him see the forces of the world in full harmony with this experience, a complete way of life of *bhakti* is just not possible. A few moments of blissful experience of divinity, in fact, can't show the durable presence and tremendous power of a divine will if it disappears after manifesting in few moment of a person's life. There would be good reason to attribute such momentary experiences to chance. But biographies of *bhaktas* show beyond rational doubt that people in very large number have led such life in past, and in present also many of them (who are alive) are continuing in it. Moreover, they who lead such a way of life, advise, preach and instruct others to adopt such away of life and to attain the supreme bliss of the presence of the Lord. They attach supreme value to such a way of life and hold that nothing else is more important in human life than this. Obviously the *bhaktas* have to give supreme value to such a way of life since it is their experience. However, the practical possibility of this way of life almost force on each one of us to acknowledge the presence and strength of a divine force of will operating clearly in the life of *bhaktas. Bhaktas* lead a life of *bhakti* only because, in their view, their Dear Lord grants them the blissful life of His constant proximity and contact. In the view of any non-*bhakta* also this way of life becomes possible only because a tremendously powerful divine will force enables and supports the *bhaktas* constantly to achieve it.

The gist of above discussion can be presented by stating that in love and especially in *bhakti* the creative power of divine will force manifests in its purest form and operates in every movement of the *bhaktas* in the direction of depth of *bhakti.* Not only the *bhaktas* but others also can and do understand its function in every turn in the *bhakta's* life if they sincerely try to understand *bhakti.*

In a previous chapter it was explained that one can understand *bhakti* only by acknowledging the presence of divine in the life of the *bhaktas.* It would be a mistake to take this chapter as a repetition of that chapter. The object of this chapter's discussion is to bring forth the force-aspect of *bhakti* which is hardly ever highlighted in such a discussion. Without an attempt to understand this aspect as an exclusively important aspect enough scope is left to misunderstand it as a sort of inner play of autohypnosis of the *bhaktas.* To point out that *bhaktas* are not lost in a useless game of autohypnosis, it is necessary to consider the force aspect *bhakti* seriously.

8

Bhagavâna—the Dear Lord of the *Bhaktas*

Kṛiṣṇa! *Bhktas* love their Lord- *Bhagavâna.* Thousands of ontological attributes are enumerated by the *bhaktas* in the Lord the sum total of which are deemed to be infinite and incomprehensible. All this remains merely a mythology and we fail to understand the actual status of the Lord of the *bhaktas* if we fail to *see* a simple fact that He is an object of his love. This is so plain a fact that we always tend to ignore. Due to this habitual or delberate overlooking we miss a valuable truth of human life and consequently get a denatured understanding of *bhakti, bhakta* and his *Bhagvâna. Bhagvâna*, who is the object of the *bhakta's* emotion, is taken to be an object of his imagination. Although this distinction is discussed in a previous chapter to some extant, it is necessary to discuss it in all its aspect in detail so that a proper understanding of *bhakti* –a very valuable human experience could be achieved.

Wherefrom The *Bhakta* Get The Idea of His Lord -The God

Like most of the other ordinary human beings, a person, who becomes and recognized as a *bhakta* at a latter stage of his life, is brought up in some religious tradition. The very first idea of God is given to him by his tradition. The possibility of a person becoming a *bhakta* in a strict secular environment is very thin although it can't be completely ruled out. This rare possibility also deserves serious attention but that will be discussed later. First it would be necessary to understand how the traditional seed of this idea germinates and grows in some of the individuals of that community although it is equally given to all the individuals.

The Traditional Image of God is a Seed That Germinates in The Heart Of a *Bhakta*

All old communities of human beings are generally religious communities. Every religious community, if it is not an atheist community like Buddhism or Jainism, has an image or images of God/ Gods. Such image/images is/are carved in every individual of the community of successive generation by the previous generation in course of their upbringing. A sort of emotional attachment with this image develops in every individual because it becomes a part of his given identity. This emotional attachment is very implicit in nature because an individual does not immediately feels it. He comes to know about it only if some one speaks ill of it. He gets hurt internally. This is a very common scenario in a country like ours where communal violence is a familiar phenomenon. People belonging to one religious community don't necessary lead life strictly according to religious code but get hurt sentimentally when an individual of a different religious community speaks ill of their religious faith. Hearing any derogatory remarks from the member of some other religious community seems to the people of any religious community as a personal insult. In such unfortunate situations it is disclosed that the object of religious faith becomes the integral part of the person's identity. This kind of emotional attachment with the object of religious faith could be called a negative attachment in view of the fact that it surfaces only during situations of confrontation with the opponents. Some individuals, however, somehow develop a positive sort of emotional attachment with the image of God given by the tradition. This may happen due to family influence or it may happen without that either. How this happens is of great importance for the psychologist and, to some extant, for the historians. But it is of central importance for the philosophers to understand the nature of this attachment at every stage of its growth. When this emotional attachment takes the shape of personal relation then it becomes easily recognizable as *bhakti*, but, as it is made clear in the very first chapter, in any other form of emotional attraction also it is love for God in a latent form. Even in the form of awe this feeling for an image of God contains in it all the attractions that become love in an explicit form and could grow as *bhakti*. Its growth in the heart of a person is almost a matter of chance since no conditions could be specified for its growth. But such chances, when looked at closely, indicates that the hidden hand of providence was working behind them.

In plain language it could be said that the divine emotion of *bhakti* emerges and grows Completely by the will of the Lord of the *bhakta*. But this creates a problem for any ncn *bhakta*s who want to understand this statement without being influenced by the emotionof *bhakti* since he finds no intelligible way from the presence of *bhakti* in the *bhakta's* heart to reach the reality of God as a person whose will produces it (*bhakti*) in his heart.In his approach to see an intelligible connection between the two the duality is presupposed that is not actually there in *bhakti*.In the overwhelming emotion of *bhakti* the *bhakta* sees his Lord *in*. particular image of Lord the God: he does not see that image is here before his (mind's) eyes and God as a real person, as the source of it, is standing separate from that image somewhere over there. If the image does not produce any attraction in the person then he is not a *bahkta*. Then that person sees only one thing –the image. For him the source of that image, as picture, may be an artist and the source of it, as a traditional concept, is the tradition. The question of accepting any supra-mundane real person as the source of attraction for that image just does not arise. Only when a person feels an emotional attachment for an image of God and if some of its feature make him feel somewhat supra-mundane then only we can say that the person is experiencing the emotion of *bhakti*. A traditional image of God may produce many emotions in a person's heart but unless it produces the feeling of what he would call supra-mundane, it can not become a God's image for him and he can't have *bahkti* for it. If the image performs this functions in the hart of a person then it does not remain an ordinary image for him but becomes itself partly divine since it becomes a manifestation of divinity itself. He does not see two things at any stage of the growth of this experience- an image and that of which it is the image. In the initial stage he sees the divinity reflecting in and through it. Divinity is a matter of feeling: it is not an idea in *bhakti.* By looking at that image or even remembering it the *bhakta* feels that it is not earthly: there is something supra earthly in it that envelops him with grace and grandeur. It is through this image that he comes to know divinity for the first time in his life. All talks of divinity and supra-mundane remain barely conceptual for most religious people. Only with an emotional attachment with the image of Lord the person attains its experiential meaning. Such a person is called *bhakta.* This brings about a change in the outlook of the *bhakta.* He, now, looks at the events occurring around him as the manifestation of the will of the Lord (who he has experienced in that image as a real supreme person). World does not and cannot remain a world governed by pure material laws: it becomes a manifestation of his Lord's will.

Gradually the *bhakta* comes to realize that not only the events of his personal life and those of world are being governed by his Lord's grace but also the event of emergence of *bhakti* in his life is the greatest gift that his Lord has given him. This realization of *Bhakti* as the great gift of Lord takes him still deeper in this experience of *bhakti.* In a previous chapter it is already discussed that later the attention of the person is shifted to a domain of experience where the person becomes directly aware of the content of experience (which is always present implicitly in all other experience of any occurrence but he never remains directly aware of this experience as a matter of experience). In this awareness the *bhakta* experiences a tremendous attraction for his Lord as the source of the invaluable blissful gift of *bhakti.* The image of Lord that was the manifestation of divinity for him now becomes the manifestation of the source of divinity i.e. Lord the God, who is the very source of all that is divine, comes directly in the contact of the *bhakta* in and through the image. By experiencing the emotional attachment with the image of Lord the *bhakta* comes to know the divinity. By becoming aware of the value of *bhakti* he sees the Lord in the image who made him know the divinity. The first experience is a first and direct experience of divinity. It is direct because it arouses the feeling of divinity in him. The second experience (the awareness of *bhakti* as an invaluable gift also is an experience) also is a direct experience of divinity but it is, in a way, more direct than the former in the sense that now the *bhakta* is immediately aware of his feeling of divinity itself. This is a purely internal experience since the immediate object of this experience is the very content of experience itself. which is within the experience and don't stand out there separate from it. This is an immediate experience of divinity (because experiencing of the feeling of divinity means to experience its direct content i.e. divinity itself). So, now, the *bhakta* in a pure internal experience directly encounters divinity that features in the image of the Lord. Now the image of Lord as a concrete image is not the object of his experience. The essence (i.e. the experiential quality) of divinity that figures in the image becomes the object of his experience. So by becoming aware of the fact that he has been given a valuable experience in the form of *bhakti* the *bhakta* comes to realize that he is face to face with his Lord Himself. He comes to know for the first time that his dear Lord Whom he was searching all the time was always present in his very feeling of divinity of *bhakti*. *Bhagvân*— the dear Lord of the *bhakta* is the embodiment of divinity present in the experience of *bhakti*. What else could He be? God is either a metaphysical term and figures meaningfully as a presupposition in the theistic metaphysics. But then 'God' is merely a concept; it is not an experiential reality. *Bhaktas'* God –his *Bhagvân* is not a concept. He the supreme real person Who graces the life of *bhaktas* with the divine gift of *bhakti* and overwhelms him by revealing Himself in it (in *bhakti*) as the embodiment of divinity. Although the *bhaktas' Bhagvân* is experienced by him not out there standing in external space, He is experienced purely internally, but that does not imply that He is dependent on or product of the emotional psychic state of the *bhakta*. *Bhakti* is a fully awake experience of the *bhaktas* in which he is not projecting anything but simply opens him to whatever comes in the experience. It is important to understand that the *bhaktas* through *bhakti* enters into a different world.

The *Bhaktas* Enter in to The World of *Bhakti*: The Dear Lord of The *Bhaktas* is The Foundation of That World

Bhaktas, through *bhakti*, enters in a world of emotional experience (the *Bhâva-Jagata*) of *bhakti*. His *Bhagvân* is the foundation and the centre of all the varieties of the *bhaktas bhâva*-s of this world. This is a world of pure experience and not a world of imagination. As such the reality of this world is unquestioned despite the fact that it is not a world of external space and time. *Bhagvân* –the dear Lord of the *bhaktas* as the centre of this world is eternally present in this world and it is quite natural that the *bhaktas* begin to feel the presence of Lord in the first experience of divinity when he enters into the orbit of this world and sees Him face to face when he fully enters in this world. If we enter into the gravitational field of any planet then we can't help feeling its gravitational pull and we will be definitely seeing the objects present on that planet (unless we close our eyes) when we land on it. Same happens with the *bhaktas.* Traditional images of God and teaching to remember Him bring us near and put us in the orbit of the divine world of *bhâva.* If we are not lost in our mundane affairs then we definitely feel the emotional pull towards this world. It is quite natural and like a natural law it has some sort of constraint in it that no one can avoid by will. Talking about and remembering about God in the given traditional image directs our attention towards its meaning as any word of our language does. Supra-mundane feature of God's image is the essential meaning of it towards which our attention is drawn as a natural phenomenon when we remember God by the word used in our tradition for it. This happens to every individual of that tradition. But very rarely only a few could go beyond it and enter into the gravitational field of the divine world of *bhâva.* The reason is simple: most of us are lost in our normal mundane problems that shows that the gravitational pull of the materially human world is functioning on us and under its influence we ignore the pull of the divine world. If a person does not ignore the pull of the divine world by convincing himself with inadequate gratuitous arguments then he is pulled towards it. Naturally this also, is a very difficult job. To have such a strong will and pointed concentration to feel the pull of divine world is a divine quality that no one can claim to have earned purely by his own efforts Two points are to be discussed in detail in this regard. First, how far the world of *bhakti Bhâva* be called a real world and second, in what way divine will influences a person beyond its field of actually palpable influences so that some individual's attention is drawn towards it despite mundane disturbances.

The Reality of The World of *Bhakti Bhâva*

Is the talk about the divine world of *bhakti bhâva* merely a figure of speech? This is an important question that needs to be understood very clearly. For us, ordinarily, the spatio-temporal physical world figures as the only real world. If anyone talks of anything or event that can be called a thing or an event of this world in any sense then we think that it is-talk of the real world. Not all theories of physical sciences could be directly experienced in sense experience but we take them to be real because they in a specific sense, tell us about some deeper laws or regularities of this world. For most of us the technicalities of nuclear physics are beyond comprehension but we accept that they are true of this real world. While accepting it as a habitual belief we hardly ever try to find an answer about the reality of the world of mathematics. What would be our answer to the question if we are asked about the reality of the world of Arithmetic —a science that we all use in our daily life? We will be hesitant to give either a positive or a negative reply at the first glance. We can't say that it is not real because we can't accept it to be only imaginary either. But to escape this dilemma if we accept that it real then we don't see anything in our spatio-temporal physical world that could be called number or any event that could be called arithmetical operations. This problem arises because of our irrationally narrow understanding of what we call real. Without Mathematics our scientific knowledge of the physical world, which we all accept as undoubtedly real, would be impossible. Realization of this simple fact helps us understand that reality is not only multi-faceted but it is multi-tired too. The world of Arithmetic in particular or that of Mathematics in general is very much a real world but it is not a physical world. Principles of Mathematics and Mathematical operations are applicable and applied to the physical world but Mathematics itself does not talk about physical reality.

The world of Mathematics is acknowledged to be real if we have to choose between the binary of 'Real' and 'Imaginary or

Fictitious'. However, if the choice is between the binary of 'Real' and 'Ideal' then surely we will acknowledge it as the latter. The world of Mathematics is an ideal world (or a world of ideas) as opposed to the real. But we must take note that real is physical in this context. The reality that we attribute to the physical world is essentially because the objects and events of this world are objects of experience. Mathematical entities like numbers, functions etc. are not the objects of experience: they are objects of intuition and mathematical derivation. We have to think for the latter and don't have to feel or experience them. They are abstract entities and although they are not imaginary, they are not acknowledged as real, (in the backdrop of the binary of 'Ideal- Real') because they are not experiential.

The world of music and dance is not an abstract world in the sense of the world of mathematics. Melody of music and beauty of dance are not concrete things like material objects but they are definitely the objects of experience. Music is the ups and downs of sound waves but it is recognizable as music because of the specific quality that we call melody. Can we say that in music only sound waves are real and melody is not real? Can we say that melody is an imaginative projection of the community of singers and listeners? We are sure that the reply is negative. In music sound waves are real but their reality is of physical dimension. Melody of music is (ordinarily) not possible without the physical presence of sound waves. Yet, melody is neither the fluctuation of sound waves nor is it determined by that. It is a reality of a different dimension that constitutes the world of music. The reality of melody is proved by its palpability. A person having taste and education *feels* the melody of music, enjoys it and appreciate it. An ordinary person not well educated in music cannot appreciate the nuances of it but he also *feels* it and enjoys it. So melody is a matter of experience and not a matter of pure imagination. Whether a piece of music is melodious, very melodious or superb, is a matter of evaluation that is done on the objective qualities present in that piece. Cultural differences in the standard of appreciation are not and can't be made a plea to reduce the objective reality of the melody of music to a matter of production of cultural taste.

The case of music is very helpful to consider the objective reality of the world of *Bhakti bhâva*. In music we hear the sound. The physical reality of sound waves is proved by the fact that they hit our ear drums and produces auditory sensation. But in music we don't sense primarily the sound but sense the melody. Melody is sensed only when the physicality of the sound is not being attended. If we try to *catch* the sound of the music we will miss its musicality altogether. We recognize music as music only when its melody attracts our attention in such a way that our attention is withdrawn completely from the fact that it is sound. We can't attend both simultaneously. If we stick too much to attend only to sound as purely given reality then we will never be able to listen music. Fortunately that is not the mental condition of most of the common people. We listen a sound as sound and we can also listen the music carried through the sound waves by our attention drawn by its melody (withdrawn completely from the physicality of the sound). Melody, therefore, is objective reality. We all experience it although this is an aesthetic experience that is not a sense experience despite the fact that it involves sense experience.

The audibility of music made many western thinkers hold the view that it is a sensuous experience. If we attend to the feature that music is listened *qua* music only when its attention is withdrawn from its sensuous-ness then it would more appropriate for us to hold the view that it is supra sensuous or supra-natural. This realization does not allow us to jump to the conclusion of spirituality of music. However, it helps in liberating us from the habitually developed and uncritically held opinion that realty means physical reality only. All our judgments about musical compositions presuppose that it is actually heard or, at least, it can be actually heard. It is presupposed in such judgments that the composition, although it is composed or created by a musician, once it is created by him, it stands independent of his mind out there in the sense that it is accessible to everyone and everyone finds that it is an object of a particular kind of evaluation. If we examine the meaning of 'composing or creating' in this context closely, we find that there is at least one acceptable sense in which it stands for a sort of discovery. It is true that a musician composes a piece of music and without his effort perhaps no such composition can come into being but what he does in this process is to *find out* the charm of combination of various notes. He can't produce the charm by any arbitrary forceful juxtaposition of notes. He can only *pick up* one or the other, or the better juxtaposition. Needless to say that it is not a passive reception; it involves the exercise of the musician's physical and mental efforts in various ways and at various levels. The greater is his effort the better melody he could obtain. But in view of the aforesaid use of his effort, it is clear that it is a sort of discovery in an appropriate sense of the term. It is neither wrong nor a bare figure of speech to say that the musician discovers melody in the world of music and brings it to us through his musical performance. The melodies are real objects of the world of music. The world of music is a real world. It is 'real' as contrasted to the 'imaginary' because the musician is not quite free to produce melody by any arbitrary exercise of will. It is also 'real' as contrasted to the 'purely abstract' in the sense of ideal or conceptual because it is experiential.

The world of *Bhakti bhâva* also is a real world in the sense the world of Music is a real world but it is real in a still deeper sense. Before coming to that sense it is necessary to elaborate how the world of *bhakti* is real in the above two sense.

It is obvious that the world of *bhakti* is not a conceptual or ideal world. Metaphysicians may be interested in speculating about the concept of God or gods and divinity etc. but *bhaktas* are least interested in such pure conceptual exercise. They want to avail the experience of *bhakti* to come in and live in the contact of dear Lord. Envisaging Lord's image and to meditate upon the concept of holiness are given some place here only in close connection with the experience of *bhakti* but too much rational exercise is despised and discouraged. The common opinion that the *bhaktas* get stuck up with an image of God and try to develop an intimate connection with it at the imaginary level is a common misconception. *Bhaktas* aspire to avail the emotional attachment with the image of Lord. His connection with his Lord that he strives for is not imagination but that of emotion that is an experience. In the traditional texts of *Bhakti* greatest importance is given to this relation and it is clearly stated in very many words on many occasions that it is very rare and can be obtained as divine gift only by the grace of the Lord directly or by getting it from the company of the *bhaktas* in whose congregation it keeps flowing like a stream[1]. So it should be very clear that *bhakti* is not a matter of imaginative construction but it is primarily and essentially a matter of experiencing the attraction for the image of Lord. With this experience the *bhakta* actually enters in a world that is very different from our ordinary world of mundane affairs. It is almost similar to a musician's entering in the world of music to find a melodious composition. The musician lives bodily in this physical world but his whole attention is drawn to an altogether different world withdrawn completely from the physical world. . In fact we have to decide whether the presence of a person's body should be the basis of claiming *his* presence in the physical world or his conscious presence at different world should be seriously regarded as *his* presence in that world. It is neither wrong nor merely a figure of speech to say that a musician enters into the world of music when he is engrossed in a composition If we give due importance to the fact that the musician's whole attention is drawn to a different realm altogether then we can actually understand the realistic import of the statement that *he is not in this mundane world but shifted to a different world*[2]. A *bhakta* also, lost in the experience of emotional attraction towards his Lord, does not remain in this world but gets shifted to a different world. Needless to say that this statement should not be taken to mean that the *bhaktas* are transported to some other planet because all other planets are physical worlds despite their very different atmosphere and chemical structure. *Bhaktas* are shifted to a different world altogether means that (i) they are shifted to a different realm of experience in which the objects and events are not physical in nature and (ii) in this happening his whole attention is withdrawn from the objects and events of physical world and gets drawn to those objects and events which are of very different nature. A full domain of such objects and events emerges before his attention

The world of *bhakti bhâva* can't be accepted to be founded on any physical object or physical energy. It is already stated in previous chapters that despite the fact that physical conditions can be delineated for the emergence of *bhakti* in the heart of the *bhaktas* it can't be claimed that those conditions *cause* it to emerge.

No physical conditions can be the cause of emergence of *bhakti* in any sense of the term 'cause'. The object of emotional attraction of the *bhaktas* alone could be acknowledged as one that generates *bhakti* in the heart of the *bhaktas.* Without an object towards which the *bhaktas* are emotionally attracted *bhakti* is just impossible and if an objects generates this attraction then it has to be acknowledged as the adequate basis or source of it. That object is the embodiment of those divine qualities that manifests in the image of the Lord (that the *bhakta* has in his heart). That object is his Lord Himself. The embodiment of the divine qualities that figure in the image of Lord is fully consciously felt in the divinity of *bhakti bhâva* by the *bhaktas.* The presence of Lord is directly felt in *bhakti.* So Lord is also the source of *bhakti* The source of *bhakti* alone could be the foundation of the world of *bahkti bhâva.* Hence Lord is the foundation of the world of *bhakti bhâva.* The reality of the world of *Bhakti bhâva* is experiential for the *bhaktas* and it is intelligible to anyone who has not decided in advance not to accept it real. There seems to be no good reasons for not accepting it real for all practical purposes if talking about the world of Mathematics and that of Music with a realistic import is acceptable to all. Emphasis on the reality of the world of *Bhakti* is being laid just to remind ourselves that whatever happens here needs to be taken seriously because they leave lasting impressions not only the life of the *bhaktas* but that of others too, and its importance could be actually evaluated only if we seriously acknowledge it to be a real world of experience. For the *bhaktas* the reality of this world is not only unproblematic but indubitable too since the reality of the material world, for him, is dependent on the reality of the former. In order to understand *Bhakti* from the *bhaktas'* stand point this point needs to be taken seriously.

Bhaktas enter into the world of purest form of love in *bhakti.* Entering into it they could *see* that his dear Lord's will is working behind all that is happening in that world (i.e. the world of *bhakti*) and in other worlds including the physical world. This is not a thought of the *bhaktas:* they don't obtain this truth as a result of rational contemplation. They feel the divine hand in every happening. This is a positive and objective feeling that all the *bhaktas* share. No one in this world ever doubt or find reasons to doubt this truth not because they have logically strong reasons for it but just because they directly feel it. The way I and others don't doubt and find no good reason to doubt that there is a paper before us on which something is printed, the *bhaktas* also don't doubt and find no reasons to doubt that everything is happening due to Lord's will. Agreement about this and several other truths show the reality and objectivity of their world and of its foundation.

Like ordinary people they also know that natural laws operate behind all events of the physical world. But in the light of their experience of *bhakti* they also see something that ordinary people don't see since they don't find any relevance to see that. For the *bhaktas* , in the light of their experience of *bhakti,* the question – 'Why are there laws operating in nature?', is a very important question. If we analyse this question, we find the question—'Why has the world come into existence at all?', is presupposed in it. This more fundamental question is of utmost importance for the *bhaktas* because they understand that this world could not have come into existence if a divine will (i.e. their Lord's will) would not have brought it into existence. Ordinary people don't find any relevance to ask this question. For them this world has come into being accidentally without any purpose behind it. Knowing well that it came at one point of time they don't wonder that they can help asking this question. They get satisfied with the scientific explanation of how could it happen and don't find it relevant to question as to why all that happened that made it come into existence. But for *bhaktas* it is a wonder that they get satisfied with this enquiry only and does not find it necessary to ask a 'why' question in this regard. 'Why' is not relevant for the common non-believer. The answer to 'how' is enough and is the end of their inquisitiveness. But every common man can understand that there is no logical inconsistency in asking such a 'why' question. Well, the question presupposes a willful intelligent mind for the answer. But that is only presupposed in the question: that is not assumed to be already proved to exist. The presupposition can be proved to be irrational only if it is shown that the presupposition to raise the question is accepted to be proved by questioning (as is done in Ontological argument). But that is not the case. The answer is given by the actual experience by the *bhaktas.* This experiential answer (that all this came into existence due to God's will) can be proved to be false or unacceptable factually only if (i) the *bhaktas* don't experience any such person and (ii) if their experience do not fully coheres with rest of their experiences. But *bhaktas* experience the presence of their Lord in *bhakti* and this experience not only coheres with rest of their experiences of the world of *bhakti* but also brings an over all harmony in all his experiences of all other worlds in which even the opposites stand well synthesized. So to ask *why this physical world came into existence*, is not an irrational question and an experiential answer to it is available also. Well, the answer is not available in sense experience but to make such a demand itself is quite irrational. Claims made about the truths of music could be tested in the world of music only and not in the world of sense experience. Truth claims made by the *bhaktas* are to be tested in the world of *Bhakti* only.

Although the claims made by the presence of Lord as the answer to 'why' questions regarding the physical world could be tested in *bhakti* only, a common man can understand this point very well and can come to realize that 'why' questions appear to him irrelevant or even meaningless only because in the name of cognitive experience he knows only sense experience and wants to judge the cognitive content of all other experiences at the level of this experience. Obviously this conceptual understanding alone can't make him know the cognitive content of other experience. For that he will have to enter in to the world of that experience. But with this understanding he can at least realize the fault of the opinion that 'why' questions about the existence of the physical world (or any other worlds also) is preposterous or meaningless. He can realize his irrationality present in dismissing the rationality of the *bhaktas'* view. This makes him open to find out the kind of experience that gives relevance to the *bhaktas'* talk that God's will is functioning behind all that is happening in the physical world or in any other world.

It is clear from above discussion that talking about the world of *Bhakti bhâva* is not irrational even from a cognitive point of view. Talking about the world of *Bhakti* is not only emotionally but also cognitively meaningful for the *bhaktas* and this point is intelligible to any non-*bhaktas* too. Any ordinary common man can understand that when a *bhakta* says that his dear Lord is the unbound ocean of benevolence he does not mean to refer to something similar to Pacific or Atlantic, but he also understands that he (the *bhakta*) is giving vent to his uncontrollable love for his Lord who's presence he is actually feeling and he actually feel that there is no limit to his Lord's benevolence. So the cognitive import of the *bhaktas* is well acknowledged by a common man despite the fact that he (the common man) doesn't feel the presence of the Lord. For a common man there is one problem with the *bhaktas'*: In his present state he does not feel God's presence. This becomes a very strange problem for many philosophers: they want to explain the *bhaktas'* assertion without accepting its cognitive import. By making some peculiar attempts to do it successfully they think that they have done a marvelous job. They fail to notice completely that they have denatured the *bhaktas'* assertions. In order to understand *bhakti* from the *bhaktas'* stand point it is neither necessary not appropriate to go via the philosopher's views. We only need to understand what is the problem of a common man in this regard. As it is stated – it is the problem of unavailability of the reference to which the *bhaktas'* experience could be related. The only actual solution to this problem lies in the realization that such a reference could be found in the world of *Bhakti bhâva* only. This realization a common man can attain at his own level of experience as he can realize, (i) that the actual function of a mathematical theorem could be known only by rising to the level of Advanced Mathematic, and (ii) that to find that some note can't be placed next to some other note in order to produce melody–could be known by entering into the world of music only. This is, common realization. This realization paves the way of apprehending the world of *bhakti* the way the *bhaktas* understand it. The *bhaktas* experience it and understand it. A common man does not have the experience of *bhakti* but can't understand *what* (the specific content) the *bahktas* understand but he can understand the *way* they understand it because there could not be two conceptually different ways of understanding any one phenomenon[3]. In the light of above discussion it is clear that there is nothing peculiar about the experience of *bhakti*: A common man can understand it even if he has not experienced it. A *bhakta's* talk about his dear Lord, therefore, is not and cannot be beyond a common man's comprehension and does not need any special interpretation for it.

Entering into the world of *bhakti* the *bhaktas* know how benevolent their Lord is. Everybody has heard from the ancestors and read in the scriptures that Lord is the creator and sustainer of this whole universe. *Bhaktas* get the experiential meaning of these sayings. They come to understand that every natural phenomenon that is necessary for the survival of life, consciousness, intelligence, memory and devices to preserve the accumulated bulk of knowledge occur independent of human will. It is easy to envisage that if any of such vital phenomena were dependent on the human will then either the human race would have been extinct long-long ago or would not have been surviving in the present develop shape. Heart-beat, respiration, blood circulation, nervous functions and all psychic functions that are necessary for a psychologically healthy normal human beings are happening as an independent routine course of nature. Every body understands how vital and important they are! But hardly anyone ever feels thankful for all these. The *bhaktas* feel extremely thankful for their Lord for all these invaluable gifts. In noticing the fact that nature never compels human beings even implicitly to feel that they are being obliged, the *bhaktas* see their Lord's immense grace. They become further overwhelmed to find that it is also their Lord's invaluable boon to them that they could see Lord's grace that most of the people fail to see.

A common man also, who is not a *bhakta,* can understand what the *bhaktas* feel. He can understand that all the involuntary life-supporting organic activities, favourable environment and necessary natural occurrences make a genuinely intelligible opportunity for everyone to feel thankful for all these happenings but hardly anyone feels that it is an occasion for thanksgiving. This feeling can't be generated by a person's will. But in the absence of feeling that nature itself is a Supreme Person or that there is such a person behind nature the feeling of gratitude can't take any actual shape since we don't feel thankful towards inanimate objects and non-persons. Having this kind of genuinely human feeling warrants a feeling of presence of a supreme person behind all these occurrences. This warranted feeling is spontaneously obtained by the *bhaktas*, in their *bhakti*. They feel the presence of their Lord behind all the events of all the worlds. The traditional and scriptural belief that everything in the world is happening due to God's will becomes intelligible in view of the realization that all natural and organic-psychic events, which are necessary for the survival of all forms of life and the presence of self-consciousness in humans, are quite independent of human will. But the intelligibility of this belief remains merely a possibility till it acquires an experiential meaning. *In bhakti* this belief gains an experiential content (like the perceptual belief that gains experiential content in one's sense perception) because the *bhaktas* directly feel the presence of their dear Lord as the foundation or source of their *bhakti.* A common non-*bhakta* does not have that experience but he can and does understand the meaning of — *feeling the presence of Lord as the source of the experience of bhakti* —the way a *bhakta* understands it. It is already explained in above discussion that a common man could understand that the Lord of the *bhaktas* is not an anthropomorphic God but at the same time he also understands that term' God' is used by the *bhaktas* to refer to something that they actually experience. A common man does understand that for the *bhaktas* God–their Lord is the embodiment of the experiential essence of divinity that manifests in their divine experience of. *bhakti.* So a common man does understand the *bhakta's* talk of his dear Lord.

Bhagvân – the dear Lord of the *bhaktas* is held by them to be an independent reality and their experience of *bhakti* is dependent on His independent existence and autonomous will. It is obvious that this belief can't have an experiential content but that does not force on us to come to the conclusion that Lord is only an imaginary construct of the *bhaktas.* No special argument is needed to support the *bhaktas'* position.

The reason to believe that any person whom we come across regularly does exist independent of our experience is very simple. When we meet a person our experience with him presuppose primarily that we are meeting a real person. All his verbal and non-verbal responses acquire significance for us only because implicitly it is assumed that he is a real person and not a phantom or something unreal. No interaction with anyone could be at possible at the first instance if we have doubt that he really exists. However, if in some peculiar situation we have to enter into an interaction with such a person then it could not have that significance for us that any normal interaction with a person actually has. Doubt can't be the primary backdrop for any interaction. Only the undoubted acceptance of existence of a person becomes that backdrop. This is very important philosophical truth. We should never forget that *truth is presupposed in all our actions and even doubt presupposes truth. Truth never presupposes doubt.* Doubt about ant situation arises only if some hindrance comes in the way of our apprehension of truth. We can't doubt that the person who we meet regularly is not a real person just because we don't have any reason to do so. Reason as method to reach indubitable truth is accepted by some philosophers since it presupposes such a truth. Doubt for just doubt sake is blatantly unintelligible and irrational and is proved to be so. So we can't doubt about the reality of a person unless there arises some reason to do so. If some reason has arisen for that then we have ways available to us for its rectification after which his reality is restored or if he is not a real person but something else then also we have methods and ways to establish the truth of its unreality. Once a doubt has arisen then we can't take rest till the truth about either its reality or unreality is positively established. It is to be noted in this regard that not merely for establishing the truth about its reality but also about its unreality we have to give positive proofs. Our failure to establish the truth about its reality can't be accepted as good reason to believe its unreality. In other words, if a doubt has arisen about the reality of a person and we fail in all our possible efforts to show that he is a real person then it only shows our incompetence and doesn't logically prove the truth that the person is not a real person. In order to prove the unreality of that person, we will have to give independent proof. By showing the results of the actions done by that person in our absence and by ascertaining that those actions were done by no other than that person alone we can give a positive proof that the person is real person and exists independent of our experiences. It is not very clear what could be taken as a positive proof for the unreality of a person. All our efforts to show that nothing is found as the result of the action done by such a person only shows our failure in this regard and do not positively establish the person's non-existence independent of our experiences of his meetings with us. At the best we can only say in this situation that the possibility of unreality can't be logically ruled out. But such a logical possibility of unreality stands with all the things and events that we practically accept as real. Such logical possibility of unreality does not debar us from accepting them real for all practical purposes because we have a direct or indirect experiential basis for holding that they are real.

In the light of above discussion it is not difficult to reach at a definite solution of the problem of doubt regarding the reality/ unreality of the *bhaktas'* Lord as the supreme person. *Bhaktas* don't have any doubts regarding their dear Lord. Any agnostic's doubts about the reality of God as a supreme person can be legitimately accepted as a logical possibility and can keep the mind's open to appreciate any concrete proof that can positively establish His unreality. But, as it is clear from the above discussion, this logical possibility does not debar any one from accepting the reality of God as a supreme person for all practical purposes. However, an agnostic's criticism that the existence of God as a person can't be established in sense experience is something more than the above stated logical possibility of unreality in this regard and it only shows that *he wants* the proof of reality only in the sense experience. This is the demand of the agnostic. It does not follow that it is a rational demand. The reality of mathematical entities and the reality of melody can't be proved purely in the in the sense experience but we do accept their reality and never think that either mathematics or melody is just a matter of subjective fancy. The reality of the *bhaktas'* Lord as the supreme person also is given in the world of experience of *bhakti.* In this world the existence of Lord as the supreme person is indubitably given as the very basis of the experience of *bhakti* that is very much a human experience and even at the level of sense experience no common man ever denies the reality of this experience as he does not deny the reality of experience of music or that of mathematical intuitions. The Lord of the *bhaktas*—their *Bhagvân* is directly known to them as the very source of their immensely blissful and overwhelming experience of *bhakti. Bhakti* makes the *bhaktas* see the presence of Lord's will behind all events. When at the depth of *bhakti* he comes to see it as the greatest divine boon the he also sees that his Lord is present in it as the very experiential essence of its unbound tremendous attraction. *Bhakti* has the uncontrollable charm in it because *Bhagvân* Himself is present in it. *Bhagvân* manifests Himself and comes in the orbit of human experientiability in the experience of *bhakti.* The *bhaktas* are the blessed ones — the dear ones of the Lord in whose heart He reveals Himself as the essence of the charm of pure love. As an independent reality – as an independently existing supreme person He manages all at will to generate the divine *bhâva* of *bhakti* in human hearts. Given the tremendous material forces working in the universe due to His will no one can attain this invaluable gift of *bhakti bhâva* unless *Bhagvân* Himself don't care to generate it in the hearts of his dear ones. Only *Bhagvân*, whose will makes everyone's heart beat and generates ideas and emotions in everyone's mind, is capable to generate the sublime *bhâva* of *bhakti.* For the *bhaktas*, *bhakti* is the proof of Lord's unbound benevolence and ineffable grace. In the direct perception of Lord's will working behind all the macro and micro phenomena as the laws operating in them the *bhaktas* get a glimpse of Lord's omnipotence. Miracles are not special proofs of Lord's unbound power for the *bhaktas*: they are only the extensions of Lord's will that manifests in the laws since the presence of such laws itself is not less a miracle for them. Existence and sustenance of anything without any law is unthinkable but the answer to the legitimate question—why should there be any law at all, is obtained experientially only in the will of the Lord –the Supreme Person. *Bhaktas* also know that if there is any power in anything anywhere in the universe it is due to the Lord's will only. Power in physical, psychic and of any other kind is only the limited manifestation of Lord's power of will. Fire has the power to give heat and burn because it is the law. But the presence of this law itself is due to Lord's will. There is no logical necessity involved here. It is an empirical truth that fire burns and gives heat. Logically it is not impossible to think that fire could not have burnt and could not have given heat. That such a power is there in fire is in a sense accidental. But accidents can't become laws. This law like behaviour of fire, its power is due to the will of the Lord that has created a world where law reins, not chaos. So Lord's omnipotence is experienced by the *bhaktas* in the all the powers of everything in the universe. Not only physical powers but also the psychic powers of reasoning, perception, sensitivity etc. are present in human beings and in other species too only as the manifestation of Lord's power of will. Lord is omnipotent because, the *bhaktas* see, all kinds of powers emanate from Lord only.

Bhagvân –The Lord Has Several Divine Attributes and The _bhaktas_ Get The Glimpse of Them

Lord's omnipresence is seen by the *bhaktas* in His presence in their thoughts, feeling and will. In fact no one else than the *bhaktas* can understand the actual import of Lord's attribute of omnipresence. Only in the experience of *bhakti* a person comes to know that there was not a fragment of a moment when his dear Lord left him alone. Only a *bhakta* knows that he forgot his Lord innumerable times and made overt or covert egoistic claims. But his benevolent Lord never minded and never forsook him. Had his Lord forsook him even for a moment he could have perished immediately because how could have he survived away from Lord's will that manifests in his life force and in the conditions of its support! The *bhaktas* know that his Lord is present where he is present and He is also present in all other places where he is not present and could not be present. In the extension of the manifestation of His will Lord is present in every smallest particle of the universe. But the most surprising thing that the *bhaktas* alone experience is the fact that even in the moments when He is not directly available to them His presence is actively felt in His absence. A *bhakta* is that blessed one who spends such moments as the absence of their dear Lord and in their pain of separation He remains present and overwhelms them with the ineffable joy of love. What else could be the meaning of omnipresence! He is omnipresent for his dear *bhaktas* because He actively makes His felt absence marked uniquely by *His* absence. So he is present in His absence too. Apart from the indirect knowledge of the presence of Lord in the directly felt absence many incidents of every individual *bhakta's* biography make them reason to hold about His omnipresence. Such innumerable incidents, which make the biographies of the *bhaktas*, interesting for any common man, show that even in those situations of which a *bhakta* is not at all aware, his welfare and his progress in *bhakti* is protected in such a way that can be done only by the Supreme Person—the Lord. A *bhakta* does indeed doubt about his Lord's omnipresence but such incidents put him also to surprise and overwhelm him with the care that Lord shows through these incidents.

The glimpses of the omniscience of Lord is got by the *bhaktas* in discovering that He knows even the most secret desire of their heart and satisfy them without showing His hand in it. As if what the *bhakta* wanted was fulfilled as a natural course. In fact Lord's omniscience is only an aspect of His omnipotence. All powers are Lord's power. So the power of knowledge is also is a power of Lord. Lord is the source of all knowledge and all kinds of knowledge obtained by human race is only a small wave of that unfathomable ocean of knowledge.

The attributes of Lord that are slightly known by the *bhaktas* are His essential attributes. In other words they are the constituents of His being. Lord is a person—the Supreme Person and in a person such attributes must be present in more or less quantity. 'Person-hood' essentially includes self-consciousness, intelligence and power of will. In a finite person like us all these three attributes are present in finite quantity. In the Supreme Person these are present infinitely. For the *bhaktas* Lord Himself is the ultimate reality of the universe. It is quite natural to acknowledge this reality as *'saguṇa'* because it is more appropriate to call any person, finite or infinite, *'saguṇa'*. A person can't be called a person at all if he does not possess the power of will. Whether he uses this power or keeps it unused is not of central importance. Possessing such a power is of central importance since this attribute (the attribute of *having the will power*) gives a person his person-hood. So there is sound reason behind the *bhaktas'* claim that Lord as the ultimate reality is essentially *'saguṇa'*. Lord is not a concept or an abstract principle that could be called —'*nirguṇa*' (attribute-less). *Bhagvân* –Lord of *bhaktas*, therefore, is acknowledged as the '*Saguṇa Brahman*'. When Lord 's will power remains unmanifest (As in the state just after mythological annihilation and before the beginning of the process of creation) then He could be called '*nirguṇa*' since in this state it becomes impossible to point to this essential attribute either. But this is a state of non-manifestation of the attribute of having the power of will; it is not the state of its *absence*. So the *bhaktas* have a point in maintaining that even in this state the essential attribute of Lord is there in His being and His '*nirguṇa*' state can't be acknowledged as opposite of his *saguṇa* state that is His essentially nature. Thus the pure transcendent form of Lord also is essentially *saguna* although He, then, could be called *nirguṇa*. *Bhagvan*—Lord in the *saguṇa*' state is the pure transcendent '*Brahman*[4]'.It is quite intelligible that acknowledging the *saguṇa*' state of Lord as His essential nature give impression that he is confined to the limitations since *every determination is negation*. But this misgiving can be stopped if we understand that in all the attributes only the infinite nature of Lord manifests because there is no qualitative or quantitative limit on His attributes. If the attribute of knowledge is assigned to Lord then it does not exclude the situations of ignorance from Him since He is the very basis on which the dichotomy of knowledge and ignorance stands. This basis, which is prior to the dichotomous or relative knowledge, is a state of knowledge itself. A doubt in any area of knowledge discloses a specific area of our ignorance. We, then, come to know that there is something about which we don't know. To know this is not to know that is not known but it is a knowledge of the specific items about which we don't know. To relate certain items of ignorance to a specific are of our knowledge is a higher order knowledge and it is prior to the growth of our knowledge about those items. Without this prior knowledge no growth of knowledge is possible. The basic or a-priori knowledge that becomes the basis of this identifying the specific items of ignorance and enables the growth of knowledge in that regard, is the knowledge of Lord. Since this knowledge that includes ignorance in itself and gives specific direction for the growth of knowledge can't be a limited knowledge and can't pose limitation on Him. This attribute of Lord, therefore, doesn't make Him finite but becomes the way to manifest His infinitude only. This issue s of great importance since it gives rise to an unpleasant dispute regarding *saguṇa* and *nirguṇa* concepts of Lord's essential nature (*Swarupa*). This issue needs some elaboration.

Dissolution of the Dispute of *Saguṇa* and *Nirguṇa Swarupa* of Lord : The *Bhaktas'* Way

For the *bhaktas* Lord can't be attributeless. *Nirguṇa* only means that He is beyond the limits of rational mode of understanding that essentially creates binaries. The *bhaktas* don't reject the description of Lord as *nirguṇa* but don't like to describe Him in that way. He may give some statement of reconciliation of the two but his way to bring about that reconciliation is not rational but emotional.

A *bhakta* wants to remain in the constant proximity of his dear Lord. He attaches himself with his Lord in some personal relation like servant, friend etc. and enjoys the ecstasy of this emotional proximity. His attention, which is withdrawn from all other directions, remains absorbed in the charm of his Lord's deeds and beauty of His form. He experiences his Lord in his *saguṇa swarupa*.

When the *bhakta* doesn't get such a *darsana* in his *dhyâna,* he becomes very restless. The separation of a lover from his beloved is extremely painful. The *bhaktas* feel similar pain, but in the most intense form. He can't stand it and weeps and cries for a glimpse of the Lord. In the absence of Lord the memory of the charm of His form absorbs the *bhaktas'* attention completely. He forgets everything else and burns in the desire to see his Lord in the same form again. In a sense a *bhakta* gets more absorbed in the form of the Lord in the state of separation than he does in His proximity. In the state of this separation the *bhaktas* experiences his Lord in *saguṇa swarupa.*

In the highest stage of *bhakti* the *bhakta* sees his dear Lord in every object and event of the world in and around him. This also is an experience: it is not a thought. The *bhakta* of that stage *does not think* that God is the ultimate basis of everything and in that sense He is present everywhere. He experiences the presence of Lord in everything. What this experience is like? On listening that it is ineffable we just drop to envisage that. This is a very unfortunate state of affairs. Ineffability of the *bhaktas'* experience is taken as epistemic ineffability by most philosophers. That is big philosophical mistake. This ineffability is not due to the impossibility of understanding of the situation. What the *bhaktas* experience is not unintelligible to him. The *bhaktas* this stage don't experience anything that is literally unintelligible (such as a sequence of meaningless of letters or sound). *Bhaktas'* experience of the presence of their Lord is not an encounter with sheer meaninglessness.

The ineffability of the *bhaktas'* experience is not the case of partial understanding either. It is not the case that they face a situation that they are unable to comprehend fully. Partial understanding leaves the person confused. He knows that he has definitely witnessed an object or an event but could not follow what he should call it in its totality. It is a variety of psychological ineffability resulting from the failure of the person to understand a situation in its totality. Ineffability of the *bhaktas'* experience is also a psychological ineffability but different from this variety.

As it is stated in above discussion *nirguṇa swarupa* of the Lord is the *swarupa* that encompasses all the necessary divisions or dichotomies for any possible human knowledge. If we look at a figure then we can see it only if it sufficiently contrasted from a background.. W e can't see a figure if the figure and the background both are of the same colour. A figure must stand out of the background to be known as a figure. The form of the Lord that charms the *bhaktas* (why only they but everyone is bound to be attracted if he could see) also is seen by him in a backdrop; may be that backdrop is just void around Him. Lord manifests in the form and the *bhakta's* attention is immediately drawn towards that. But the void that serves as backdrop also is nothing else but Lord Himself. A *bhakta* knows that every law operates the way it operates due to the will of the Lord. He knows that in every law Lord is present in the form of the will that makes that law operational. Lord is present in the law of 'figure and background' also that enables the *bhakta* experience his Lord in the charming form. So the *bhakta* knows that his dear Lord, by attracting his attention only towards His form (and not towards the background of void) is enabling him to see him. This awareness of the *bhakta* is the awareness of Lord's presence in the background also; this is the awareness of the *nirguṇa swarupa* of his Lord. Despite this awareness his attention is drawn to the charming form –the *saguṇa swarupa* so the *bhakta* accepts this as Lord's will. He acknowledges it as his Lord's approval to enjoy His (Lord's) *aiœwarya* and enjoys it loosing himself completely in it. But he also gets great joy in acknowledging that all this becomes possible because his Lord so wills It would not have been possible if Lord had not willed so. The power to will refers to Lord's *saguṇa swarupa.* Hence the *bhaktas* hold that Lord has the *nirguṇa swarupa* because He wills so. It is just another way of hoding that Lord is *nirguṇa* also because He is *saguṇa.* If lord were not *saguṇa* (i.e. if He were *nirguṇa* essentially) then He would not have been able to manifest Himself in both *saguṇa* and *nirguṇa rupas.* The fact that Lord has both the *swarupas* establish that He is essentially *saguṇa* and to think that *saguṇa rupa* is merely illusory is great misunderstanding. To consider the *saguṇa rupa* even as secondary is equally a misgiving. The *bhaktas* prove to be wiser than most of the so called *jnânis* who despise the *saguṇa* worshipers as idolaters tied to finite forms. This is a widespread misunderstanding about the *bhaktas* and *bhakti* that, very often, gives rise to the erroneous presentation of the image of the *bhakta* as an emotional fool and *bhakti* as an indulgence into this sort of foolishness. The innocence and humility of the *bhaktas* should not be mistaken theiras ignorance and stupidity. In the biographies of the *bhaktas* we come across several incidents where such a mistake put the so called *jnâni* to shame and humiliation. The incident of the inestimable pain in stomach of Sri Totapuri, who initiated Sri Ramakrishna Paramhamsa into the *sâdhnâ* of *nirguṇa Brahma,* is well known in this regard[5]. This incident is usually stated as a message of victory of a humble *bhakta* over an arrogant *jnâni.* However, this tells us much more than just this. In context of the present discussion regarding the *saguòa* and *nirguòa* a few points are of great philosophical importance.

Sri Ramakrishna Paramhansa never said anything against Sri Totapuri's belief in the supremacy of *Nirguṇa Brahma* although the latter ridiculed the belief in Mother Kali. Totapuri, despite having the experience of *nirvikalp samâdhi,* mistook Kali the mother goddess as an imagination of Sri Ranakrishna. This situation itself raises several questions regarding many beliefs about this dichotomy that is wide spread. We can't enter into them at present. However, it is clear that even a person of high level of experience of *Nirguṇa Brahman* may have misunderstanding about *saguṇa swarupa* of Lord. Not all the *jnânis* suffer from this misunderstanding but some of them definitely suffer from this. The opposite is also true. Some *bhaktas* also try to reject the *nirguṇa swarupa.* This rejection may be of at least two sorts. A *bhakta* may be intelligent enough so that he can refute all arguments of the supporter of *nirguṇa* and disarm him completely. Actual instances of such case are available in the biographies of the *bhaktas.* But these biographies also tell us that such an attempt made by a *bhakta* is condemned by the *bhaktas* too because they know that it is only a ego trip in disguise[6]. But a *bhakta's* innocent assertions about their unbound love for their Lord leaves even the *jnânis* spell bound and helps them correct their misconception about the *saguṇa swarupa* of the Lord if they have one. Very many instances of this sort of silent but powerful rejection of theory of *nirgṇa* are also available[7]. *Bhaktas* utterances combined with his spontaneous behaviours say and show that Lord is essentially *saguṇa* and it is a sort of assertion that hardly anyone could deny. People (including the *jnânis*) could not refute the *bhaktas'* assertions since they are so lovable that no one could think of rejecting.

Lord's Moral Attribute as Love for which the *Bhaktas* Live and Die

Lord's moral attribute is His divinity that is the source of all conceivable highest moral qualities of character. This is directly felt by the *bhaktas* in the ecstatic experience of His love – in *bhakti.* Lord is love. Perhaps it would also be appropriate to say that Lord is the very basis of the experience of love that is essentially sublime.

The *bhaktas* realize, in direct and in indirect ways, the will of Lord that manifests in his *bhakti.* Emergence of *bhakti* in his heart despite extremely adverse conditions becomes possible only because Lord wants that people should feel its divinity. It is clear to the *bhaktas* that Lord wants pure sublime love should occupy human hearts and it is clear to all who understand the *bhaktas.* To obey the will of the Lord is the only and highest duty fo them. Anything that is against pure love is not acceptable to Lord. Hatred, violence and dishonesty etc. are opposed to love but basically these are only the outcome of what is actually opposed to pure love.

Inclination towards materiality is the basic evil that is opposed to love. Love is marred by passion. It is very unfortunate that love very often confused for passion. Human beings experiences both and know that love, at least in one of its form, is the experience of dissolving of one's identity in the identity of the person whome one loves. Passion is sharply contrasted with this experience.

Passion in all its forms strengthens one's ego. It is always a demand and always a demand that is directly connected to 'I', 'me' and 'myself'. Demand may be of very many sorts. There could be a public demand with which we are nowadays very much familiar. But even if a public demand gets some how connected to some one's ego it becomes his passion. Passion expresses itself in possessiveness and that generates all other maladies like hatred, jealousy, violence and so on. In generating *bhakti* –the pure love in the heart of the *bhaktas* Lord disapproves all these. But Lord can't forcibly generate love in the hearts of the people because anything generated forcibly can be anything but not love. This impossibility does not delimit the omnipotence of Lord not because it is logically impossible. Our logical limit of intelligibility itself is a manifestation of His will. Lord could have put some different sort of limit on our understanding but then that would have been our logic. The fact that we understand that Lord could not forcibly generate love in our hearts because it would be logically impossible –shows that Lord wants us to understand love only in this way. He has given us the understanding of love in which it can't be conceived a feeling that could be forcibly generated. Since passion and its outcomes—hatred, jealousy etc. are the natural opposites of love Lord can't forcibly stop them to crop up either (because for so doing He will have to forcibly generate love that He can't do). Love that presupposes freedom on the part of the person is definitely shown as Lord's will, thus makes the basic condition for his moral life and enables them to choose their course of life either in favour or against love. *Bhaktas* choose love. Everyone else also can choose it. Who chooses love, Lord's will supports him as it supports the *bhaktas*. In *bhakti* one comes to know in what sense Lord is the source of moral values. He is the giver and sustainer of person's freedom, giver of wisdom to judge between moral and immoral and also giver of moral strength. But apart from these a very important factor, which is ordinarily overlooked in discussions of morality, the feeling of happiness in performing a moral act is attained in *bhakti* and this also is to be ascribed to Lord alone. A moral act could not rightly be called moral if the person performs it with a feeling of burden. In love for Lord a person performs a moral action without any sense of pride or with the feeling of any burden. He does it very happily because he has actual reason for so doing. So Lord is the source and foundation of moral life itself. A religious believer in general and the *bhaktas* in particular find that morality without Lord is impossible. Agnostics try to find a different foundation for morality. Remaining within the so-called secular framework one may be satisfied. But one realizes something centrally important is missed in morality if the presence of Lord in human life is accepted at least at the conceptual level in the form of a postulate. There is no morality without Lord. It is this necessary connection that at times mislead some thinkers to identify religion with morality and to commit the mistake of reducing the former into the latter. Religion is an experiential relation with the divine: morality is its spontaneous outcome. Both are inter related but different. *Bhaktas* live and die for the love of their Lord. They don't care for their conduct in the world but in their love of Lord they produce the highest instances of moral excellence without taking note of the fact that it is being done by them. Any fixed notion of morality becomes stagnant and often proves to be inhuman. Love for Lord is never static. So the *bhaktas* set the norms of morality that proves to be revolutionary and liberating for mankind.

In the light of above discussion we can understand what *Bhagvân* is for the *bhaktas.* We can now understand why it is not correct to say that *Bhagvân* is a construct of the *bhaktas'* imagination and why it is correct to say that the *bhaktas* are created by *bhagvân.*

Bhagvan is the essential foundation of the world of *Bhakti bhâva. Bhakti* is a fact that we all accept. The essential foundation of *bhakti*, therefore, can't be denied. This acceptence is not an acceptance of Lord as mere postulate for philosophizing: Lord is the foundation of *bhakti* and is directly known in *bhakti* both as an object and as the foundation. *Bhaktas* know the Lord not as a concept or a principle. They know Him as the Supreme Person who has infinite attributes— many of them are directly known by the *bhaktas*. Each of the attributes of Lord discloses His infinitude and does not delimit Him.

References

1. लोकेऽपि भगवदत्रगुण क्षवण कीतर्नातत्र। मुख्यतस्तु महतत्रकऋपयैव भगवदत्रकऋपालेशाब्दा ।।.37.38 Narad Bhakti Surtra
2. Certain clarifications are necessary in this regard. The idea of a different world may appear to be Platonic. In a sense it is Platonic that it exists independently of the physical world as ideas don't belong to the physical world. But it is not Platonic in the sense that it is not a world of ideas or though but of experience. It may appear to be Husserllian in nature, but it is different from that either because this world it is acknowledged to be independent of the consciousness. Consciousness does not constitute these world but only reveals it. Moreover, in the present discussion of the world of Music it is not stated that music can't be listened in the physical world. Music is made and heard in the physical world by common people but we have to acknowledge that that nost common people have the capacity to hear sound and also have the capability to notice the 'musicality or melody' in some sequences of sound and this distinction is necessarily involved in all events of hearing and recognizing music qua music. S when we say that the world of music is different from the physical world we must note that it means that normal human capability to understand music overlaps his normal capacity of hearing any sound. The difference is involved in the overlap of the world of Music over the physical world of sound.
3. If a person p1understand a phenomenon S in one way and p2 understands it in a different way then unless there be a third independent way of understanding S we can't say that both understand the same S in two different ways. So to talk about the conceptually different ways presupposes that there is one unanimous way of understanding it.

   If understanding of different people were different with regard to any S then it would not have been possible to meaningfully make the statement that two or are in complete agreement with regard to their understanding of S. Our agreement with regard to our disagreements about any point also show that we all understand any S in the same way. This helps us realize our common mistake that we make in saying that your understanding may be different from mine. The same istake is committed in making a difference between a person's understanding of his experience and the third person's understanding of his experience. Had there been such a difference then two person's could not have ever been come to an agreement in this regard that is mostly expected by the person who's experience is under discussion and that is actually reached at. We do at times say –' Now you understand me'. Meaningfulness of such sentences show that the first person and third person distinction with regard to understanding is not acceptable at all If a *bhakta* experiences a phenomenon and understands it then anyone else also will understand it in that way only. It would be insightful to remind ourselves in this regard that all men understand labour pain but by the very nature of the pain they can never experience it. Only a pregnant woman can experience such a pain and understands *what* she is experiencing and she understands it the way any woman or any human being could understand it. So it becomes actually possible for any man to understand it. The experience of *bhaktasi,* however, is not riddled with this sort of difference within them. Hence it could be said without any difficulty that it is a species of human experience and any human being is capable of attaining it subject to the practical factors arising in different cases.

4. रामसच्चिदानन्द दिनेशा नहि तंह मोह निरा लवलेशा ।
सहज प्रकारा रफप भगवाना नहि ताहि विज्ञान विहाना।।
3rd caupayi after Doha 115 in the Balkanda of Sri Ramcarit Manas.
5. This incident is depicted in the Sadhaka Bhava of Sri Ramakrishna Lila Prasanga. (Sri Ramakrishna Ashrama, Nagpur........)
6. Shreenivas, a disciplle of Chaitanya, was very sad over the derogatory remarks of a *Nirguṇa Advaitvādin* Swami Prakashananda over the Kṛiṣṇa *bhakti of his master.* Shreenivas tried to reject hisview by logical arguments. It didn't yield him the desired result and his master Chaitnya also disliked his move and asked him to stop that. Jeeva Goswami —a young disciple of Chaitanya was scolded by Sanatan Goswami, his uncle and an

elderly *bhakta* disciple of Chaitanya, for defeating a *pandit*,who put a challenge before the *pandits* of Vrindavana See—*Chaitanya Charitanrita by* Prabhudatta Brahnacari (Geeta Press, Gorakhpur)

7. Chaitnya Mahaprabhu, when met Prakashananda at Prayaga did not replied to the arguments of thelatter but rected a shloka grom the *[a]atapadi Stotra* written by Samkaracharya with the heart flowing devotion for the Lord. It touched the core of the heart of Prahashananda and next day he surrendered at the feet of Chaitnya. In Sri Madbhagvat also the change of heart of Uddhava on hearing the Gopis' utterances for their love for Sei Kroshna,is an instance of the same.

9

Understanding an Aspect of *Bhakti*-Movement

Krişņa! Scholarly investigation, which generally proceeds on pure rational line, at times, throw certain questions that appear very strange to innocent hearts. It would sound ridiculous if someone asks –When did, for the first time in history, a human being started loving someone? But the curiosity about the first use of the word 'love' does not appear to be strange because some period can be specified in reply regarding the beginning of the use of this word. This is a curiosity purely regarding linguistic history. It does not imply that human being in general or the people of that linguistic community particular got the experience of love for the first time in that period only. Love is not regarded as a primary emotion. At least the selfless love, in which the lover desires to loose himself in the being of the beloved, is not accepted to be primary emotion. Such love presupposes a developed cultural background that itself presuppose the growth of language to a height where the sublimity of love manifests in literature. Despite this understanding about this connection between sublime experience of love it is not customary to draw the conclusion that the community of that language users underwent this experience for the first time only about the period of the first use of the word 'love' (or its equivalent in that language). It is well acknowledged that history of use of a word does not necessarily refer to the beginning of that experience which is referred to by that word. However, an attempt to trace the beginning of the use of the word '*bhakti*' in a particular period of Indian literature and drawing the conclusion that this religious practice of Hindus started in that period, is not looked at with any doubt. It is, on the contrary, regarded to be very scholarly.

Hardly anyone can afford to hold the opinion that there is anything wrong in acquiring scholarship in the grammar of '*Bhakti*' or investigating the social conditions in which that religious phenomenon grew that is referred to with this word. In view of the fact that religion is not a personal affair of anyone and religious experience or types of it also are not personal but social in a deep sense, the reason behind the attempts made to locate the beginning of *bhakti* (as a religious phenomenon) with the beginning of the use of '*Bhakti*' (as a word to refer to that phenomenon), is quite intelligible and correct too. However, an implicit assumption works behind such attempts. It is assumed that the ecstasy and grace felt by the *bhaktas* are only subjective mental states that are significant and valuable for them personally but have no importance or relevance to understand *bhakti* either as a social phenomenon or as a movement. This assumption is only a particular case of the more general assumption that personal feeling or subjective mental state of a person does not affect his or others social life unless it manifests in some of his interaction with others. This is further connected to the assumption that any person learns to value anything as a part of a community that gives it value and he could value some of his subjective mental states also only because he learns to value it as a part of the community that gives it value. Although it is not explicitly propagated in the form of a universal statement but for all practical purposes it is, implicitly, accepted to be so. This is an unexamined assumption. At least in its universalized form it is not tenable. An elaboration of this point and extension of its implication for understanding the case of *bhakti* as a social phenomenon and as a social movement is needed here.

Conceptually a distinction between the notions of 'social' and 'objective' is very important. Very often wrong conclusion is drawn if this distinction is not made Ordinarily.the instances of the two are not separable but it is possible to make a distinction between them at the conceptual level. In almost all cases of the process of value ascription is learned by a person only within the community in which he grows and it is almost impossible practically to show any instance of leaning of value ascription that is not a learning within a community. But the practical impossibility to show that the process of giving value to anything is learnt by an individual apart from his community, does not prove that the objectivity of value apprehension or ascription *means* social approval for a value. It is important to note in this regard that this impossibility arises due to the fact that the objectivity of learning of value apprehension and/ or value ascription manifests in a social or collective practice. It means that social or collective practices of value apprehension or ascription becomes possible *because every individual can objectively apprehend a value and ascribe it to something.* To hold the view that this process is objective *because it is learnt by the individual only socially* is to put the cart before the horse. The notion of objectivity is logically prior to the notion of social although psychologically the latter comes first. Even if this understanding of distinction between the two are not universally accepted in the context of *bhakti* there is a good reason to hold that the *bhaktas* give value to their experience of emotional love for Lord because they find it objectively that it is valuable and not the other way round. In the following paragraphs of this chapter attempt is made to accomplish this task by analyzing some events of some well known *bhaktas* of 15-16th century of India.

Jaideva : His *Bhakti* and His Life

It is customary to begin the discussion of *Bhakti*-movement with the life and works of Acharya Ramanuja, Madhwa, Vallabha and others. It is done so because they gave a philosophical framework to *bhakti.* For the masses abstract philosophical theories have never been of much interest. To understand *bhakti*- movement as a movement it is perhaps more important to look at the life and works of those *bhaktas* who made *bhakti* popular without preaching an intricate system of metaphysics. Jaideva is one among them.

Born in a brahmin family of the Kenduvilva village in the Veerbhum district of Bengal. Jaideva's life is full of miraculous events. The stories about the events of his life are popular in the folk of rural Bengal and fondly told and listened by the people as an example of the life of a *bhakta* in which miracles take place frequently as Lord's grace. A couple of such events need to be stated to understand what actually influences people in the life of *bhaktas*.

It is told about that Jaideva's father had borrowed some money from a local money-lender named Niranjan but could not repay the debt in time. As usual the money-lender came to Jaideva and asked him to repay the debt of his father. Jaideva had not enough money with him at that time so he said that with the blessings of his Lord he would return the money. Niranjana, the money-lender, who was a purely money-minded miserly person, did not relent and asked Jaideva very rudely to give the right and title of his parental property and house to him. Jaideva did what Niranjana asked him to do. Now, the story goes like this: While Niranjana was becoming happy over his easy grab of Jaideva's property his daughter came running to him and frantically informed him that his (Niranjana's) house is on fire. Stunned by this news Niranjana ran towards his house. Jaideva also followed him and without any fear entered into the burning house. Fire extinguished immediately. This incident moved Niranjana completely. He appologized from Jaideva and tore away the documents of right and title of Jaideva's house and property. Niranjan became a different person after that.

The story ordinarily appears to be common story of miracle. Similar stories of miracles are found associated with other *bhaktas'* life also. The miracle aspect of this story is highlighted mostly both by the common folk and by the educated modern people for quite opposite reasons and purposes. A rural fellow, ordinarily, states this story and emphasizes the miracle to show the power of faith in God to whom the *bhakta* is dedicated. The modern man highlights the story, ordinarily, to show the irrationality of faith in God. Whether miracles happen or not is an issue here that draws our attention easily but a more important point surfaces in this story that does not easily catch our attention. In this episode Jaideva's behaviour was not like any common man's behaviour. Let us try to look at his behviour and examine it closely.

Jaideva was *not angry or not even disturbed* over Niranjana's unjust demand. He rather happily conceded to fulfill his demand. This is not the normal spontaneous behaviour that we can expect from any person in ordinary circumstances. Several questions arise about it and we should try to find and entertain all answers that are rational. Is it possible for a person to respond to such an unjust the way Jaideva responded (or said to have responded)? What does 'possible' mean here? These two questions need to be addressed first of all.

It is expected that on an unjust demand that could bring crisis to a person, the person will be disturbed very much and his feeling of disturbance would reflect in his spontaneous response either in the form of anger or panic. It is not expected that he would remain cool under ordinary circumstances. He may only pretend to remain cool in such a situation if he has to impress on others that he does not bother for such incidents. The behaviour of pretension can be distinguished from genuine behavioural response. It is practically possible to distinguish pretension from the genuine response if we closely observe However, conceptually they are very different from each other in respect of the presence or absence of the internal strain that the person feels in pretending and not pretending respectively. In order to show in overt behaviour what he actually does not feel, he has to pass through a strain. Whether it could be practically detected or not is an empirical matter but it is clear that such strain is present in the behaviour of pretension and by admitting this as the criterion of distinction at the conceptual level we can identify a person who is pretending to be what he is not.

Can the cool behaviour of Jaideva be seen as act of pretending? Do we have reasons to believe his? There could be negative reasons to believe so and there could be positive reason also to do so. When no positive reason is in the sight that could be held for a person's unexpected behaviour then it seems rational to believe that the person is only pretending. When we fail to find a reason for a person's unexpected behaviour in a perticular situation then we are tempted to believe that he is only tying to show and impress on others that he is not influenced by those conditions which make a person behave the way that is normally expected. This is a negative reason to believe that someone is only pretending. Very often we make use of negative reason to reach at a conclusion in our daily life. It could be acknowledged as rational procedure to decision regarding someone's behaviour only if in the bulk of available knowledge we actually find no positive reason for that. However, non-availability of positive reason for a person's unexpected behaviour can't be deemed as a definite ground for ascribing negative reason unless there be a positive reason for making use of a negative reason. It might be a failure in the part of the investigator only. Some people get easily tempted to make use of negative reason to jump to a conclusion about a person's unexpected behaviour but that discloses more about their preoccupation regarding that person's behaviour than enabling us to reach at an objective conclusion. If someone draws the conclusion that Jaideva was only pretending to be cool and unperturbed on the ground that there is no positive reason to understand why he behaved in that unexpected way then it would not be clear whether it is a fact about Jaideva or about the prejudice of that person against Jaideva.

At the conceptual level we can't make use of negative reason as a criterion to distinguish pretension from genuine response in the case of unexpected behaviour. At the conceptual level we can't claim that Jaideva was only pretending unless we rule out the possibility of the absence of strain in his behaviour. Since Jaideva is not present and we have no record available either to decide whether his behaviour was stained, we can't rule out either of the possibilities. (i) We can't say that Jaideva's cool and composed behaviour on the unjust and alarming demand of Niranjan was *not* a strained response, and (ii) we can't say that that Jaideva's cool and composed behaviour on the unjust and alarming demand was *not* a spontaneous (i.e. unstrained) response either. Ordinarily we have no good reason to rule out either. But some people rule out (ii) on the ground that thereis no supporting reason for (i)They fail to see that on logical level both (i) and (ii) stand on the same ground and whatever ground could be given against one to support the other can be reciprocated in respect to other too. The impossibility of refutation of either opens up possibility in favour of both. It is to be noticed that both (i) and (ii) could not be true together if they are held as universal propositions but as existential (particular) propositions both can be held true together. The impossibility here is a practical impossibility (not logically impossibility). Factors like— non-availability of good evidence to ascertain about the nature (strained or spontaneous) of his behaviour etc. make it impossible in the practical sense. In the light of above discussion it is clear that the view that Jaideva's cool and composed behaviour on an unjust and alarming demand was his spontaneous response is rationally not untenable. This logically amounts to holding that it is rationally tenable but that is only accepted as a formal possibility of its rationality To make it empirically meaningful this much is not sufficient at all. However, it is clear that no illogicality or irrationality is involved in holding the view that Jaideva's behaviour was his spontaneous response in that situation. This is enough incentive for searching for the positive reason for this ordinarily unexpected behaviour.

If someone values something then on its loss, even with the fear of its loss, he gets disturbed. This is a natural response that is expected from any normal human beings. But it is possible that what is valued by most of us may not be felt as valuable. This also is possible and this could happen for various reasons. It is possible that a person may not be interested in that thing which is valued by most people. Most people value wealth. It is indeed valuable to lead a life of good standard. But some people don't value it in comparison to political or administrative power. For them wastage of money is not disturbing at all if it brings them power. We also know about people who like sensual pleasure most and for that they don't mind squandering their wealth. So it is not difficult to envisage conditions when a person does not value that which is ordinarily valued by most people and that becomes the reason of their not being disturbed if it is lost or feared to be lost. This is a level where we understand the reason of ordinarily unexpected behaviour of a person because we understand the comparative values of both—ours (ordinary normal people) and the other person's (whose unexpected behaviour is under consideration).

If the level of values are not the same then the comparison between the values become very difficult and a person unfamiliar with the level of value of another person can't fully grasp the reason of his unexpected behaviour. Many artistes and litterateurs are found to be leading life of poverty and ill health. They are mostly lost in their work and don't care for money and even for health. A layperson may find it difficult to understand they get a deep enjoyment from their work- an enjoyment that could be experienced by those who work in that field. He can understand that for the artistes and litterateurs give more or supreme value to his work but he can't envisage exactly the nature of enjoyment that makes his work valuable to him. So for a layperson an artiste's behaviour of indifference for money or health turn out to be very strange.' Artists and poets are crazy people'—is a comment that a layperson very often pass sarcastically against them. Such comments show a layperson's failure of understanding the reason for the artists and litterateur's indifference to money and health.

With education and growth of taste in art and literature a common man begins to understand that an artist or a litterateur gets great joy in his work of creativity that is not physical in nature and it occupies him very much. In comparison to this joy money or even health is a very inferior value. Spending time to earn more money or to look after his health seems to him the wastage of time. When a common man understands the nature of joy that the artist or a poet gets in his creation then he also comes to understand that their behaviour of indifference for wealth and health that appeared to him strange earlier, was their normal response. 'Normal' here does not mean a statistical average: it means spontaneous response in a particular situation. He can, then, understand that it is quite normal for the artist and litterateur that they don't give value to wealth and health. Without money and health they face several trouble and get irritated too but that does not mean that they value these things. Their irritation in poverty and ill health is basically for their deprivation from their chosen work and the lack of necessary condition for their work They value only their work and anything that comes in the way of it becomes the reason for their irritation.

Jaideva was not a poet: he was very much more than that. He was a *bhakta*—a lover of Lord Sri Krishna. For Jaideva physical wealth was not less valuable in comparison to the joy that he got in the *bhakti,* rather the joy of *bhakti* alone was valuable for him.

So his indifference to physical wealth was not a matter of comparison. Physical wealth was a sort of disturbance or hindrance for him since it engaged him for some time in its looking after and deprived him from the joy of Krishna *bhakti.* So when Niranjana asked him to give all his property and house he was not disturbed; rather felt the sort of relief that someone gets when saved from some unpleasant task forced on him. He was thankful to the money-lender. On hearing that Niranjana's house had caught fire he held himself responsible for it (*bhaktas* believe that they are always saved by Lord from the evil doers but the evil doer, who intends to do harm to them, has to face the wrath of their Lord). So to save Niranjana from the wrath of his Lord he jumped into his burning house. This unexpected extra ordinary behaviour of Jaideva does not remain unexpected if we see it in the backdrop of his *bhakti* that was an actual experience of supreme value.

The miraculous part of this episode (extinguishing of fire with Jaideva's entry) turns out to be very trivial for consideration if way pay attention to all that Jaideva felt and did in this situation. Whether the fire actually extinguished or not does not make Jaideva's act extremely respectable. It would have been respectable even if fire were not put off and Jaideva would have been burnt in it. In that case it would have been deemed as an exemplary act of sacrifice for others help. This would not have been deemed to be a respectable act in the sense of an act prompted with divine force even if it were done by Jaideva with internal strain. In that case it would have respected as a great heroic act but not necessarily carrying the touch of transcendence in it. It was the spontaneity of his act that made his act extra ordinary and respectable in the sense of bearing a touch of divinity in it. People were influenced by Jaideva's act and respected him as a *bhakta* due to this spontaneity of his act. This spontaneity is acknowledged as the presence of divine will operating in his heart as *bhakti.* Any ordinary person can do this sort of heroic act but his act could not be an unstrained and spontaneous. He would do such an act passing through a great strain. This forbearance makes him respectable in the sense of a hero. Respectability of Jaideva as a *bhakta* lies in acknowledging by him and by others that he did not feel any pain or strain in so doing This is admitted as the operation of divine will in him that raises a person from the level of physical influence to non physical level of existence. A *bhakta* is known for his *bhakti* with his Lord and the presence of *bhakti* in anyone's heart is acknowledged, explicitly or implicitly, as the grace of Lord Himself. It is almost a reiteration to say that a person's influence on others can be regarded as an influence of *bhakti* only if it is related to *bhakti*. So to understand Jaideva's influence over others and the contribution of this influence in the movement known as *Bhakti* movement, it is necessary to relate his behaviour with his experience of *Bhakti* as an experience of Transcendence. Without taking the element of Transcendence into consideration we can't understand *bhakti* as *bhakti*, and *Bhakti* Movement as a movement that got its origin and force in *bhakti*. A very important point of practical, significance needs to be elaborated at this juncture.

Bhakti Movement is known to be sort of reform in Hinduism. An humble but firm stand was taken in this movement against caste system and gender discrimination. The force working behind the discrimination along caste and gender line was a force of religion. If a force could mobilize the masses against it then it would have to be acknowledged as one that had greater hold over people. *Bhaktas'* way of life and their message also influenced people due to its religiousity but people felt that what the *bhaktas* were doing and teaching was a sort of *deeper or real* religion in sharp contrast with the institutional injunctions and commands of religion. This feeling that was at the level of individuals gradually resulted into the belief of the larger chunk of the people. Larger number of people began believing that *bahktas'* way of life and message, despite their indifference and implicit defiance of certain Hindu code of conduct, represented authentic Hinduism and the institutional injunctions and commands of Hinduism were inauthentic, superficial and dead. This belief grew day by day, gathered force and to shape of a mass movement of reform. *Bhaktas* never explicitly took an agenda of any reform in Hinduism. Most of the *bhaktas* said nothing against caste system or discrimination on the ground of gender. Those who spoke about the qualification (*adhikâr*) of *bhakti* expressed an attitude of indifference but did not directly question this system of discrimination. They just did not care for that. But this attitude was felt by the people as the spontaneous manifestation of a living authentic religion and easily disengaged them from reinforcing these discriminations in their daily life.. This turned out to be a movement of reform. This reform in the way of the larger chunk of the people took place due to *bhaktas*' influence over them but it (this reform) was a natural outcome of what people *felt* as the presence of divine in *bahkti* : it was not a *planned objective* of the *bhaktas.*

People relied on what the *bhaktas* said because they felt the presence of divine in their *bahkti*; they felt that in their *bhakti bhaktas* rise to a level of existence that is not mundane at all. This was a sort of direct experience, yet some people doubted and tried to test the *bhaktas*. Stories about the miraculous passing of such tests by the *bhaktas* are abundantly available in the folk-lore about the *bhaktas* and in their biographics too. Life of Jaideva and his wife Padmavati are full of miraculous events of passing such tests. These miracles (true or fabricated) suffuse our vision and blind us towards an important fact that the *bhaktas* never made any special effort to pass such tests even if they had knowledge about it. They never tried to prove that what they told about their experience about their Lord was true. Their spontaneous responses in a particular situation (that was prepared or chosen for their test) made people realize that what the *bhaktas* did was actually their effortless response (as if it *happened through them* and *not done by them*) although it was quite unexpected from any ordinary person n that situation. This shows that unquestioning attitude of the *bhakta* regarding matters related to his Dear Lord. This unquestioning attitude was a direct consequence of the *bhaktas* close emotional connection with Lord that they experienced in *bhakti.*

It seems from some events in the *bhaktas'* life that they also, at times, doubt about the existence of Lord. This doubt is very different from the doubt of the atheist or agnostic. *Bhaktas'* doubt is not a matter of curiousity. It is not his interest to know whether his Lord exists or not rather it is his concern about it; it is a demand to reinforce the experience of *bhakti*. It s an attempt to renew his emotional relation with his Lord. This reinforcement is just for the sake of joy of renewal and does nor presuppose that the prior relation had withered or died. There is a well known story about 'Geet Govinda' written by Jaideva. While writing a copulate of the hymn Jaideva could not decide what should he write as the last line of it. Padmavati— his wife, seeing that he is getting late for his meal, asked him to stop for a while and to start writing after taking meal after his bath. Jaideva went out for his bath. Soon Padmavati found that he returned without bathing and asked her to give the incomplete Geeta Govinda. He said that while he was going to take bath suddenly the appropriate line flashed in his mind and he rushed back home just to complete the copulate by adding that line. After finishing the copulate Jaideva asked for water from his wife to take bath . After taking bath and having finished his lunch he went into his room to take rest for a while. Then Padmavati went to take her meal. While she was eating she saw her husband returning after taking his bath, Wondering how his wife started eating before his lunch (this was Padmavati's routine to take her meal only after her husband) Jaideva enquired with Padmavati about that unusual behaviour. Padmavati stated about the whole event . On listening this Jaideva went into his room and fond that no body was there. He then realized that his dear Lord came in his form and did what he was hesitating to do. Jaideva was hesitant in writing the last line that was coming to his mind since he thought that it would perhaps give impression of his arrogance in respect of his relation with his Lord[1].

Doubt never comes in the heart of the *bhaktas* in the form of disbelief and the doubts that come in the minds of the people only reflect their own dispositions. An atheist can never reach any certainty about God's existence and also fail to see that he is not in fact trying to know but to have confirmation that God does not exist. On the other hand some people, who are not *bhaktas* but feel attraction towards them and try to see a point in what they say, get confirmation of the presence of divine in *bhakti*. When such people put the *bhaktas* on test and get a positive result regarding the presence of divine in the *bhakti* of the *bhaktas*. their finding should be taken seriously because they are ready to accept a negative result although don't wish for it like the atheists.

Chaitanya: His *Bhakti* and His Life

Chaitanya was a *Krişņa*! intoxicated *bhakta*. All *bhaktas* are God intoxicated but among them the intoxication of Chaitanya was perhaps the highest. Understanding of Chaitanya's *bhakti* in the backdrop of his life gives so much insight into the life of *bhakti* that many misgivings are shattered.

Biography of Chaitanya is well known..Born in Navadweep (or Nadia) in Bengal he was earlier called by the name Nimai Pandita. Because of extraordinarily fair complexion he was called Gauranga (literally mean having limbs with white complexion). His father's name was Jagannath Mishra and mother's name was Sachi Devi. This *bahkta* of Bengal born in 1406 A.D. was endowed with extremely sharp intelligence and power of reasoning that is ordinarily deemed as not very favourable for *bhakti*.

Nimai was a young handsome and well known teacher of Grammar and Navya Nyaya (Indian school of Logic that got its birth in the 'Nyaya Sutra' of Gautama but later developed in 13—14th century by Gangesha Upadyaya of Mithila). Like many other *pandits* of Nadia Nimai also ran a school where Grammar, Nyaya and Vedanta were taught to the students. Nimai *pandita* had the temperament of rigorous rationalist. His ability to analyze any theme with great subtlety and power of argumentation brought him great fame. He once defeated Keshawa Bhatta – a *digvijayi pandita* from Kashmir, who came to Nadia and put a challenge before the *pandits* over there. It is also said that he had written a commentary on Nyaya Sutra but flown it the river Ganga to please his friend Gadadhara, who felt that no body would like to read his commentary on the same if Nimai's commentary would be available to them. All these give some idea of Nimai *pandita's* logical capacities.

The elder brother of Nimai, who was much older than him, renounced the world in his youth and left home only when Nimai was only a young child. Inspired by his elder brother Nimai also expressed his desire for renunciation more than once before his mother but she did not allow since she did not want to loose her only son after the renunciation of her elder son.

Nimai got conventional initiation into *sanyâsa* in Gaya by a *sanyâsin* Sri Ishwara Puri when he had gone there for offering *pinda dâna* to the departed soul of his father. After this the *bhakta* nature of Nimai *pandita,* who was given the new name of Krishna Chaitnaya, bigin to unfold very fast. Krishna Chaitanya or poularly known as Chaitanya Mhaprabhu amidst his disciples, spend the later phase of life mostly in Puri (Jagannathpuri).

In the personality of Chaitanya all the characteristic features of *bhakti* that are depicted in Sri Madbhagvata and other sutras on *bhakti* manifested profusely. Chaitnya became the living embodiment of *bhakti.* During the Chariot festival (*Ratha* Yâtrâ) of Lord Jagannath he used to dance before the chariot so frantically as if he was not within his body. Not only his close disciple but anyone witnessed him dancing and singing devotional songs could got a clear glimpse of the powerful emotion of love for Lord Krishna erupting in his heart. Hardly anyone was left untouched by his *kirtana* and even by his bare presence. He influenced all whom he met. His influence made the *Hari–Nâma Sankirtana* popular in Bengal and in the whole of north-east provinces of India, He traveled the whole of India and with him the message of Krishana *Bhakti* spread through out the land. Not only Hindus but also many Mohammedans got initiation into the '*Hare Râma Hare Krişņa*! *mantra* and become his followers. The names of Swami Haridas (who was by birth a Mohammedan and earlier known by some other name) and Chand Kazi are well known.

Life of Chaitnya is full of incidents of his deep and extremely intense emotional love for Lord Krisna. It is a significant to note that despite so many miracles associated with his life, his *bhakti* dominated the miracles and was not dominated by it. People were touched by his *bhakti,* and miracle, if at all any, was neglected or noticed only as an aspect of *bhakti.* An incident needs to be presented here.

There was a *sanyâsin* in Prayaga (now Allahabad) who was a strong supporter of *Advaita* theory of Vedanta as propounded by Shankaracharya. His name was Swami Prakasahnanda. He believed in the pure formless (*nirguņa*) *brahman* and the identity of *jiva* and *brahman. He* opposed Chaitnya's faith in Lord Krishna as the ultimate transcendent *brahman* and ridiculed way of worshiping through song and dance. Once Chaitanya came to Prayaga. He was invited by Swami Prakashananda with false modesty. He wanted to ridicule and humiliate him publicly. Chaitanya went to see him and very humbly sat on the floor near the door. Prakashananda enquired with him about the reason to believe in Lord Krishna as transcendent *brahman* and duality of *jiva* and *brahman*. Influenced by the popular opinion about Shankara's *Advaitavâda,* Prakashananda also believed that Shankra was against the belief in *saguṇa* God. He thought that his question would render Chaitaya disarmed with any logical reply because in his view *Advaita* theory of Shankara was logically unbeatable. But nothing of the sort happened that he expected. With pure humility Chaitanya first expressed his ignorance about the scholarly interpretations of great *Âcârya's* words and then quoted a copulate from Shankara's *'Şatapadi Stotra'* that is addressed to Lord Vishnu and means:

'O Lord! Even if it were true that there is identity between You and me it is clear that I am yours (i.e. I am dependent on you) but You are not mine (i.e. You don't dependent on me), as the waves are said to be the sea-waves but sea is never said to be the wave-sea (i.e. made pf waves)'

Tears started flowing profusely from Chaitanya's eyes and he fell unconscious on the floor due to unbearable out burst of emotion. Prakashanand and others were touched by the simplicity of his response and witnessed for the first time in their life how much a person can get lost in *bhakti.* Prakashanada was moved completely. He was very much ashamed of his dealing with Chaitnya. Some people hold that Prakashanada wept in isolation at night and in the morning he went to Chaitnya fell on his feet, asked forgiveness and requested to take him in his refuge. Chaitanya accepted him as his disciple and gave him the new name Prabodhananda. Many scholars disagree with it and argue that Prabodhananda—the disciple of Chaitanya was a different person.

In above incident of Chasitaanya's life the issue whether Prakashananda turned into Prabodhanad(disciple of Chaitnya)is not of much impo tance. It is important to see that an argumentative *sanyâsi*, who did not learn to value even the sublime emotion of *bhakti, was touched and moved by* Chaitanya's Krishna *bhakti.* This reminds us of the event of dialogue between Uddhawa and Gopis as described in Sri Madbhagvata.

Uddhawa—a friend of Sri Krishna, who was a *jnâni* and believed in the reality of *nirguṇ brahma* only, was completely overwhelmed and moved with the emotional love of the innocent simple hearted gopis of Vrindavana. Before their love for Lord Krishna he felt the pettiness of his dry theoretical knowledge[2].

The event depicted in Sri Madbhagvata can be ignored as mythology. Event in Chaitanya's life is not a myth: it is history. Some people do not give importance to this historical event For them there is nothing historical in it nor is there anything of importance. To understand *Bhakti* Movement it is important to understand both– that it is a very important event of human life, and it was of historical importance.

Living in the physical world human life is conditioned with and constrained by several material conditions. These constraints very often force us to ignore and turn our heads away from so many things of sentimental values. These constraints turn up in very many ways and in very many forms. All human beings are familiar with them. There is no need to elaborate this point. However, there is a need to understand that our physical conditions make us insensitive to some extent. This insensitivity works as a kind of defense mechanism against the possible psychic and physical damage that can happen to us due to the presence of innumerable shocking factors present around us. In view of this benefit we accept this limit over our sensitivity as a mark of normal human behaviour. This limit over sensitivity, however, becomes a practical hindrance to *feel* even those innumerable situations around us that are favourable for our life. This normal incapacity to do that results into our failure to appreciate their actual importance. Our failure to appreciate the actual importance of either the alleged mythological event of 'Uddhawa-Gopi dialogue' or that of 'Chaitanya- Prakashananda dialogue' is an instance of this normal incapacity. We ordinarily wonder what so special happened to Uddhaw on meeting and talking to the Gopis! We wonder about it because primarily we can't appreciate the psyco-physical condition of the Gopies when Krishna left Vrindavana. Similarly we wonder about what happened to Prakashananda on witnessing the total response of Chaitanya. This is so because we primarily fail to appreciate the condition of Chaitanya on being told about the complete identity of *jiva* and *brahman* and that *saguṇa* form of *brahaman* is itself a product of *māyā*. Any amount of interpretation of this incident can't help us in understanding the condition of Chaitanya. As it is stated earlier, it is our incapacity to feel certain situations spread around us that results into failure of understanding their actual importance. Hence it is necessary to make ourselves aware of these common insensitivities.

We all know that all our vital functions of organism that keep us alive are not run by us. We also understand that it is good that these are not within our control because the moments of sleep or forgetting about them would have proved to be devastating for survival. Despite our full understanding about the fact that our survival for such a long span (say 70—80 years) is being managed by the well regulated mechanism run by innumerable forces independent of us, we don't get overwhelmed with joy. Is this not an occasion of joy that we are getting pleasures and benefits of the body without taking any worry about its smooth functioning? Most of us don't find any occasion of joy in it. Thousands of such and other situation of human life in general and hundreds of situations of every person's life in particular could be enumerated to show that we are not sensitive to them although they are all of great importance for survival and for life as developed human beings.

Love is a joyful experience for every human being. Ordinarily we all want to be loved by all. To say that no one likes anyone's hatred and everyone likes everyone's love is so trivial a truth about human nature that hardly needs to be highlighted or stated. However, most of us don't care for those situations in which we get love without our explicit demand. We become insensitive to those responses of love, which, we feel, are taken for granted. We become insensitive to all those valuable gifts, which we get and keep getting without any effort. We are reminded of their values when they become suddenly absent from our life and value them for a while if they are returned to us but, usually, forget them again. We remember the value of those only things, responses or relations for which we have to make effort. Mostly our values are the value of achievements. We value those things, experiences and relations which we have to achieve. We become insensitive to the value of those things, experioences and relations and forget them, which we don't have to achieve but which are necessary for our existence and identity as self-conscious human persons. Values of achievement are not vital or existential since one can survive without them and maintain one's identity as self-conscious person too. On the other hand, values of survival and maintenance of self-conscious identity as a person are necessary for all humans despite our insensitivity towards them. Although we remain insensitive towards them we become suddenly conscious of them and suffer a great deal when they are not available to us.

There are certain experiences in human life which have the features of both sorts of values. They are values of achievement in some sense and, in some sense, they are also the values of survival and maintenance of identity as self-conscious person. We are, ordinarily, not sensitive to them since we don't loose anything if we don't try to achieve them. But they don't become available unless we aspire for them.

Bhakti, is such a valuable experience of human life that possess both the features in it. Nothing (in the sense of existence and identity as self-conscious person) is lost if we don't achieve it. But we deprive ourselves from a valuable experience if we don't aspire for it. Like those valuable gifts that are necessary for our survival we don't give any importance to the experience of *bhakti,* neglect it or forget it completely. We can afford to do so because, it seems, nothing is lost in so doing. Like the valuable things for which we aspire to achieve, we achieve it only if we aspire for it. We loose something vital if the experience is not available to us. It is a survival value in a very important sense. We loose a part of our identity as a self-conscious persons if we would not have been gifted with this possibility and capability to experience divinity. *Bhakti* is an experience of divinity. A human person with complete absence of the capability to feel divinity would be no better than a good computer. *Bhakti* is a valuable experience in the sense of achievement also since it enriches the life of the person.

In the incident of meeting of a *bhakta* with a person who is against *bhakti* (due to any reason good or bad) something very special happens. The powerful experience manifesting through the involuntary behavioural responses of the *bhakta* influence the person facing him. If the person is just open then he feels this influence. There is nothing mystical about it . Tears trickling from anyone's eyes influence everyone and a smile on someone's face also influences everyone. Seeing someone's face and seeing someone crying produce different types of responses on any person. In the former one just sees a face but in the latter one is at least touched if not moved. This is a normal human response and no mystery is associated to it. A person, who sees the *bhakta's* tears of great joy, not only sees it but also gets influenced by it. If he is not familiar with the religious back ground of the *bhakta* then he would not know the object or person to whom the tears are associated to but he can understand that these are the tears of joy and this understanding involves in it the understanding of what is called joy. Joy can't be grasped as a situation that does not give joy. So the *bhakta's* experience that manifests in his involuntary responses is bound to influence anyone who is just open to him. A person can't be influenced by the *bhaktas'* involuntary responses only if he is nor attending those responses. Due to several reasons people can fail to attend *bhaktas'* voluntary responses in which their experience of divinity manifests. In general, this happens when our attention is drawn to something else or we just don't want to attend those responses due to certain preoccupation regarding our idea of divinity. A powerful response can easily draw anyone's attention. But if one is determined for not attending *bhaktas'* responses then with the power of one's will one can keep oneself away from it.

In normal condition if a *bhakta's* involuntary responses are powerful enough then one can't fail to notice them. By noticing them one comes to know what the *bhakta* is experiencing like. One can, then, understand the value of *bhakti* as an achievement. If the responses are powerful enough then one can have some idea of it's magnitude and depth of this valuable experience. But if the responses are more powerful than one's expectation then one feels deprived and demeaned before the *bhakta*. This is an understandable state of affairs. There is nothing very strange in it. Swami Prakashanda's feeling of regret is, therefore, quite intelligible a state of affair Lost in the smugness of his theoretical understanding of *Advaita Vedanta* he never expected that divinity (of his opinion) could manifest in *bhakti* of *saguòa* and *sâkâra*. Observing a powerful manifestation of divinity in the responses of Chaitanya's *bhakti* of Lord Krishna Swami Prakshananda was at once put to shame on the realization of his fault and felt how poor he was since he lacked the experience of divinity that he witnessed in Chaitanya. It is not strange if he was deeply touched by the responses of Chaitnya.

The effect of Chaitanya on Swami Prakashanda, if grasped the way it is presented in above discussion, gives us the insight of the actual force working behind *Bhakti* Movement. But the functioning of that force could be grasped only if *bhakti* is accepted to be a human experience of deep survival vale and also of achievement value. The story of Prakashananda's transformation into Prabodhananda – a disciple of Chaitanya indicates more towards the survival value since a change can be postponed in case of achievement value but it can't be postponed in case of survival value. One can live without something that is additional to living but one can't live without that which is necessary for existence. Whether Swami Prakashananda converted into Prabodhananda or not may be a matter of historical importance (in the sense that it would have influenced his followers also) but to understand the historical importance of this conversion it is necessary to accept the survival value of *bhakti* for human life.

Chaitanya's whole being was a sort of embodiment of living *bhakti*. The presence of Chaitanya was so powerful that it made people (especially to those people who gave no importance to *bhakti*) understand both of its values. A sort of intense attraction was felt by most people who came in his contact. This was the attraction the powerful experience of *bhakti* that manifested through the involuntary spontaneous responses reflecting in Chaitanya's personality. This attraction is found in the personality of all the *bhaktas* in some amount and is felt easily by any ordinarily sensitive person. A person, who is closed to this dimension of human experience, can and does ignore it ordinarily. But if this experience emerges in someone very powerfully then it becomes very difficult even for a closed person to ignore it. He may, then, deny the effect by rational argumentation but it will be very clearly felt by him. In

Chaitanya the force of attraction of *bhakti* was so big that it blasted the self-imposed restraint of many people

Swami Prakashananda's episode is of great importance but it is known more within the community of Chaitanya's disciples. The incident of Chand Kazi's transformation into a Krishna-*bhakta* is widely known by people outside that community also[3]. These incidents show the effect of *bhakti* at the level of ordinary human life. Denial of the effect of *bhakti* is, directly or indirectly, a denial of the fact that it is a human experience, which, like any other experience, affects the experiencer and others. Since this is an experience of divinity it has its distinct qualitative content. Its typical effect on the experiencer and others lies in its typical content. But that is so with all other human experiences. There is no reason to deny either that it is a human experience or that it affects the experiencer and others, if we don't deny that about other experiences. Such denial shows only an irrationally closed attitude of the people who hold such attitude. With any such irrational attitude we can't understand the actual nature of *Bhakti* Movement.

Jaideva's *bhakti* and Chaitanya's *bhakti* manifested different colours of the *bhakti* of Lord Sri Krishna. The way of life of love for the Lord that reflected in these *bhaktas'* life influenced people effectively because divinity was *seen* at the earthly level in *bhakti.* It was this feature that involved people completely gave them the vision and way to welcome and accept the people of lower caste and other faiths as brothers and sisters without any fear of the violation of divine injunctions prevailing from the times of Vedas. Neither Jaideva nor Chaitanya ever spoke a word against caste system; they, rather supported it, yet the way of their life showed how the cruelties and inequalities that are known features of a religio-social system disappears practically in *bhakti.* This was not the specialty of Krishna-*bhakti* only. It was shown in the life of Rama-*bhaktas* and in that of the saints who are known as the follower of *nirguṇa-upāsana.* Swami Ramamnanda, who preached only *bhakti*, proved its ethereal liberating and all-encompassing power through the life of his disciples. They (his disciples) not only belonged to different casts but also experienced divinity in and through the *bhakti* of either Sri Rama or Sri Kishna or of the formless embodiment of divinity referred to as *nirguṇa.*

Ramamnanda: His *Bhakti* and His Life

Ramananda's preaching of *bhakti* influenced the people of northern India in a very powerful manner. He was born in a brahmin family of Prayaga (now Allahabad). The time of Swami Ramananda is believed to be the end of 13th century A.D. It is not confirmed that he belonged to the *bhakti* tradition of Ramanujacharya but it is evident from the works that are ascribed to him by his disciples that he brought certain features of Rama *bhakti* from south.

In his *Ānanda Bhāṣya* Swami Ramananda has propounded the supremacy of *Saguṇa Brahma* and held Him as the efficient and material cause of the universe. He has established the duality of *jiva* and *Brahman* and held that *bhakti* is the only way to achieve *moksha.* It is important to note that Swami Ramananda has given an inferior place to *Nirguṇa Brahman* in comparison to *Nirguṇa Brahman.* Rama, for Swami Ramananda, is the supreme transcendent reality and He is essentially *saguṇa.* After creation and after its end *Brahman* remains in an un-manifest *nirguṇa* state This state is acquired by *saguṇa Brahaman* on will and it is withdrawn by His sheer will.

Swami Ramananda taught the path of *prapatti* (complete surrender) at the feet of Rama. *Prapatti* is the essence of *bhakti.* Complete surrender becomes possible only if the person gets *bhakti* for the Lord by His grace. Complete surrender is not an act that one can do Till the doer of the surrender remains a doer surrender can't be really *complete.* If one decides to surrenders oneself at the feet of the Lord one could offer oneself only partly since the part which does the act of offering is not being offered. Complete surrender could happen to someone but can't be done by him. It is a happening that occurs to some one very rarely. This happens only by the will and the grace of the Lord. In *prapatti* the will of Lord operates in the heart of the person in the form of intense desire to dissolve oneself at the feet of Lord and the awareness that this intense desire has aroused in his heart due to the will of Lord becomes the ecstatic experience of grace of Lord. This awareness, however, is not within the control of the person. This awareness itself is the gift of Lord to the person. The ecstasy of loosing oneself completely at the Lord's feet is the only aim of a *bhakta.* A *bhakta* enjoys *bahkti* at two levels: first, at the level of a deep unfathomable emotion (*bhâva*) and second, at the level of taste (*rasa*) of that emotion. Neither of the levels is attainable by the exercise of personal will because that becomes the hindrance. So the ecstasy of *bhakti bhâva* and that of *bhakti rasa* that the *bhakta* experiences are the proofs of presence of divinity in their hearts. *Prapatti* is the key to meet the Lord. So Swami Ramanand emphasized on it. His emphasis on the role of *prapatti* is not a demand from the *bhakatas* to do *prapatti.* We saw it is not a matter of *doing.* The emphasis on *prapatti* demands from the *bhaktas* to make themselves aware of the tricks of ego and to beg most earnestly from the Lord to take him in His refuge. Swami Ramananda did not denounce the '*varṇa* system' that had degenerated into the unjust and inhuman caste system. He never spoke against the prevailing social attitude regarding the superiority of brahmins but proved through his deeds that whosoever had got the gift of *prapatti* in Lord, was acceptable to him irrespective of his caste Raidas was a cobbler by caste, Kabir was a weaver and Sena was a tailor. Swami Ramananda accepted them all as his disciples. This apparent contradiction dissolved due to the power of love for the Lord that motivated him to do so. How this apparent contradiction dissolves—needs elaboration.

How is it possible for a person to accept the caste system with respect and also accept a person with love of the so-called low-caste? This question becomes further complicated by the consideration that the person, who respects caste system and is said to have accepted a person of low caste as his disciple, himself belongs to the priestly class.

A person, who belongs to upper caste by birth but does not like caste-system personally, can accept anyone as his disciple with full affection but in that case we can't say that he has respect for the caste system. It is not enough that he does not express his disrespect for the system. To have respect for caste system requires from a person to show respect for priestly class and to treat the persons of the fourth class (i.e. *sudras*) as inferior to all the three classes. If the person himself belongs to the priestly class then he should treat that person as inferior to himself in all social matters because that is a part of the practice of the system. The feeling of hatred or aversion to the person of lower caste is not necessary because that is an internal matter. Whether one feels hatred or aversion for the person of the lower class is not of much importance. But he must behave with him in a way that is deemed to be a treatment of giving lower status to that person. This is necessary for accepting any treatment as a mark of respect for the caste system.

An outsider, perhaps, can do both because the imperatives and injunctions are not obligatory for him. He may respect caste-system for some of his merits in his eyes. He may have affection for a person belonging to lower caste. He may have personal reasons for his affections for that person. Since he himself does not belong to any caste it is not obligatory on him to identify and treat that person essentially as a person of low origin and to treat him accordingly.

A person who belongs to the caste system can give respect to the system only if he treats the lower caste people as lower or inferior in social status. He may accept a person of lower caste as his disciple but may not give him affection. How is it possible for him to treat his disciple of a lower caste as a person of inferior origin and to give him affection too? It is a very delicate point and it ordinarily evades our attention. If treating one with as a person of lower origin necessarily implies a *feeling* of aversion for him then it is impossible for anyone to do both simultaneously. The question arises does this really imply? Apparently the answer seems to be positive but actually it is not so. Neither logically not practically there is any necessity for connecting a person's treatment showing that one belongs to lower origin to his feeling of aversion. To do the prior is a matter of observance of social behaviour and the later is a matter of person's internal feeling. We know that very often we perform several rituals and formalities without any feeling attached to that. Such formalities are deemed as true responses of formal courtesy. The absence of feeling does not necessarily mark the spirit of formality. After all the slogan of duty for duty sake does not involve the person's emotional involvement with his duty. It is, therefore, possible for a person (belonging to priestly caste) to treat a person of lower caste showing in his behaviour that he belongs to lower origin and simultaneously have a feeling of deep affection for him. There is nothing strange in it. It could be deemed as a matter of forced compromise either with the respect of caste system or with one's own feeling of affection. It may be son in some cases but it is not so in all cases. At least we can envisage this possibility without any logical contradiction or without any practical difficulty. We find number of examples in the history of Modern India also in which a Hindu treated one of his dear Muslim friends with great affection but observed all the restrictions in his behaviour that was imperative on him according to the Hindu traditional living of that age. Swami Ramananda had respect for the caste- system and observed in his behaviour all that was imperative on a Brahmin in his age but accepted the lower caste persons as his disciples with great affection. The logical and practical possibility of doing both is explained in the above paragraph. However, Swami Ramanand had another reason also that enabled him to do both simultaneously without contradiction. That reason is very important for understanding the nature of *Bhakti* and its impact on *Bhakti* Movement.

Bhakti is a transcendent phenomenon that occurs in the historicity of human experience. We ordinary people lead our life in historicity and end up with that. Transcendence supervenes in the historicity of human experience on very many places necessarily. This is a necessary feature of human life because life at the self-conscious stage essentially involves transcendence. We may, if like, notice the occurrence of transcendence in our day today life or we may no do that. Most of us waste our life without noticing the presence of transcendence. Anyone does some work in which self- consciousness is actively involved and in so doing, encounters the presence of transcendence in his life. A *bhakta* is a person who is deeply self- conscious. Transcendence manifests in his life and enriches him with the great wealth of divine ecstasy. As we have seen earlier also, a *bhakta* wants nothing accept the joy of *bhakti* itself. For him his Dear Lord is present in the very experience of His *bhakti*. For him that is the supreme value. Everything else may have value below that. Swami Ramananda was an *Âcârya* of *bhakti*. *Bhakti* of Lord was the greatest wealth for him. It is the wealth of transcendent divinity. His treatment of anything of the world of historicity was in accordance with his feeling of highest esteem for the transcendent divinity. For him the *varṇa* system was a manifestation of divine command in historicity. As such it was respectable for him. However, the presence of *bhakti* in anyone's heart was a proof of the presence of divinity irrespective of his caste. As such affection for anyone, who had *bhakti* in his heart, was a spontaneous response for Swami Ramananda. Body, caste etc. are the objects of mundane world where historicity reigns. At the level of historicity Swami Ramananda paid due respect to the laws regulating them. These laws where deemed to be manifestations of divine command but were regarded to operate the worldly life only. The presence of Bhakti in anyone's heart was the descend of Lord himself in the eyes of Swami Ramananda. This descend of transcendence in human heart is not for any worldly reasons; it is for elevating the *jeeva* from the level of historicity to the level of pure transcendence. A *bhakta* judges everything either transcendent or historical from the point of view of this pure transcendence only that operates in historicity but remains untouched by it. Since, it operates in and through historicity, a *bhakta* gives importance to the historical aspect of life but he does so only with the view to elevate himself and others from it. Swami Ramananda treated his disciples of lower caste such as Kabir, Raidas and Sena as people of inferior origin with respect to the priestly class but he had no feeling of aversion for them at all. In view of the fact that *Bhakta* Ramananda led a life of transcendent divinity in historicity, we can understand that there was no reason for a feeling of aversion in his heart, for his disciples, despite his overt treatment to them as inferiors. This peculiarity has to be underlined for understanding *bhakti* in the practical life of man and it is more important to understand this feature to grasp the actual spirit of *Bhakti* Movement.

The *bhâva* of *bhakti* affects the person and others who are in his surrounding. Any other emotion does the same. But the emotion of love for the Lord influences the person and others in some special way. In this *bhâva* the person experiences the transcendence and the same is transmitted to others. Historicity becomes the base on which transcendence lands. Transcendence gives a new importance to historicity when it descends in it. In *bhakti bhâva* the person experiences the transcendence and the historical conditions in which it descends on human heart, acquires a new historical significance with it touch. Caste- system also got a new historical significance with the touch of *bhakti.* Without the touch of *bhakti* caste- system was nearly a degenerated form of *varṇa*-system. It was proving to be oppressive and dehumanizing. Some enlightened souls started speaking against it. The saints of *Nâtha*- Sect spoke aloud against caste-system. But as it was stated earlier, believed as a divine ordain it bounced on the *Nâtha* saints themselves and made them loose their popularity amidst the Hindus. *Bhakti* on the other hand, respected and maintained the caste- system but enabled the spread of transcendence. This effect of *bhakti* was not theoretical. People actually felt that the *bhaktas* and especially Swami Ramananda brought a palpable message of divine, despite their respect for caste-system. People got a new insight to lead life according to caste-system without necessarily oppressing or demeaning others. This was the strongest reason for the popularity of *bhakti* as a movement. This feature is hardly given any due concentration in the discussion of *bhakti* or *Bhakti* Movement. *Bhakti* would not have become a movement had it not shown this feature. The *Nâthas* and Buddhists rose strongly against the old Hindu orthodoxy and lost their popularity very soon. *Bhakti* could have met the same fate too if it had not proved its power to encompass the orthodox with the unorthodox. Ramananda's life of *bhakti* and his work that spread through his great disciples proved this divine power of *bhakti.*

Kabir: His *Bhakti* and His Life

Kabir- the disciple of Ramananda, is perhaps the most unique *bhakta.* In a sense he is not a *bhakta* since he does not worship Lord in any form. He is the follower of the path of *nirguṇa.* Kabir was the most powerful saint of 15th century A.D. who showed his revolutionary spirit in the normal sense of the term and suffered a lot for that. The revolutionary spirit of Kabir highlighted by the authors and historians of *Bhakti* Movement to an extent that his image transforms into a revolutionary of socio-economic cause. It is not clear how far this image of Kabir is true but it is certainly false that he was a secular- minded person with an agenda of social reform.

Kabir was not an atheist despite his following the path of *nirguṇa upāsnā*. He was perhaps the first illiterate saint who talked about *nirguṇa,* which is ordinarily talked of by Great Sanskrit *Âcâryas. Bhakti*, which is ordinarily deemed to be the path of idol or form worship, was not the path of Kabir. Yet, he was a *bhakta* because his path was the path of love for the Lord. This point is very important to understand Kabir as Kabir. Several couplets of Kabir are popular which prove this point. [4]

The abstract notion of *nirguṇa Brahman* is too intangible to be grasped and accepted by common folk. But the *nirguṇa* of Kabir gained wide popularity. This is a point to be noted for understanding Kabir's *bhakti.* It is held by the historians that path of Kabir was a mixture of several effects like that of Siddhas, Sahajayanis and *Bhaktas.* Although the path of self- realization ultimately gives an encompassing vision to the follower of the path, a rational reconciliation of various paths can hardly be a path of actual self-realization. One should not forget that Kabir had taken the initiation into Rama-*Mantra* by Swami Ramananda. This can be taken as a strong proof of the fact that Kabir was a follower of *Bhakti* Path. The object of his *bhakti* was not a Personal God like Krishna or Rama. The Rama of Kabir was not the Rama of Tulsidas literally. However, his *nirguṇa Brahma* was not merely an abstract principle nor was it the *Śunyatā* of Buddhism. His *Sunna Mandal* also is different from that *Śunyatā.*

There was something in the heart of Kabir. That *something* was the experience of that which is experienced by the *bhaktas* as *bhakti* or pure emotional love for their Lord. Kabir himself admits the supreme importance of love in attaining knowledge of transcendent formless *Brahmn*[5]. *Bhakti*—the experience of emotional attraction towards an image of God gives the *bhakta* an awareness of the powerful presence of what is referred to as — 'Holy', 'Divine' etc. The experience of 'Divine' is also an experience of eternal present. It would more appropriate to say that the experience of eternal present (without past or future) is an essential aspect of what is felt as divine. A *bhakta* experiences the presence of his dear Lord (Who is an embodiment of all divine attributes) and the ecstasy of contact with Lord leaves that content of present in his awareness as the only object (of awareness). Apart from that ecstatic present his sense of time (running from past into future) is lost completely. It is explained earlier that a *bhakta* very soon comes to understand that the presence of his dear Lord manifests not only in the form but also in the background in which the form becomes visible. He also understands that the very law of figure and background is also a manifestation of the will of the Lord. Certainly, manifestation of Lord in the fundamental laws operating in experience of form cannot itself be a form; it has to be formless. However, that formless is very positive presence of Lord since it is the positive manifestation of Lord's will. This experience of the positive presence of Lord is equally ecstatic and timeless. This timeless presence of divinity is achieved by *bhakti-* the love of Lord. It can be attained by other means also but *bhakti* also is a way to attain this experience. Kabir achieved the experience of *nirguṇa brahma* through this way. The Rama of Kabir is not the Rama in human form but it is the transcendent *nirguṇa brahma* in the above sense. Kabir is a bhakta because he is in love with this *nirguṇa brahma.* His response to *nirguṇa brahma* is the response of a lover- a mature lover. He has emotional relation with it although this emotion manifests in his overt behavioural responses somewhat differently from that of the *bhaktas* of *Saguṇa brahma*. The *bhakta* of *Saguṇa brahma* maybe found to be weeping and crying loudly as an outburst of love of Lord. The *bhakta* of *nirguṇa brahma* also experiences the love of the Lord but he does not weep or cry overtly. It would be completely wrong to think that the *bhakta* of *Saguòa brahma* are hypocrites or pretentious, or the *bhakta* of *nirguṇa brahma* is insensitive. It would also be wrong to value one and demean another. Both are the experiences of love for transcendence and the fact that they are having it is intelligible (conceptually as well as practically) to them and others also. It would be very different from the situation when the persons have the plain experience of divinity without any emotional attachment with it. Whether it is possible or not is a different question all together (perhaps the answer is negative). Sharply contrasted to this later situation (at least at the level of conceptual possibility it can be envisaged) it can be said that Kabir was also in love with Lord (The Supreme Divine Person). To say that he was not in love with Lord in his *nirguṇa brahma* nature, would amount to put his position beyond intelligibility. Love for the Lord in his *saguṇa* and *sâkâra* nature is itself *saguṇa* and *sâkâra,* i.e. manifested in overt behaviour also. So a putative *bhakta* weeps, cries, sings and dances in the love of the Lord. *Saguòa Bhakti* is that form of in which it emerges in the heart of the *bhakta* as a strong feeling of attraction for the Supreme Divine Person and it spontaneously involves his overt behaviour also. *Saguṇa* bhakti means the feeling of love for the divine that manifests through the palpable qualities (*guṇas*) of *bhakta's* behaviour. Contrasted with it *nirguṇa bhakti* means the feeling of attraction for the Supreme Divine Person that does not manifest in the palpable qualities of *bhakta's* behaviour. Hence, the bhakta of *nirguṇa* does not feel like weeping and crying and dancing in high excitement. Since, he does not feel like that he may think that doing such things in the love of Lord is unnecessary and hypocritical. But if we understand the heart of *saguṇa bhakta* then we can't accept this opinion as true. However, our understanding would help us resist passing a judgment against the *nirguṇa bhakta's* opinion about the *saguṇa bhaktas* because we know that it is but natural for him to form such an opinion. Kabir's dislike for expression of love for the divine in overt behaviour must be seen in this light. His dislike for explicit manifestation of *bhakti* in overt behaviour is a result of his deep love for the *nirguṇa* nature of the Supreme Divine Being. It is; therefore, appropriate to say that Kabir was also a *bhakta.*

Understanding Kabir as a *bhakta* in the light of above discussion does not only emancipate us from many misgivings regarding *bhakti* but also discloses a new aspect of it. Whosoever came in the contact of Kabir felt that his attention was deeply pulled inwardly towards a formless locus of divinity. This pull was clearly non-rational in character and was felt by all who came in contact-whether they were his opponents or followers. An additional dimension of *bhakti* was disclosed on common folk. People could understand that the divine pull that they feel in their daily life on witnessing many events of love, compassion and sacrifice in and around them is also a specimen of the pull that the *bhakta* feels in his heart for the Lord. A life of simplicity in which the ritualistic worship is absent also becomes the life of *bhakti* if the person feels an emotional pull towards the divine. The emotional inward pull is the characteristic feature of the life of *bhakti.* Even if this pull is not directed towards any tangible image of the Lord it is a *bhakti* for him. It would be important to note at this juncture that an inner pull felt by the *nirguṇa* saints like Kabir was non- rational in character. It was not the kind of attraction or pull that one feels towards the argument of theory of the person who has defeated his opponent in intellectual duel. Hardly any intellectual came in contact with illiterate Saint Kabir. His presence and his words enthralled and enchanted the people around him. His *sâkhis* also left the same effect on the people. His words leave an emotional spell on the listener. Needless to say that it is the influence of *bhakti* and not of rational consistency.

Kabir's words could influence common folk because it essentially carried with it an emotional power. The kind of scientific rationality that is ascribed to Kabir by some modern historians is not very helpful to understand his influence on the masses. Common people are never influenced largely by reason but they can very easily be influenced by emotion. Kabir's over all influence over the masses support more the view that his words carried with them an emotional influence.

It would not be wrong to say that Kabir was a *bhakta* and not a *jnâni.* This statement should not be misinterpreted in the backdrop of an assumed confrontation between *bhakti* and *jnân*. In a sense there is a confrontation between the two and in another sense there is not confrontation between them at all. Given this condition we must clearly understand that in the former sense Kabir was a *bhakta* who is contrasted to a *jnâni,* but in the latter sense he was both. With Kabir the socio- religious awareness that was gathering force became much stronger. The caste-system and ritualistic way of life that was given a central place in Hinduism lost its hold over the people due to the influence of Jaidev, Chaitanya and Ramananda and it was further emaciated with the *nirguṇa bhakti* of Kabir.

Guru Nanak; His Life and His Work

Nanak was born in Talwandi (now know as Nankana Sahib) in 1469 A.D. Guru Nanak's life is well known as the founder of Sikhism. The movement that was gathering force in different parts of India in the form of *Bhakti* Movement grew as a new faith in the northwestern India. Sikhism evolved from Hinduism in the sense that Guru Nanak Dev was born in a Hindu family, and also in the sense that despite the presence of several features of Islam in it, it was never recognized as a branch of Islam. In the teachings of Guru Nanak Dev the philosophy of *Viśiştadwaita* reflects clearly. However, the discrimination on the basis of caste and ritualistic brahmanical form of worship was given no place in it.

The teaching of Guru Nanak Dev apparently gives an impression that he was a preacher of *jnâna mârg.* As it is said earlier *jnâna* and *bhakti* are not opposed to each other in one sense. If we follow that sense that then the above statement has no relevance at all. But in another sense in which the two are opposite it is not only relevant but also necessary to underline that the path that Guru Nanaka showed to his disciples is not against the emotional surrender before the Supreme Person (Lord.). A heart filled with love for the Supreme Person can embrace everyone with due respect for their faith. This feature is abundantly found in Guru Nanak's teaching and he proved it practically in his life too. A theoretical reconciliation can't have this feature.

Guru Nanak's teaching and his life added a very special dimension to the movement generated by *bhakti.* Guru Nanak himself led a life of a *grihastha* (one who leads family life) and instructed clearly to his *śişyas* or *sikhas* (literally means disciples) do so. Although many of his predecessors also led a family life and did not take *sanyâs* but many of them did that. They preferred to remain involved in the *bhakti* of their Lord uninterrupted away from the disturbing duties and activities of family life. Guru Nanaka put curb on this tendency. He did not allow his *sikhas* to become *sanyâsins*. It is evident from the fact that one of his sons Srichanda, who followed the path of *śanyâs,* had to sesparate himself from the community of the *sikhas*. He was also an enlightened soul and some people followed him. His path is known as '*Udâsî*'. However, Guru Nanaka never allowed his *sikhas* to do that. The reason is very important. Transcendent Divinity that descends in human experience in *bhakti* needed its manifestation in and through the gross mundane level of human life. The sublimity and the ahistoricity of *bhakti* can manifest, survive and give strength to the in the *bhakta* in the thick of the family responsibilities and pure worldly activities. This truth was proved by Guru Nanak by raising the community of his *sikhas*. The power of divinity is a real power that not only helps the person to face the difficult situations of human life but also transforms every act into an act of worship and prayer. This transformation culminates in the acts of supreme heroic sacrifice without fear to establish those divine qualities that make human beings truly human.

In the life of Guru Nanak *bhakti* established its connection with human action. Divinity unfolded the connection of *bhakti* with *jnâna* in the life of saints like Kabir. In the life of Guru Nanak divinity of man unfolded its connection with all his actions. This statement needs clarification.

Knowledge, emotion and action are inseparably connected to each other in every human beings life.. Knowledge of the situation arouses emotions in man and manifests in his actions. In this sense Kabir's *bhakti* that seemed to manifest directly through his *jnâna* also translated itself into his actions. The typical way of life of Kabir essentially follows from his *nirguṇa bhakti.* However, through the teaching and life of Nanak *bhakti* entered the mundane historically conditioned will of his disciples and transformed it into divine will. A *bhakta* knows that his freedom of will is a valuable gift that is given to him by his Lord. He understands that his Lord has given him and everyone the power to choose freely among available options. One who is not *bhakta* chooses anything either for his own personal gain or in the light of his principle that covers everyone within the scope of its application. In any case the choice is guided by mundane conditions. A *bhakta* becomes aware of the fact that his power to will is a gift of Lord. He finds that in his desire for love of Lord also this power is operating. This desire withdraws his attention from all mundane affairs and directs it towards the very content the experience of love. The manifestation of Lord's will may take a different form also. Instead of withdrawing the attention of the person from the mundane affair and directing it to the love of Lord it may manifest in the awareness of the fact that even in the will to perform a mundane action Lord's will is operating. This awareness brings about a qualitative change in the nature of will to perform the action. Because of this change the will to act for anything mundane is *felt* to be operated by divine will. In this changed situation person's ego does not remain the motivating force of action that ordinarily functions behind any such actions. The action performed is drastically changed due to this changed situation that arises due to the feeling of divine will operating in mundane actions. Either the action is impeded or stopped or expedited. All that was done earlier for the sake of satisfaction of the ego earlier looses its force. That which is done not for the sake of ego but for spreading the love for the Lord gets increased and accelerated. Every ordinary action, thus, transforms into a worship or prayer. This situation occurs in some *bhakta's* life. Withdrawal from the mundane and turning of *bhakta's* attention towards experience of love for Lord is an experience of *bhakti* but feeling the presence of Lord's will operating in all mundane actions also is an experience of *bhakti.* In the life of Guru Nanak *bhakti* took this latter form. Guru Nanak taught this very form of *bhakti* to his *Sikhs.* In his successors this form of *bhakti* became more and more distinct. The action-oriented nature of Sikhism is constituted basically by this form of *bhakti.* Other geographical and historical factors prevailing around Punjab was the not the reason for the emergence of a new religion in the form of Sikhism. Geographical and historical reasons generate political awareness. They cannot be the reason for spiritual enlightenment. *Bhakti* that descended in the heart of Guru Nanak illumined the world in and around him with divine light. It was natural for him and his successors to choose a course of action that was completely in accordance with the perception of the world that they attained in divine illumination. The heroic sacrifices of many Gurus were the natural manifestation of this divine manifestation. In the life of Guru Nanak and his successor Gurus, divine power that manifested in the experience of the *bhakta's* life proved its real historical effects very clearly. It would be ridiculous to interpret Sikhism on any material lines. The spark of divine light emanated from the personalities of the Gurus and dazzled the whole world.

With the life of Guru Nanak and other Gurus the period of *Bhakti* Movement is deemed to be over historically. Hardly any historian believes that the force of that movement kept working down the centuries and showed its presence in the life of Sri

Aurobindo and Mahatma Gandhi till the end of nineteenth century. A few facts about the working of this force would be presented latter in this discussion. Before that a synoptic look of the life and *bhakti* of the saints of western and southwestern parts of India will be presented.

The Life and Bhakti of Other Saints

In the southern and southwestern parts of India many *bhaktas* spread the message of *bhakti* through their teachings and life. The names of all these *bhaktas* are not known to all of us. Many of them were the sons of the soil and they are known only in the oral tradition of the locality. The importance of these unknown *bhaktas* cannot be undermined just because their names are not recorded in the books of history. The actual living of the people was influenced by them. It is difficult to even innumerate the name of them all. For the purpose of our present discussion only the lives of a few well-known *bhaktas* would be presented now.

In a small village called Narsi Baini near Hyderabad the well-known saint, Namdev was born in thirteen century A.D. He is the revered *bhakta* amidst all the *bhaktas* of Maharashtra but his influence spread up to north east of India and Punjab also. He was the *bhatka* who witnessed the presence of divine in all the objects and events of the world. Every event in his view was a grace of God. Once a part of his hut caught fire and he started shouting with delight that with this he will be relieved from the duty of cleaning the hut and wished that the whole of the hut should be burnt. It is said that by the end of the night not only the fire was extinguished by itself but also the whole hut was set right. This may appear to be an exaggeration and also an assertion of miracle but it is explained in the above discussion that, it is neither. It does not make much difference whether this incident actually happened or not but the stated response of Namdev is a matter of great importance for understanding *bhakti* and its effect on the people. He led a life of complete dedication to Lord. Remembering the name of Lord, ceaselessly, was his worship to Lord that he performed doing all sorts of activities of day-to-day life. Namdev, who saw this world in the light of *bhakti*, denounced the ritualistic pomp and shows of worship. Whosoever came in his contact or listened his hymns was enchanted by the presence of divine in his heart. Namdev's life and his *bhakti* left a lasting effect on all the *bhaktas* and social reformers of Maharashtra.

Tukaram, another *bhakta* born in Maharashtra is highly respected in the well-known saints of Maharashtra. Tukaram was born in a low caste family and was a worshipper of Lord *Vithovâ*. *Vithovâ* is known as a form of Lord Sri Krishna. Tukaram's life and *bhakti* gave a living message to the people that experience of divine in *bhakti* is possible to all and it is not restricted by the barriers of caste. Maharashtra, where the feeling of caste and the disparity between upper and lower caste was so acute, the message of Tukaram proved to be revolutionary. He awakened the people against their dogmatic rigidity and dehumanizing practices in the name of caste.

Gujarat, the western part of India has the pride of giving birth to the father of the nation, Mahatma Gandhi. Mahatma Gandhi, the saint turned politician or the politician turned saint (whatever we like to accept) had something very deeply saintly in him, which he inherited from the saints of his land. Narsi Mehta's influence on Gandhi is very clear. Narsi Mehta was born in the Junagarah town of Kaṭhiawad. He was a *bhakta* of Sri Krishna. He wanted to remain engrossed completely in the ecstatic joy of *bhakti*. He was not a *sanyâsin*. He led a family life and many events of his life are suffused with miracles. These episodes of miracles state how divine presence actively operates in a *bhakta's* life.

Narsi Mehta was a *Vaişņava* (the worshipper of Lord Vishnu) and in that sense he was a worshipper of *saguņa brahma*. However, his *Vaişņavism* is defined in his very popular devotional song in a way that does not give any impression of idol worship at all[6]. It does not mean to say that he was not an idol worshipper or against it, it means that the narrow sense of idol worship that is wrongly imposed on the *bhaktas* was never the spirit of any living *bhakta*. The *bhaktas,* who worshipped the Lord in his *saguņa* nature, loved the attributes and form of the Lord very much; they were infatuated by them but never thought that their Dear Lord has these qualities in concrete physical form. It is this attraction for these enchanting sublime qualities that manifested in the song of Narsi Das. The life and *bhakti* of *bhakta* Narsi Mehta influenced the people of Gujarat deeply and its fragrance spread beyond the boundaries of that state also.

The Movement of *Bhakti* Still Continues

The definition of history as the study of the records of past event is an outdated definition. History nowadays is regarded as the observation of the forces arising from the past and functioning in the present also to give direction to human civilization. Adopting the spirit of this definition it would not be wrong to see the functioning of the force in present that arose in the early fourteenth, fifteenth century A.D. or even before that. It would be very difficult indeed to pinpoint the initial period of the beginning of this force. Even if it is admitted that the period of Narad Bhakti Sutra and other Sutras is not very old we can trace the seeds of bhakti in Ramayana and Mahabharata, which are regarded to be the oldest epics of Sanskrit after the Vedas. It is very difficult to pinpoint the period of beginning of *bhakti* but to confine the period of the functioning of the force of *bhakti* only till the end of fifteenth century does not seem to be quiet reasonable. The force that was working till the end of fifteenth century in the life of Guru Nanak, Kabir and others, is still visibly working in and around us. Saints of modern age of India like Sri Ramakrishna Paramhamsa and SwamiVivekananda, Sri Ramana Maharishi, Sri Aurobindo and many others are the living proofs of this fact. This force of *bhakti* that was giving new shape and order to the society in and through the life of Sawmi Ramananda, Kabir and others was also seen to be giving martial power to the Sikh Gurus to fight against the tyrannical powers. The same force was felt by Sri Aurobindo and by Mahatma Gandhi, which we know, gave a decisive direction to the Indian freedom struggle. It is not the purpose of this chapter or this book to relate a history of modern India from the point of view of the force of *bhakti* operating behind it. That is a very serious task and can be undertaken by someone. For our present purpose it would be sufficient to indicate that Sri Aurobindo's active participation in freedom movement did not yield much fruit but after his self-exile in Pondicherry, where he lived a life of yogi, his participation in the same movement at the spiritual level contributed heavily to bring the movement at a fruitful end.

His declaration on 15th August 1947from All India Radio about the coincidence of this date with his birth date describes what he actually saw at the Supra Mental level of consciousness. Except for the devotees of Sri Aurobindo and The Mother other people generally don't take this statement seriously. Sri Aurobindo also made several statements which are purely about the political situation of the world and that of India but these statements sprung from the Supramental state of consciousness that he used to attain in meditation and which illumined his mind and transformed his body too. Due to our apathy to understand seriously anything above physical realm we are easily tempted to accept all such talks as irrational and dismiss them without due consideration. It is pointed out many times in earlier discussion that this attitude is irrational and we should remain alert of this sort of deeper irrationality that surreptitiously keep operating in our life and make us miss many valuable experiences. With this much understanding about the truth of any statement that it is proved either true or false within a particular domain of discourse and can't be rationally either accepted or dismissed without doing so. The truth of Sri Aurobindo's statements regarding political conditions of our national and that of the world is to be tasted in the realm of Supramental state of human consciousness. The physical consequences of these truths can be observed at the ordinary psychic level of individual consciousness also if the individual is not under any influence against these truths in advance.

Sri Aurobindo: His Life and His *Yoga*

Sri Aurobindo's life and his message gives a clear indication of the continuous functioning of the Divine will force in human life for its evolution into the higher states of consciousness. He is of the view that this evolution can't take that mechanical course that it had taken till the state of development of self-consciousness. Beyond the state of self-consciousness (which is the state of evolution of individual mind) evolution is not possible without an active involvement of the individuals. Individuals have to prepare themselves for this further evolution by actively engaging themselves in all round growth of body and mind and by opening them for the descend of Supramental force with the sense of complete surrender before it so that it can come down and transform them from mortal creatures to a divine immortal soul. Active involvement of the individual in the form of complete surrender is the essence of Sri Aurobindo's Integral Yoga. In the Integral Yoga of Sri Aurobindo the traditional *Jnâna, Bhakati* and *Karma Yoga* all are combined. It would not be correct to say that this path of Yoga is identical with, or even similar to that of Chaitanaya or Jaidev but it would be equally incorrect to admit that a non-rational acceptance of the divine foundation of all existence is basis of Sri Aurobindo's Integral Yoga. His own life also as a yogi and his attraction – a psychic pull, towards the Super-mind is the reason and motivation for this acceptance. To call Sri Aurobindo a *bhakta* may sound very strange initially but in the light of understanding *bhakti* as a non-rational attraction (that is felt ordinarily as an emotional pull) towards the Supreme Divine Person helps us in seeing a point of significance in it. By Super-mind Sri Aurobindo refers to a transcendent timeless reality that is not material but a state of consciousness above the known state of self-consciousness and it is the seat of infinite knowledge and power of will. What else is the *bhaktas'* Lord (Supreme Divine Person)? An emotional attraction for an image of the Lord is a form of *bhakti* but that is not the only form in which it manifests. We have reached an understanding of *bahkti* as stated above. From this understanding seeing in Sri Aurobindo a continuation of *Bhakti* Movement is not a forced imposition of *bhakti* on a *yogi.* It would be rather an injustice to him. If we dont admit it.

Sri Aurobindo was an activist earlier. He was an activist later also. His activism manifested first as a revolutionary. He wanted to achieve freedom for his country earlier. For that he had adopted the path of armed revolution. But this desire was basically a desire for the freedom of human consciousness from the shackles of materiality and to help it to evolve into its Supramental state. This desire manifested in his life as a yogi. This desire was not an unconscious escape from the shadows of his earlier desire in which he apparently failed. Love for the Motherland and the desire of freedom for it neither died nor suppressed in his later life as a yogi. It only got a broader and stronger base for fulfillment and got combined with the vision of truth regarding the fundamental divine nature of all existence. Both the important elements were absent earlier in his life as a putative revolutionary. He had to make his important contribution in the freedom struggle in a more significant way. A great historical moment of decisive importance had arrived for both –for the people of the world and for the people of his Motherland. World was facing world war and India–the war of independence. His contribution for both would have been negligible if he had stuck up to the ordinary path of political revolution. He might have gained fame but the more important task would have been left incomplete. A big battle between the forces of darkness and light, which physically also manifested in the shape of world war, was going on in that period. Sri Aurobindo witnessed it in his meditation and contributed forcefully in the favour of light, life and goodness[7].

Mahatma Gandhi- His Life and His Work

Very little is common between Sri Aurobindo and Gandhi. Gandhi, from the very beginning was a follower of non- violence. Sri Aurobindo, on the other hand, did not initially believe in the philosophy of non-violence for the freedom of India from British rule. Despite these apparent dissimilarities both contributed heavily not merely for the political freedom of their motherland but for the liberation of mankind form the oppression of evil forces that functioned within and without, and for this both made themselves the tool of divine will. That divine will, which manifests in the form of *bhakti* in the heart of the *bhakta* and brought significant changes in the life of the people around them, also manifested in the shape of a political movement in Gandhi's life.

Gandhi belonged to the land of Narsi Mehta who was a well-known *bhakta* and who had already defined *bhakti* in terms of realization of higher virtues in human life. Both the parents of Mohandas Gandhi were deeply religious and that left lasting impression in his heart and head. The importance of truth in life was got by him by heart at a very young age when he witnessed the play- Satya Harishchandra. Needless to say that if a young child learns a lesson of truth from 'Harishchandra', his idea of truth can never be theoretical in the sense of being non-religious. His growth from a young boy to a college going youth and then an educated young man aspiring for the degree of 'Bar at law' in England consistently shows a growth of divine will in his heart. His autobiography and other biographies also make it clear that his life was being shaped by an unknown force to become a concrete model for the manifestation of divine will power. In the situations, which can definitely inspire a young man to take revenge from the race, which humiliates him, he learnt the lesson of tolerance. In the situations of explicit physical assault and social humiliations he looked for his inner strength to retaliate it in a befitting manner without adopting the evil means. *Satyâgraha* that he put into practice for the first time in South Africa against the British policy of apartheid was never thought of by anyone in the 20th century. How this thought came to his mind and remained not merely a thought but turned into a mass mobilizing force- deserves serious consideration. Can we ascribe it to the socio-political situation of the time? Can this type of ascription give us a satisfactory answer? There is an easy option, which is adopted by some people, to accept that Gandhi was a very cunning politician who knew how to use religious forces for achieving political aims. Again the question arises-can we really accept this? A cunning politician is bound to be an ambitious fellow whose motivation is only the seat of political and administrative power. This ambition was completely absent in Gandhi's life.

It is simpler; even if it is not easier for many of us, to accept that the divine force was working in the life of Gandhi and made him do what he did. Not only his life but also his death gave this message very clearly despite the fact that his dream to get an undivided independent India was not fulfilled. The divine will that pulls the *bhaktas* attention towards itself and manifests in various forms was also working in the heart of Gandhi. At any phase of his political life, his political activity was never merely political. His actions always sprung from his deep faith in God. How can we understand the nature of his faith if we think that faith is something constructed by human thought? He used to chant the *Râma Nâm* but he hardly ever worshipped the idol of *Râma*- the bow wielder. Bhagwad Gita was always his guide and his source of inspiration but we don't know whether he did anything that the worshippers of Lord Krishna used to do. His interpretation of Gita that he practiced in his life is not theoretical. His chanting of *Râma Nâm* was an actual remembering of the name of the divine from the core of his heart and it was proved undoubtedly at the moment of his death. It is very difficult to find an event of Mahatma Gandhi either from his personal life or from his political life that did not spring from his unshakeable faith in God. It would be mere repetition to say that Gandhi's faith in God is not theoretical or rational because faith cannot be so. Faith is nothing but another way of describing the situation of the *bhakta's* heart that feels a deep non-rational pull towards the divine and gets the evidence of divine in the very experience of that pull. In this sense there is no difficulty in accepting Gandhi as a *bhakta*.

India's freedom struggle cannot be separated from the life of Mahatma Gandhi. The life of Mahatma Gandhi was a life of a man of true and deep religious faith. Deep religious faith is another name of *bhakti*. Therefore, it follows almost logically that the life of Mahatma Gandhi was the life of *bhakta*. Whosoever, came in the contact of Mahatma Gandhi also felt the presence of divine will in his heart. Person's whose life was completely in politics, they also felt it very often and got disturbed. Common people felt the presence of divinity in him more clearly and got easily captivated by his simple and unscholarly words. The great impact on common Indian people, most of whom lived in the villages, were mobilized by Mahatma Gandhi because of the functioning of divine will that flew through his words and personality without any resistance. Thousands of students left the colleges and could not complete there education ever just on the one call of Mahatma Gandhi. Women of India, who were taught for centuries to remain inside home and do the domestic duties only came out in huge number forgetting all their restrictions. Even the British rulers were startled over his influence over Indian people. Some of them bowed their heads before him in reverence and some of them saw in him the spirit of a true and devout Christian. The fearlessness of Mahatma Gandhi that made him stand erect against the most powerful rulers of the world at that time and which made him write and open letter to Hitler advising him to turn away from his inhuman deeds cannot be said a human power of virtue if we do not include divinity in the essential meaning of humanity. His works of social reform truly bear the spirit of the *bhaktas* who did not theoretically denounce the age-old system of caste but never did anything dehumanizing, Mahatma Gandhi also never refuted caste-system but stood firm against untouchability and fought a war against it till the end of his life.

Bhakti dwells in the heart of the *bhaktas* and makes his heart the abode of divine on earth. With the presence of *bhakti* some *bhaktas* are motivated to choose one course of action and some others are motivated to choose another. Some course of action appears to be socially relevant in view of the social situation of a period. When some *bhaktas,* motivated by the divine force of their *bhakti,* choose such a course of action then they become famous as great social reformers but they do not actually have an agenda of social reform in their head. In this respect they must be contrasted with all the social reformers of secular mind. On the other hand those who choose that course of action, which is not apparently seen as socially important then they are not given any credit for social reform and revered only as saints within a particular religious community. In the light above discussion regarding the nature of *bhakti* and its various manifestations in human life, it is clear that what *bhakta* feels gets necessarily translated into his spontaneous behaviour and action. *Bhakti* can never be a compartment of human life. It emerges in the very foundation of his being, gives him overwhelming joy at a psychic level, and brings about a qualitative change in his spontaneous responses and gets translated necessarily in some of his deliberate actions. Divine force of will that manifests in and though *bhakti* is the very basis of human existence and when it descends in human heart it involves his whole being, his thought, his words and his action. Those actions are *bhakta's,* which appear to be not of direct social relevance, such as dancing and singing of Chaitanya, innocent activities of Sri Ramakrishna Paramhams or in the silent sitting of Sri Raman Maharishi, also have a deep social importance. In and through the life of these saints people get awareness of another dimension of human life, which is as social and public as any other social activities are. As the aesthetic joy of watching a beautiful performance of dance is very much objective and public, the joy of *bhakti* also is objective and public. Every individual feels the ecstasy of an art performance individually, but that does not make either the performance or the joy, private. Similarly, the ecstasy of the *bhakti* is felt by the *bhakta* in whose heart it emerges, there is nothing private about it. An art performance may have a social message in it but apart from that it gives the message to the people about an atemporal dimension of their life. This latter message is not less important socially, since it internally inspires people to rise above the limitations of materiality. This message is very clearly and distinctly given in the experience of *bhakti* and this message is not merely an inspiration but becomes the transformation of the *bhakta* and all others who understand the feelings of the *bhakta.*

If human beings are merely the lumps of material sorts, then there is nothing wrong in acknowledging this truth. However, if one single individual on earth evinces the descend of divinity in his heart in the form of *bhakti,* then every other individual is equally entitled to achieve it. Not to achieve it would be a matter of incomponsable loss to every individual, in particular and the whole of humanity, in general. Whether we give due consideration to this truth or not shows only our level of understanding human life. The fact of the great loss remains the same and cannot become less if we are ignorant of it or do not want to pay attention to it. *Bhakti* is a divine gift. It descended on many individuals' hearts and still overwhelms many among us. Our ignorance of the divine dimension of human life cannot compensate for this great loss. A serious attention is needed to understand the importance of *bhakti* in human life. This understanding alone can help us understand the nature and actual importance of *Bhakti* Movement.

Kṛṣṇa! *Bhakti* is everything for a *bhakta.* He does not want anything more than *bhakti* and cannot be satisfied with anything less than *bhakti.* In fact for a *bhakta, bhakti* is as valuable for him as his dear Lord is. Nothing can be more valuable than the Lord but that which manifests his Lord cannot be less valuable for him than Lord himself. A humble attempt is made in the preceding chapters to understand *bhakti* the way *bhakta* understands it. The attempt is not yet complete. In fact it cannot ever be completely complete. This work begins with an effort to dispel some common misgivings regarding *bhakti.* It then proceeded to take into consideration some of the important aspects of *bhakta's* life, which are influenced by his love of Lord, directly. At the end the object of *bhakta's* love-*Bhagvân* gave his glimpse as the soul centre of *bhakta's* world and also the centre of all the worlds- possible as well as actual. Many more questions and issues are to be addressed to understand the extension of *bhakti* in various dimensions of life. Each issue requires to be dealt with separately in as much length as the length of this work. Obviously they would figure separately if Lord wills. Here, at the end, only a few things are to be put forth which could not be given enough space in the earlier discussions.

Bhakti and Reason

Repeatedly it is said in the earlier discussion that *bhakti* itself is a gift of Lord. It is stated that no emotion can be aroused just on will and *bhakti,* which is a very delicate and high level of emotion, cannot be aroused by any effort or technique at all. Until God will no one can have the divine emotional attraction for Him. An emotional attraction for the Lord is not the result of any human action but it is one of the finest rewards that Lord has given to his dear ones. Two questions arise about this issue.

First, if *bhakti* is a gift of Lord, is not Lord blameworthy for not giving it equally to all human beings? Prima faci a negative reply can be readily prompted by the *bhakta*. However, the manner of this negative reply would depend on the intention with which the question is posed. If it is posed by a person with a heart filled with pain that he is not fortunate enough the feel of Lord then the reply is negative in the sense that the presence of pain in the questioner's heart shows that he has got the love for the Lord. Who can ask this question, who can feel pain on the thought that he is deprived from the love of Lord? Only a deep lover of Lord can have this quality and only he can ask this question. So the very presence of this question in his mind, if it is aroused of the feeling of deprivation from Lord's love, shows that he has already been gifted with *bhakti*. If, on the other hand, someone asks this question without any pain of deprivation of Lord's love then it is merely a verbal question, without having any sense of value for *bhakti*. In that case if he is deprived of this divine gift he is not deprived of anything valuable in his own eyes. *Bhakti* is valuable for *bhakta* and for them who understand it. Understanding of *bhakti* necessarily involves a sense of its immense value. If only by listening from the *bhakta* about the value of *bhakti* someone asks the question why has Lord not given him this valuable gift then his question is vacuous because he does not actually find any value in what he is asks for.

Second, if someone asks this question to put blame on the Lord that he is unjust then he is only conflating many ideas just to make a false point. If someone puts the blame on the Lord of being unjust, then he presupposes a notion of justice independent of *bhakti* and that of his Lord. Either he has the notion of socio-political justice in his mind with which we talk about *bhakti* in our ordinary context or he assumes that Lord could have done better justice if he had followed the notion of justice, which he assumes in his mind. This point needs some elaboration.

When someone blames Lord that he should have given *bhakti* to everyone in equal amount he assumes that what Lord has done is not the best of all possibilities. He further assumes that the person knows more than and better than what Lord knows about people. It implies, therefore that he places himself above God. In any theistic system of thinking this is purely illogical and irrational let alone be blasphemous. Even if one has not any emotional attachment with Lord and one is only considering the concept of Lord as a rational presupposition of theistic life the implicit assumption makes his question about Lord's justice irrational. Leibniz's argument that God has made this world as the best possible world can be brought in this regard. The answer to the question containing a blame on Lord's justice, lies in the fact that it is the best thing that Lord has not distributed *bhakti* equally to all and to do so would have been the best thing. If everybody would have been given the ecstatic experience of *bhakti* then *bhakti* would have lost its charm that it has at present in it. In that situation *bhakti* could not have been recognized as *bhakti* at all. Distributing *bhakti* unequally among the people Lord has not proved himself partial or unjust rather He has proved himself the best planner since he had actualized that best possibility in which the greatest value of the experience of *bhakti* becomes evident to all who actually aspire for it. Moreover, Lord has left some room for human effort also in achieving *bhakti* and enabled every human being to exercise his freedom also in this regard. Had God given the reward of *bhakti* to all equally then there would have been no role of human decision and human effort in this regard. It is clear that between the options of presence and absence of human choice, the presence of human choice is definitely a better choice. Making room for this choice God has done the best possible thing. If he would have done everything that were pleasant for human beings but would not have given freedom to exercise his free will then he would have made human beings only idle creatures and the world would have been a monotonous, non-developing world at least in the moral sense. Enabling men to exercise his choice to achieve his reward of *bhakti* he has brought into being that world which is the best possible world.

Since, *bhakti* is complete surrender at the feet of the Lord, it appears as if human effort and reason has no role to play but it is not true. It is true that reason and emotions are ordinarily opposite to each other. Reason tries to control emotions and does not allow it to overpower human life and if emotions become stronger then reason is suppressed by it. Yet, both are deeply related to each other and we cannot think of one without the other. It is needless to say that for the arousal of any emotion function of reason at initial stage in different forms is very much needed. Recognition of situation, individuation of an object or a person as the centre of that emotion, assessment of the situation and the behaviour of the person and ascription of certain factors or qualities to the person or the object of emotion require the function of reason. The role of reason, therefore, in the emotion is undisputedly accepted. The role of emotion in the governance or control of reason needs to be explained, since it seems strange or preposterous.

Our actions are ordinarily regarded to be guided by reason. In the moral domain emotions are not given any place. What ought to be the case is not our primary concern here. In this discussion we are not going to make an ideal according to which human actions are to be followed. Our concern here is to see if there are human situations in which emotions not only have an upper hand but also guide our rational choice. What do we do in a situation of a dilemma? When we have opposite reasons for any action and both have equal weight then reason cannot serve as our guide.

Do we completely postpone actions when we face a dilemma? The answer is negative. Despite the equal weight of reasons for or against a particular action we have to and we do choose one action. A theory of priority comes forward to support the view that even in an enigmatic situation people have rational choices for or against an action. This theory can be accepted for certain situations but it cannot be accepted as universally true. We can understand human situations where one has to use his free choice without any clear reason for it. Believing in God is such a human choice where human reason is not of any help. We all know that no one can become or be made a God believer on the basis of rational argumentation. No one believes in God purely on the basis of reasons or proofs given in support of God's existence. Belief in God is a non-rational phenomenon in the sense that people believe in God first and give reasons in justification of their belief, later on. However, if we are placed in a situation of choosing between theism and atheism we cannot take help of reason because we know very well that the set of arguments in favour of theism is as inconclusive as the set of arguments against it. Strictly, rationally in the logical sense of the term we have no ground to say that one is more rational than the other. But we know that ordinarily we do not accept this logical sense of rationality and claim that atheism is more rational and theism is irrational or less rational. Most atheists and very largely a big segment of common people also assume atheism as more rational, since they associate it with secularism in social context and science in the cognitive context. In social contexts we find that religious commands and injunctions make undue interference in our social and personal matters for which it has no rational ground. So, it is deemed from the social point of view that theism is irrational or less rational and atheism in comparison to that is more rational. In cognitive context we think that scientific hypotheses are based on experimental proofs and supported by evidential reason. Religious beliefs in contrast to them are deemed to be matters of pure belief without any evidential support. So, they are regarded as irrational in comparison to scientific theories and hypotheses. Despite these two reasons we know very well that neither scientific methodology nor our concern for personal and social autonomy can rationally demonstrate in the logical sense of the term that theistic beliefs are irrational. Rationality of science cannot prove irrationality of theism. Discovery of any natural law cannot be a counter argument for belief in God. This is a very common and popular sort of mistake towards which our attention hardly ever goes. Theism can be proved irrational, in the logical sense, by scientific methods only if it is positively established that God does not exist. God is not found at all in any remote or proximal research of science is completely inadequate to refute the belief that God exists. Unless it is established by scientific method that the proposition that 'God does not exist' is universally true, theism cannot be logically ruled out. It is to note that to establish theism we need only an existential proposition that 'God exists' (or 'there exists at least one situation such that God exists'). It seems at least empirically impossible to establish that 'God does not exist' is universally true. Hence, no scientific development and discoveries done as yet or in the future may logically refute theism. What cannot be logically refuted gets at least a minimum scope to be called rationally acceptable, although it is not sufficient for that. Theism has at least this minimum rationality granted since we have seen that no scientific discovery can logically repudiate it. In that situation the common opinion that theism is irrational or less rational in comparison to science is itself an irrational position.

What cannot be logically refuted by the rational methodology of science cannot be refuted by the demand of concern for public and personal autonomy. Secularism, at the most may express its indifference or even aversion for theism but that does not logically abound to refute it. So despite all our social concern for personal and public autonomy and associating rationality with a secular, modern lifestyle, theism even in modern society cannot be held to be irrational in the logical sense.

In the light of the above discussion it is clear that this common public opinion that theism is irrational and various brands of atheism either in the form of scientism or in the form of secularism is an irrational belief, in the logical sense because there is no good reason to declare theism as irrational. This discussion throws light on a fact which is very simple but ordinarily not noticed by most of us that we side with theism or atheism not because of reasons in their support or against each other but we *want* to adhere to one sort of reasoning rather than the other. I support atheism not because I have good rational grounds in its support or have conclusive rational grounds against atheism but because I like it. We can find psychological, cultural or even biological reasons for this liking but we cannot have any reason for this liking since we have seen that there is no conclusive reason for it. Why do not I like to believe in existence of God? Can be answered by pointing out my psychological make up, or by referring to the cultural set up in which I am brought up, or perhaps, by linking it to my genes. But none of these are reasons for not believing in God but are factors, which generate dislike in me for believing in God. These factors are not under my control, so I cannot call them my reasons for not believing in God, although knowingly or unknowingly these factors are exploited as reasons. Anyone can easily distinguish between reason and liking. One may have reasons for accepting something or not accepting something but one also knows that it is very different from liking something or disliking it. I may have reasons for my taking milk daily. I may be taking milk as a matter of my decision to fulfill my deficiency of calcium etc. This is the reason for taking milk. On the other hand I may take milk daily jus because it like it-maybe for its taste. It is very clear that it is not a reason but a liking for milk. I may rationalize later on my liking by arguing that taking milk is good for health etc. but I know it well that it is merely rationalization of my liking and not a reason for my taking milk. On many occasions most of us, very cleverly, rationalize our liking. We may delude others by our capacity of argumentation and we may also try to do so with ourselves but we cannot succeed fully in deluding ourselves that my rationalization is really a reason. We may have liking for atheism. Various factors must be operating behind our liking. But we understand that it is our liking for atheism and not reason for it. Similarly, some people may have liking for theism and various factors may be operating behind that also. But they also know that this is their liking and not reason. Both the parties are correct in their positions since if they defend their position regarding theism or atheism, they do it under the influence of their liking for their position. They defend their position because they like that position. It becomes wrong when one party begins to criticize the other party for the irrationality of its position. It is wrong just because one party blames the other for the demerit that cannot be there. An atheist's criticism of theists that they hold irrational things is wrong because the theists do not hold it for any reason but because they like it. Similarly, putting a blame of irrationality by the theists would be wrong. However, this latter situation hardly ever arises. Theists are generally blamed for being irrational, superstitious etc. In the modern society atheists are not blamed of irrationality by the theists. They maybe blamed by the theists for their materialistic attitude but not for irrationality. It is, therefore, worth noting that the theists are blamed for a demerit (irrationality) that is not present in them. Theists are free to defend their position by freely admitting that they *feel like* accepting and adhering to theism. They are also justified in giving reasons for their liking to theism. If they do it in terms of the joy that they get out of it. This sort of reason, which is internal to liking, deserves serious attention to understand theism. A *bhakta* believes in his Lord or does *bhakti* because it gives him the joy that only *bhakti* can give. *Bhakti* attracts some persons and it is this attraction that transforms them very often as a *bhakta* whose centre of life becomes the love of God, only. This attraction for *bhakti* or the love for the Lord can be said to be the reason for it. This psychic attraction involves the person's rational approval for its actual manifestation in his life. The attraction may be very strong and almost mechanical a person can be pulled by it and transformed into a *bhakta*. Even this be so this happens only though his rational approval because he could not have given his approval. A person may get addicted to a particular sort of intoxication. Various factors may attract him very forcefully towards that sort of intoxication but ultimately it is his approval that makes him fall in it. This kind of comparison between *bhakti* and intoxication is not appropriate from a standpoint either of the *bhakta* or from that of anyone who understands *bhakti* but it is made with a purpose to explain that one has to use his reason for final approval even if the force of attraction of *bhakti* is very strong. In actual situation of human life the force of attraction of *bhakti* or the love for the divine operates as a very mild force of attraction. This force cannot start functioning in his life unless, the *bhakta,* by his own rational efforts does not approve its functioning. Surrounded by din and bustle of mundane life and material responsibilities a person's existence is pulled from various directions and it is very difficult for anyone to follow even one material force and to accord it with rest. The supra mundane mild force of *bhakti* proves ordinarily very weak before these material forces. Till it becomes rooted in a person's life and grow adequately stronger one has to keep it giving rational approval and support, constantly. In the light of above discussion that we have no compulsive rational ground in favour of theism, it becomes doubly difficult for a person to avail the gift of *bhakti* if he does not constantly exercise his reason in support of this mild force of attraction, till it becomes very strong and takes control of his whole life. If we understand this actual situation then so many theoretical questions loose their practical relevance. Questions, such as- why did not God give everybody the boon of *bhakti* equally, if it is a great gift etc. remains no more practically significant. It is true that *bhakti* is one of the greatest gifts of the Lord but given the fact that we are also given the faculty of reason we have to understand the actual relation of reason with *bhakti*. Reason does not give direction to *bhakti* because it is not meant for that. It does not have that capacity at all. If it were forced to give direction to *bhakti* then it would amount to making *bhakti* rational. But there is nothing like rational *bhakti* so it would only result into a kind of mental gymnastics. Reason has to assist the force of *bhakti* no matter how mild or weak it is at any stage of its development in the *bhakta's* life. This may appear to be a very strange use of reason for *bhakti* and ordinarily it is not acceptable to a rationalist mind. But *bhaktas* know it very well that whatever maybe the significance of reason in mundane world it has only a role of assistance for *bhakti* in the world of Lord's love. It is also worth noting that reason is not denounced as useless at all. It has a very significant use, especially, in the life of a growing *bhakta*. The strength and the function of reason are not denied in the world of *bhakti*, only its supremacy is denied. For a *bhakta* reason also is a gift of God and is to be honoured as any.of his gifts deserve. However, *bhakti* is much greater a gift and has to be placed above reason. Even if *bhakti* is at a weak stage in a *bhakta's* life and reason very strong, it has to be given supremacy over the latter and the latter is to be cultivated to accept the supremacy of the former. It is something like the situation in which an infant regent is looked after and served by a strong grown up servant. Despite, the physical strength and physical maturity the servant is a servant of the infant and the infant regent is yet the master despite the fact that he is physically weak and immature. This analogy may appear to be very feudal in its look but it is not. It is only to bring forth the specialty of relation between reason and *bhakti.* It would be too ideal to think that *bhakti* in human life can grow without the help of reason. *Bhakti* is not an ideal situation. It is a real experience of human life. It cannot grow by itself alone. Rational approval to those situations in which it could survive and grow faster is a necessary condition for the manifestation of *bhakti* in human life. Those situations, which may prove to be injurious for growth of *bhakti*, are to be abstained by a *bhakta* and this is decided by his reason. Criticism of Lord or his *bhaktas* mars the growth of *bhakti* in a person's life. So a *bhakta* abstains from it. Too much involvement in worldly activities also create problem for the growth of *bhakti.* So he tries to keep balance between this world and the world of *bhakti.* Maintenance of this balance in order to gradually shift to the latter requires a very cautious use of reason. In brief it can be said that reason is needed at various stages in *bhakta's* life. There can't be a set pattern or program for doing this. Reason itself has to make its path and proceed on it watching the surrounding conditions.

From the stand point of the *bhakta* of a developed stage, in whose life the divine force of *bhakti* has already taken full control, this sort of cautious move of reason is a gift of Lord, and it is true also. But from the position of the *bhakta* of initial stage (who gets joy in the acts of *bhakti* but falls back to mundane world again where he has to decide his course of action with reason) this truth needs to be made a matter of experience in every action with the help of reason itself. This is not a matter of thought. *Bhaktas* have to feel that *bhakti* is the driving force in his life. For this he has to meditate more and more on the given-ness of those factors that are necessary for survival, for the exercise of will and for the favourable environment for the execution of will. To feel (and not merely to think) that *bahkti i.e.* the love for the Lord is controlling his life the *bhakta* at the initial stage has to repeatedly focus his attention on all those happenings where the given-ness of all the valuable things are easily seen. Life, self-consciousness, reason and sensibility (to feel others pain and pleasure also) are the most general but invaluable gifts with which every living and sane human being is endowed. They are all divine. Life itself is a valuable gift and although parents become the medium to bring us to life they themselves are not the source of life since they have inherited it from others. So the precious gift of life is given to us by an unknown giver. Self-consciousness is a more precious gift since it constitutes our human identity. Reason that enables us to separate useful from harmful, good from evil and mundane from divine is equally valuable. And, sensibility to feel pain and pleasure of others also is equally a precious gift. These can be ascribed to nature only if it is acknowledged that divinity is hidden in nature. Nature as a bundle of dead blind laws can't be accepted as the giver of these gifts unless the natural human feeling that these are divine is suppressed irrationally. Nature, if deemed as *natura naturance,* then alone these gifts can be ascribed to it. Nature as a mechanical force cannot be said to be the source of these divine gifts, since life cannot be thought to be evolved from lifeless matter, consciousness cannot be though to be evolved of not conscious and sensibility cannot be thought to be evolved of that which has no sensibility at all. At the most reason can be said in some sense to be evolved out of materiality but in that sense it is not a gift at all, since it can be programmed in a machine also. Apart from these general divine gifts every individual *bhakta* can and do find so many valuable things in his personal life that helps him directly or indirectly, positively or negatively to lead on the path of *bhakti.* If a *bhakta* belongs to a poor background he may find that his poverty has saved him from unnecessary luxuries that create disturbance in Lord's love. If, on the other hand, he belongs to a rich background then he can think itself as a boon of Lord and also take it as a great help to save him from the unnecessary wastage time to earn livelihood. In nutshell we can say that thousands of things are found and happen in every individual's life that would turn out to be divine gifts only if he looks at them without any bias. Along with it he also has to exercise his will to see only the positive aspects of any event. Some events may apparently be painful or even disastrous for a *bhakta* but he has the freewill to exercise his reason to find out some of its good aspects at present or in future, or somehow relate it to his past. It is impossible logically that any action or happening be out and out bad in all respects. Some good consequences even of the most unfortunate events are present with its bad consequences also. Under the painful influence of bad effects of an event one forgets or does not want to see those good consequences. However, a *bhakta* at the initial stage of his development has to cultivate in him this disposition to look at only the good effects so that the gift of the Lord even in those events he could feel.

Above discussion is only a brief account of what role reason has to play in the life of the *bhakta.* The account maybe small but it makes it very clear that a *bhakta,* especially while he is growing towards the highest stage of *bhakti,* has to use his reason wisely and constantly to nurture and strengthen the feeling of *bhakti.* Looked at this way the commonly imagined conflict between the emotion of *bhakti* and reason not only disappears but also turns out to be ridiculous. Given this understanding we just cannot think *bhakti* without a good use of reason. To think that a *bhakta* is a non-rational person, in fact, reflects only our irrationality. Even if the *bhakta* is quiet illiterate as Kabir or Raidas were, they are very wise and very rational too. They know very well how to use reason, where to use it and how much.

Can This World Become a World of *bhakti*?

Bhaktas spread *bhakti* directly and indirectly too. Somewhere, deep in his heart he also has a desire that everybody should attain *bhakti* to attain the joy of *bhakti*- the bliss of loving the Lord. This is quiet natural. Even a non-*bhakta* can understand it very well if he understands the feeling of the *bhakta.* However, for an atheist it is a ridiculous desire and for a common man, who is not necessarily against *bhakti,* it is impossible. We can admit that this is such a dream that can hardly ever be realized even partially. Given the situation around us it seems impossible to think that even the half of the population or a big chunk of it can become *bhaktas. Bhakti* descends on earth in some *bhakta's* heart and blossoms only in a small group. However, it is neither logically nor empirically impossible to think of a world full of *bhaktas,* only. A clarification in this regard is not quiet inappropriate.

There are certain misgivings regarding *bhakta* and his life in respect of modern ways of living. By the term *bhakta* a typical image of a person is formed in our mind, which resembles a Chaitnya, Kabir or Meera. All these images are medieval and seem to be unfit for modern world. If modernity means materialist outlook and selfish way of living then definitely a *bhakta* cannot be a modern person at all. But even the most modern of the modern persons would hardly agree with this definition of modernity. If modernity, on the other hand, is associated with technological advancement and not with materialist, selfish attitude then there seems to be no conflict between *bhakti* and modernity.

The age of Chaitnya, Kabir or Meera was not a mythological *Satayug.* They were also living in the age, which was materialist in a sense. They had to face opposition in their age, which were basically political or social or religious. It may appear very strange that materialists, qua materialists hardly ever confronted with the *bhaktas.* They just did not care for the *bhaktas* and their message. Many *bhaktas* adopted the path of *sanayâs* like Chaitnya but many of them kept working on their inherited or adopted profession. Kabir was a weaver and remained a weaver till his death. Same is true of Raidas. So any particular material action is not opposed to *bhakti* at all. *Bhakti* as we have seen earlier is an emotional experience of Lord's love. Anyone can fall in love irrespective of his profession; similarly in anyone's heart the love of Lord can emerge irrespective or the profession or the deeds of the person. In any action can be performed by offering it fully at the feet of the dear Lord then it is not against *bhakti,* rather it becomes an act of *bhakti* itself. In Bhagwad Gita also this message comes out of the mouth of Lord himself. If a Kabir can make his weaving *bhakti* and a Raidas can do *bhakti* while making shoes then there is no reason why a businessman, a scientist, a teacher, a student or any worker cannot transform his act into worship of Lord. This does not amount to giving the message- 'work is worship'. Understanding work as worship means to give central importance to work. Making work a worship of Lord in our sense of the discussion means placing oneself primarily in complete dependence of Lord and perform all the actions, whatever it may be, as an instrument in the hand of the Lord. It brings about a qualitative change in the life of the person who performs his action with this feeling. Two sorts of changes are to be underlined. First, certain actions cannot be performed at all with this feeling if one is not constrained for that. A person who places himself in complete dependence on Lord's will and does any action as an instrument in his hands looses all reasons for doing any action, which are done with purely selfish intentions. Ordinarily all the virtuous actions are expected to emerge in his life but even if it does not happen, whatever he does becomes free from selfish intentions. Second, in a situation of constraint a person does that action for which he is constrained but remains free from the stresses of those constraints. A *bhakta,* ordinarily would avoid fighting with anyone but if the situation constraints him in such a way that he is not given any chance to escape it then he fights with all his might but without any sense of ego or ambition of winning a fight. He feels every moment that he is an instrument in the hands of the Lord and his attention is completely drawn to the joy of this relation and not on the act of fighting.

If some work yields good results for the *bhakta* and for others also then apart from the central joy of being connected to the Lord as his instrument he also finds Lord's blessings in the goodness of the result. All that human beings do can be done by the *bhaktas* but with a very different attitude towards his deeds. The world would not be very much materially different if everyone in the world become a lover of the Lord- becomes a *bhakta.* Yet, the world will be very very different from what it is at present. A lover of Lord essentially loves another lover of the Lord. It is practically almost inevitable that a *bhakta* does not love another *bhakta.* Internal differences between two *jnânis* also are ideally denied but practically this is very often witnessed in the history. *Jnâna* wipes out ego of the person and removes the reason for conflict. However, the assertion of *jnâna* in the most humble terms either presupposes an ego on part of the assertor or forms a possible reason for conflict with another assertor. This condition is ordinarily not present in the case of *bhaktas.* From the initial stage to the stage of achieving the height of *bhakti* no *bhakta* ever claims to be a great *bhakta.* If you ask a *bhakta* – are you a *bhakta*? The most expected reply would be –'no, I am an ordinary, pity servant of the Lord, how can I bee a *bhakta,* who is so dear to Lord.' The presence of love for the Lord necessarily makes the *bhakta* feel that it is just the grace of the Lord that he has got some drops of nectar of his love but he cannot claim for anything and cannot take it as a matter of his right. So, a deep-rooted humility becomes the disposition of the *bhaktas.* An internal conflict of one *bhakta* with another *bhakta* on the ground of his claims seems to be therefore, practically almost impossible. A *bhakta* is ready to except his ignorance even before a non-*bhakta* and hardly any reasons arise for internal conflict between two *bhaktas.* However, a conflict between the *bhaktas* cannot be completely ruled out for two reasons. First, there could be a conflict between the *bhaktas* who have not been able to dissolve their egos completely in all its aspects at the feet of the Lord. The hidden ego may surface at any time in any form. It is to be noted in this connection that complete transformation of ego into one's identity as a pure instrument of Lord takes place only when the force of *bhakti* itself takes complete control of every dimension of the *bhakta's* life and elevates him to a level where no conflict is possible in the sense of ego tussle. Before this the identity of the *bhakta* as an instrument of Lord can be overpowered by material forces and force him enter into ego tussle. Second, a very different kind of internal conflict between the *bhaktas* is possible and it is described very fondly in the *Purâòas.* This is a quarrel of the lovers to offer the best to the beloved Lord. This quarrel is not merely a pretension. Actual feeling of conflict and tussle emerges in the heart of the *bhaktas.* This may take any form of various *bhâvas* and a physical manifestation of it is inevitable. However, all this is ineffably blissful for both the opponents and give great joy to others instead of spreading hatred or violence.

Modern living with *bhakti* is not only possible but perhaps most befitting too. The world of *bhakti* and the *bhakta* is a full-fledged world. No, inhibitions and taboos are forced in this world. The only driving force is the love of the Lord that is in fact a great passion and the supreme *bhoga.* A *bhakta,* as it is stated earlier, is not desirous of *moksha.* Even if he takes to *sanyâsa,* he does so for the passionate enjoyment of pure bliss of the proximity of his Lord in all its innumerable manifestations. *Bhakti* is a *bhoga* – a supreme and pure *bhoga.* Modern world is a world of *bhoga,* so far as the attitude is concerned. Just a shift of attention from world to Lord makes this world immensely enjoyable for a modern man. A modern man runs after pleasure. A *bhakta* also runs after pure pleasure of the proximity of his Lord. A modern man is possessive in his attitude and a *bhakta* too is very much possessive for his love of the Lord. Just a switching over is needed and a modern man can easily transform into a *bhakta.* Materiality, qua-materiality is not against *bhakti* and the materialistic attitude has something very important in common with *bhakti.* It is therefore not practically impossible to envisage that the world becomes the world of the *bhaktas.*

Modern man is not ready to listen the preaching of penance and renunciation. He loves his world, wants to live in it, and does not want to abandon it due to the sufferings that he has to undergo as a necessary consequence of living in this world. He wants to avoid the physical sufferings and get rid of mental stress. For this he frantically looks for something, which can give him relief of mind without necessarily damaging his body. *Bhakti* does not promise to give anything material. It promises to give only what it is, that is the love of Lord. But if one understands *bhakti* then he very well understands that *bhakti* can give everything literally, whatever the *bhakta* desires. Peace of mind and wealth of this world are generally deemed to be opposite to each other. A *bhakta* enjoys both without any problem. One who understands *bhakti* can also understand that only *bhaktas* can enjoy both can and no one else can do. It is *bhakta's* will to enjoy material wealth or not to enjoy it. If he likes to keep away wealth from him and enjoys *fakiri*, like Kabir, then he lives in material poverty. If, on the other hand, he is just indifferent of wealth and does not care to keep himself away from it either, then he leads a materially affluent life also, like Jaidev and Vallabhacharya. One who loves Lord, Lord gives him both the boons- spiritual wealth and material wealth too. Material wealth in the form of money etc. is not divine since they are not given to humans as natural gifts. They are the products of human construction. In fact they are the means to exploit the abundantly available natural resource for cleverly planned ends. They are earned by human beings by lot of physical labour and/or by cleverness. Lord's boon of spiritual wealth of ecstasy of *bhakti* and the deepest level of self-conscious life brings with it the material wealth also and the *bhaktas* don't have to earn it with the cunningness of reason. In fact material wealth follows the *bhaktas* like their shadows. One, who does not love Lord but runs after material wealth, has to keep oneself constantly engaged in chasing this shadow and to make effort to remain in its touch. It is not difficult to understand how difficult is it to follow one's shadow. One who follows one's shadow has to turn one's back towards the source of light; one has to face darkness continuously. This is the plight of the people who run after material wealth. This situation becomes compulsive if one never cares to turn his eyes towards the source of light that gives one a shadow and puts it at one's back. This is not merely an analogy; it is truth of human life. This happens in the life of all the *bhaktas* yet it seems very difficult to believe it since we don't find any material reason for it. Obviously there could be no material reason for it since it happens indirectly as the spiritual gift of Lord. However, it is not difficult to understand it at the mass level. If people don't become greedy and possessive of material wealth then even if they work with the machines and do commerce with a *bhakta's* view to find the joy of work as the gift of Lord, abundance of material wealth would be procured and available for everyone individually and collectively too. At present competition is the way to achieve the selfish motive of possessing more and more wealth for oneself. Competing with others mean to surpass others. It is basically a violent principle. If poison be contained in the root then it is foolish to expect that the fruit would be free from it. Most of the problems of materialistic attitude begin at the root. *Bhaktas* make every work worship of Lord and that is actual motive behind all his actions. All his actions are directed to no one else except Lord. Thus the reason for stress remains absent from the very beginning. The joy of excellence in the work, which in terms of material gain or production means big quantity with high quality, is the motivation for the *bhaktas* since this is what he would see as a variety of the joy of experiencing the love of Lord. A world in which material activities are run by the *bhaktas* would be a wonderful world of in which material pleasures get transformed into spiritual bliss.

References

1. *Sthalkamalganjanam mam hridayranjanamjanitrati rangabhâgam Bhaò masriò vâòi kar vâòicaraòa dwayam sarsaldalakta krâgam Smar garal khaòdanama mam °irasi maòdanam* ....
Jaideva wanted to write the line —— '*Dehi me pada pallawamudâreama*' to complete this copulatebut he thought that it is too high a demand for a petty person like him and it would be arrogant on his part make such a demand. The other Jaideva Lord *Kṛṣṇa* in his form wrote this line to complete the copulate and to wipe out his doubt completely.
2. *Sri Madbhâgvata,10,47, 63.*
3. *Chaitnya Chbaritamrita* (vol. -II) by Prabhudatta Brahmachai,, Geeta Press, Gorakhpur
4. जव मै था तब हरि नहीं जब हरि है मै नाहि प्रेम गली अतिसांकरी या मे दो न समाहि।
5. पाथी पदृि पदृि जगमुअ पृडित भयां न कोय । ढाई आखर प्रेम का पढे सो पंडित होय ।।
5. P*othi Padhi Padhi Jag Muâ Pandit Bhayâ Na Koye Dhâi Âkhar Prem Kâ Padhe So Pandit Hoye* II
6. वैसणव जन तेनै कहिए जो पीर पराइ जाने रे
7. ....Sri Aurobindo- An Introduction, pp-56, Sri Aurobindo Society, Pondicherry

Bibliography

Classical Texts

Ananada Bhashya by Swami Ramananda.

Bhaktirasamrit Sindhu by- Roop Goswami, ed.— Dr. Nagendra & Dr.Vijayendra Snataka, pub. Department of Hindi, Delhi University, 1963.

Durga Saptshati, Geeta Press,Gorakhpur.

Sri Madbhagvata, Geeta Press, Gorakhpur.

Sri Madbhagvatgeeta, Geeta Press, Gorakhpur.

Narad Bhaktl Sutra.

Ramayana by – *Valmiki,* ed.— Hanuman Prasad Poddar, Geeta Press, Gorakhpur.

Ramcharit Manas by—Goswami Tulsidas, ed.—Hanuman Prasad Poddar, Geeta Press, Gorakhpur.

Shandilya Bhakti Shiksha.

Other than Classical Texts.

Bhaktivedant, A. C. Swami Prabhupada – *Bhaktirasamrit Sindhu,* Tran. Dr.Shiv Gopal Mishra (Hindi), Bhakti Vedanta Book Trust, Juhu, Mumbai (India).

Blackstonw, W. T.—*The Problem of Religious Knowledge.* Prenice HallInc. Englewood Cliff, N. J. Spectrum Books, 1963.

Braithwaite, R. B.—'An Empiricist's View of The Nature of Religious Belief', *Philosophy of Religion,* (ed.- Basil Mitchell), Oxford Reading Series, Oxford University Press, 1963.

Brhamachari, Prabhudatta – *Chaitany Charitamrita,* Geeta Press, Gorakhpur, 1962.

Descartes, Rene—Meditations ,in *Philosophical Works of Descartes* , trans. & ed. Elizabeth Haldane & Ross, Dover Books, New York, 1955.

Gandh, Mohandas Karamcahnd — *My Experiments With Truth.* Navjeevan.

Ghosh, Aurobindo – *Life Divine,* Sri Aurobindo Ashram, Pondicerry.

Hazari Prasad Dwiwedi—*Hazari Prasad Dwiwedi Granthawali,* Vol. 3 (Hindi), Rajkamal Prakashan New Delhi, 1981.

Hick, John—'Theology and Verification', *Philosophy of Religion* (ed. Basil Mitchell), Oxford Reading Series, Oxford University Press, 1963.

,, — *Faith and The Philosophers,* Macmillan Co. Ltd. London 1964.

Kant, Immanuel- *Critique of Aesthetic Judgment,* ed.& tran.G. Di.Giovanni & A. W.Wood Cambridge, Cambridge Univ.Press, 1996.

Kabir (1918)–'Sakhi', *SakhiSamgraha* (Hindi), Allahabad.

Klyan (2003) (*Bhagvat Premank*) (Hindi), Geeta Press, Gorakhpur, 2003

Price, H. H. – "Belief In and Belief That", *Philosophy of Religion,* Oxford Reading Series, Oxford Univ. Press. 1963.

Plantinga, A.—'Is Belief in God Rational', *Rationality and Religious Belief* ed. C. F.

Delaney, Notre Dame, 1979.

,, — *Faith and Rationality* , ed. Alvin Plantinga and Nicholas Wonderstorff, Notre Dame Pess, 1983.

Ramanuja– *Vedarthsamgrah,* tran.Raghawacharya, Mysore, Ramakrishna Ashram, 1969.

Raidas—*Raidas Ramayana* (Hindi) ed. Swami Sukhanand, Agra 1925.

Spinoza, Benedict— *Ethica* trams. –W.H. White & A.H. Skirling, Oxford Univ. Press.

Sri Aurobindo—An Introduction, Sri Aurobindo Ashram , Pondicherry.

Wisdom, John – 'Gods', *Philosophy of Religion* (ed.-Abernathy & Langford), Routledge & Kegan Paul Ltd. 1960.

Wittgenstein, Ludwig— *Lectures and Conversations on Aesthetics, Psychology and Religious Belief* ed. C.K. Barrett, Oxford Univ. Press 1966.

,, — *Philosophical Invesigation* ed. G. E. M. Enscombe , Oxford Univ. Press, 1963.

Index